HOLIDAY DINNERS *with* BRADLEY OGDEN

∽ 150 FESTIVE RECIPES ∽
TO BRING FAMILY & FRIENDS TOGETHER

BRADLEY OGDEN *with* LYDIA SCOTT

Running Press
PHILADELPHIA · LONDON

*This book is dedicated
to Mom with love*

Books published by Running Press are available at special discounts for bulk purchases in the
United States by corporations, institutions, and other organizations. For more information, please
contact the Special Markets Department at the Perseus Books Group, 2300 Chestnut Street,
Suite 200, Philadelphia, PA 19103, or call (800) 810-4145, ext. 5000, or e-mail special.markets@
perseusbooks.com.

ISBN: 978-0-7624-3915-7
Library of Congress Control Number: 2011928972

E-book ISBN: 978-0-7624-4359-8

9 8 7 6 5 4 3 2 1
Digit on the right indicates the number of this printing

Cover and interior design by Amanda Richmond
Typography: Berkeley, La Portentia, and Gotham

Running Press Book Publishers
2300 Chestnut Street
Philadelphia, PA 19103-4371

Visit us on the web!
www.runningpresscooks.com

CONTENTS

4

ACKNOWLEDGMENTS

5

FOREWORD

7

INTRODUCTION

11

THANKSGIVING FEAST

107

CHRISTMAS DINNER

199

NEW YEAR'S DAY CELEBRATION

259

A SPECIAL NOTE ABOUT WARM WEATHER HOLIDAYS

270

INDEX

280

ABOUT THE AUTHOR

ACKNOWLEDGMENTS

THIS BOOK IS A CULMINATION OF THREE DECADES OF COOKING FOR THE holidays. These recipes were refined at home in my kitchen and not too long ago just a dream to publish.

I would like to thank Lydia Scott for all her dedicated work to make this book and my dream a reality. My editor, Geoffrey Stone, for his guidance, knowledge, and support. My sons Chad and Bryan, also chef graduates from the Culinary Institute of America, and Cory Ogden, the doctor of the family, for making me proud. A special thanks to Bryan for his excellent taste and wisdom of wine and to Jody Ogden for her years of encouragement and expertise. A special thank-you to Maricla Salcido for her support in testing, tasting, organizing, and typing my recipes.

I would like to express my deepest gratitude to my close friends, Maria Ferrer Murdock, Michael and Sandy DeRousse, and Carolyn Stuart for their overall influence, advice, patience, and support. Thank you to Jeremy Ball for the photographs, Amanda Richmond for the art direction and book design, Ricardo Jattan and Jackie Prophit for the styling; Sparrow Lane Vinegars, for continuously supplying their fine wine vinegars; and Wes Hagen for his wine.

Finally, I am eternally grateful for the contribution of my fellow chefs from Root 246 Restaurant, Brian Ridgeway, Yohan Denizot, and Daniel Talaima, and Iris Rideau and John Martino from Chumash Casino Resort, and to my business partners, Michael and Leslye Dellar.

And to all my friends and neighbors who volunteered their talents, taste tested my recipes, and offered their helpful and meaningful critiques.

FOREWORD

*I*T WAS IN THE 1980S WHEN I WAS WORKING WITH THE LATE JAMES BEARD that I first heard of Bradley Ogden. Each year Beard went to San Francisco to conduct a series of classes and always stayed at Campton Place. Without fail, he came back quite impressed with the quality of Bradley's ingredients, his use of inspired flavors, and his exquisite execution of the food.

Bradley's upbringing in Michigan unknowingly prepared him for his culinary journey where fresh trout, just-hatched chicken eggs, and his grandmother's homemade pies were taken for granted. "Food from scratch" would come to form the backbone of his approach to cooking for others.

He trained at the Culinary Institute of America in Hyde Park, New York, and had come to California via The American Restaurant in Kansas City, which was one of the foremost restaurants of its time in the Midwest. In Kansas City, Bradley had utilized local farm purveyors and farmers and brought that same sensibility with him to the West Coast.

When Bradley was arriving on the scene, there were other chefs on the same American fresh food bandwagon, each with an individual style. Their menus were driven by the bounty of the season (still a novelty in some areas today) with great importance given to the provenance of the produce. It was only a matter of time before this concept began to make an impact around the country. At Beard's house, where the James Beard Foundation is now located, on West 12th Street in New York City, I witnessed a pilgrimage of visiting chefs who would drop by to receive the master's blessing; Bradley was among them.

A few years ago, Bradley started conceptualizing this book. He envisioned one that celebrated holidays throughout the year. It is clear why it covers Thanksgiving, Christmas, and New Year's with a slight nod to summer celebrations. The end-of-the-year holidays are our most cherished ones, and this book allows more concentration and dedication to these holidays. It's in this spirit he shares an abundance of good food, which connects us to loving friends and family in the kitchen and around a festive table.

Holiday Dinners with Bradley Ogden is a comprehensive reference to our three most important holidays of the year. While paying homage to our traditional holiday menus, Bradley has brought the old into the new with added life and sparkle. He teases us with some non-traditional recipes like his wonderful signature dish, Twice-Baked Blue Cheese Soufflés. This book offers a simplistic approach to timely recipes for you to create for the holidays. It makes holiday cooking even more pleasurable.

—CAROLINE STUART,
Cofounder James Beard Foundation and cookbook author

INTRODUCTION

*P*EOPLE HAVE MANY GIFTS IN LIFE—MUSIC, LANGUAGES, PAINTING, and even gab. Mine is a special talent for food. I spent the summers of my youth on my grandmother's farm in Windsor, Ontario. In retrospect, this was the beginning of a fabulous career that I never could have recognized at the time. Both of my grandmothers were great cooks. I believe my mother was as well, although with seven children to look after, she seldom had the opportunity to really demonstrate what she knew. My father, on the other hand, considered himself the world's greatest cook, and was especially known for his breads and homemade ice cream. Of course, the young spindly arms of my six brothers and sister and me were the engine for his churned creations. Nevertheless, to us, it wasn't about hard labor but rather playing a game, resulting in a reward of creamy fresh flavors, from cherry to peach to strawberry, all of which we felt were awesome.

Being around good cooks was important for educating my young palate, but the other even more essential lessons were learned from the farm, regarding the importance of seasonal fresh quality ingredients. Every season held a gift of fresh new produce to be picked, prepared, and, most importantly, enjoyed. I vividly remember anticipating certain times of the year for summer tomatoes fresh off the vine, asparagus and morels in the spring, pumpkin and macintosh apples in the fall. There is nothing more flavorful than the simplicity of a farm-fresh egg or a trout taken from an icy creek and placed directly into a sizzling frying pan. Experiencing and appreciating these pure unadulterated tastes and flavors unwittingly helped lay the foundation for my cooking philosophy and successful career.

There is no exception to my love of all things fresh from the farm. These days that means regular visits to my local farmers' market to buy seasonal items, and purchasing organic and sustainable produce and meats. It's the best way to get the fresh flavors I remember so well from childhood. Still, when I come across cherries I have mixed feelings of love and dread. I'm sure this came from overexposure, brought out by the fact that I had to spend endless hours picking them in my youth. Fortunately, I've long ago learned to appreciate cherries for what they are, and find great satisfaction in cooking with them, as long as I don't have to pick 'em!

Churning ice cream might have been the extent of my culinary career except for the fact that my father read a feature in the *Detroit Free Press* about a cooking school called The Culinary Institute of America, based in Hyde Park, New York. I was only eighteen at the time, but from the CIA article, my father developed a plan. His logic was simple: "If you can cook, you can always find a job!" Another ulterior motive might have had something to do with someday owning a family restaurant. Up until this time, he had owned and operated a rock-and-roll dance hall, named the Tanz Haus. Traverse City, Michigan, might seem an unlikely location for such a venue, but he was able to book the big-name talent of the day, drawing from nearby Detroit. His vision might have been to convert the dance venue to a dining room and kitchen with me as the cook. Instead, it functioned for twenty-five years as a dance hall.

Prior to my first days at the CIA, I had never set foot in a commercial kitchen, but by the time I emerged from the CIA four years later, I recognized that I had an innate talent. It was a bit of a fluke that I fell into something I loved. I reflect on it sometimes. I might have been a draftsman, since I had studied drafting for three months. Had it not been for my father's plan, born out of desperation for fear of unemployment, I might have been just like a musician whose talent never found a stage for lack of piano lessons.

In the years since, at every one of the restaurants at which I've been involved, we have paid special attention to the holidays. It has become part of my signature, just as farm-fresh, organic ingredients have been my theme for the last thirty-five years. I've paid special attention to holiday meals because they meant a lot to me growing up. In my youth, other than holidays, Sunday afternoon was the only time we, as a family, came together for a meal. All of the other meals of the week were one-pot dishes consumed individually whenever each of us found the time. The food was good, to be sure, but there was no real celebration or intimate sense of family that I love so much.

At the restaurants, I constantly strive to create the feeling of a special family meal. Everyday at work, I imagine that patrons are coming to my home for me to cook for them. I always serve expected and traditional foods, prepared with an exciting and creative touch. At Lark Creek, for example, we offered turkeys with a twist for the holidays: fresh, natural turkeys, grilled outdoors or roasted with interesting spices. Always something new, flavorful, and exciting delivered continuously to the dining room, which patrons appreciated and devoured. Menus are always prix fixe, and engineered so that each course supported and complemented each other. Never heavy, always fresh, and definitely designed to leave room for dessert.

On hearing that I was working on a cookbook about the holidays, a friend pointed out that there were already many resources for holiday recipes, and questioned why anyone should use my recipes versus someone else's. My reply was that I create amazing American food on a daily basis and that there may be people out there who would like to put a new creative twist on their routine holiday meal. My recipes are tried and true. They are traditional, accessible, and inspiring, and have been lovingly refined and served over a lifetime of real cooking. These recipes are important to me. They are what I like to eat and share. Since they have worked so wonderfully for me in my professional career, I would like to share them with anyone who is interested in my philosophy of cooking. Some of the recipes that appear in this book have been born in restaurants, but all have been tested at my home on equipment found in virtually all homes. I would be honored to reinvigorate someone's holiday feast and introduce tempting new flavors with my recipes.

Some ingredient lists and procedures you will find here might look long and more ambitious than other recipes. Where that is true, I invite you to persist. This is the way I cook and you won't be disappointed. Quality ingredients and certain techniques make the difference between a good recipe and a great one. Where practical, I will point out a recipe or portion of a recipe that might be done in advance, and often it will be the better for it, as flavors will get the opportunity to meld and develop.

Inside I am still that little boy who grew up in the Midwest and savors the traditional, down-home flavors of good old American food, and my recipes reflect that. My repertoire has been built on this great country's food and traditions. I have always strived to improve on the familiar and make it the best it can be. I think you will agree when you prepare these recipes for yourself. Happy holidays, and bon appétit.

Thanksgiving
Feast

THANKSGIVING GATHERINGS USUALLY INVOLVE AN OVERABUNDANCE of food that celebrates the cornucopia our wonderful country has to offer. Where I grew up in the Midwest, freshly picked corn, sweet pumpkins, unfrozen turkeys, and ham were always available and extremely flavorful, since they were grown or raised nearby. Besides the seasonal food, I especially enjoy the communal atmosphere of this special holiday. Sharing a great meal, I believe, is one of life's richest experiences, undoubtedly strengthening family ties and friendships. Because holiday get-togethers are so important, I believe the food should be outstanding too. With that in mind, I have kept my recipes traditional, but with updated or flavorful twists that make the meal memorable and delicious. Take, for example, my beloved Three-Layer Pumpkin Pie (page 84). I layer different pumpkin flavors and textures, turning a traditional pumpkin pie into a showstopping dessert capable of winning any blue ribbon for its flavor and appearance. It is definitely a family favorite.

Thanksgiving is my favorite holiday because it is the one time I can say for sure that the whole family will make the effort to come together and share a meal. Memories of my youth like sweet baked ham, savory roasted turkey, and my all-time favorite food—pumpkin pie— have been recreated and perfected in the pages that follow. Since traditional favorites like turkey and canned cranberry jelly can seem unimaginative and boring, I have taken the opportunity to slightly change holiday classics with creative touches and flavorful elements. If you are planning a large family gathering, try the Sage-Butter-Roasted Turkey (page 40); or for more intimate gatherings, the Pan-Roasted Turkey Breast with Sweet Squash Matchsticks (page 44) and the Celery Root and Pear Purée (page 61) would be perfect. If a more exciting and exotic recipe is desired, the Red Curry Turkey Scaloppini recipe (page 49) will not disappoint. It is light, quick, and easy, with bold and unexpected flavors.

These are recipes for you and your family to remember and I hope they become a regular part of your holiday table. They can be arranged in a number of different dinner combinations for use throughout the years. I have put together several menu suggestions that combine all the exciting flavors and vibrant colors from this special time of year.

APPLE JUICE WITH CRANBERRY AND GINGER, 18

HOT MULLED CIDER, 20

SPARKLING PEAR PUNCH, 21

CHILLED APPLE SOUP WITH LOBSTER SALAD, 22

SHELLFISH CHOWDER, 23

ROASTED HARVEST SQUASH SOUP, 25

ENDIVE SALAD WITH TANGERINES AND KUMQUATS, 26

LOBSTER SALAD, 26

GREEN BEAN AND PERSIMMON SALAD, 27

ROASTED PEAR AND GOAT CHEESE SALAD, 28

YANKEE SALAD WITH APPLE, WALNUTS, AND BLUE CHEESE, 30

CORN AND SHRIMP FRITTERS, 31

TWICE-BAKED BLUE CHEESE SOUFFLÉS WITH CITRUS-FENNEL SALAD, 33

CRUNCHY HONEY LAVENDER ALMONDS, 35

GRILLED CHICKEN AND CARAMELIZED PEAR SALAD, 38

SPICED HONEY-BAKED HAM, 39

SAGE-BUTTER-ROASTED TURKEY, 40

PAN-ROASTED TURKEY BREAST WITH SWEET SQUASH MATCHSTICKS, 44

WOOD-GRILLED TURKEY CHOP WITH WILD MUSHROOM GRAVY, 47

RED CURRY TURKEY SCALOPPINI, 49

LEFTOVER TURKEY HASH, 52

BRAISED SHORT RIBS WITH ONIONS AND SUGAR PUMPKIN, 53

WOOD-GRILLED BUTTERFLIED LEG OF LAMB, 54

GRILLED SPICY SOLE FILLETS, 55

BRAISED NAPA CABBAGE WITH APPLE AND BACON, 57

BUTTERED BRUSSELS SPROUTS AND CHESTNUTS, 58

BUTTERNUT SQUASH GRATIN, 60

CELERY ROOT AND PEAR PURÉE, 61

CHESTNUT AND OYSTER GRATIN, 62

GRILLED CORN WITH ROASTED PEPPER BUTTER, 63

CORN AND SAGE STUFFING, 65

KUMAMOTO OYSTER AND SAUSAGE STUFFING, 66

MASHED RED POTATOES WITH GARLIC, 67

SWEET POTATO GRATIN, 68

WINTER PANZANELLA, 70

CORNBREAD, 74

CRANBERRY SCONES WITH ORANGE GLAZE, 75

DILL BUTTERMILK DROP BISCUITS, 76

PERSIMMON BREAD, 77

APPLE CRUMB PIE, 80

BUTTERMILK ICE CREAM, 81

CLASSIC PUMPKIN PIE, 83

THREE-LAYER PUMPKIN PIE, 84

PERSIMMON WALNUT UPSIDE-DOWN CAKE, 87

SOUR CREAM PIECRUST, 89

CITRUS-CRANBERRY GLAZE, 90

CHIMICHURRI, 91

JELLIED CRANBERRY SAUCE, 93

RED ONION AND TOMATO RELISH, 94

SPICY GLAZED WALNUTS, 95

LEMON-THYME-MUSTARD BUTTER, 96

LEMON-BASIL VINAIGRETTE, 96

TURKEY GRAVY, 97

ONION-BOURBON-HORSERADISH MUSTARD, 98

CORN STOCK, 99

LOBSTER STOCK, 100

TURKEY OR CHICKEN STOCK, 101

SETTING THE HOLIDAY TABLE

DECK THE HALLS AND THE HOLIDAY TABLE WITH THE RIGHT DECORATIONS to make any holiday meal even more appetizing. A simple yet stunning centerpiece, candles, and the proper flatware are all you need to festively adorn your table.

1. I like to use a simple white tablecloth with a contrasting placemat. Use name cards for a sophisticated formal touch.

2. The simplest ideas are the best ones, especially with all you have to do during the holidays, so take a minimalist approach to flowers for your table. Instead of doing an arrangement of different flowers, which can be difficult, pick one type of flower and do a large mass of them. It will look dramatic yet understated. Or, pick one color scheme, like orange, and mix all types of flowers with the same hue. Another idea is to mix bunches of herbs in with the flowers: sage imparts the perfect color and aroma during the fall. Try mint in the spring and basil in the summer. For a modern approach, place single flowers in small vases and arrange the vases in the center or down the table. A clear vase filled with colored Christmas ornamental bulbs also makes a nice centerpiece.

3. Don't forget vibrant and aromatic seasonal fruits and vegetables. Use them whole and uncooked to garnish holiday platters or to grace ornamental fruit bowls. Fruit arrangements can be stunning and made in lieu of or in combination with flowers. Try floating flowers in a bowl of water with sliced or whole seasonal fruits, such as kumquats and cranberries during the fall and winter, or strawberries and blueberries during the spring and summer. Harvest corn and seasonal gourds like pumpkins and squash also make colorful and festive harvest baskets, perfect for any traditional table centerpiece. For a contemporary look, use squash in the same hue, like pale green; coat the squash with a shiny layer of lacquer for added vibrance and place in dark brown bowls. Offset the centerpiece with white table linens and china.

4. Candles—from large decorative sconces to small tea lights—create instant atmosphere. Let the flame sparkle against your fine crystal or clear glass creating an ethereal and intimate atmosphere. For a clean modern look, fill a small glass vase or bowl with water and float a small candle, cranberries, and sliced kumquats in it.

5. Use your best silverware or simple silver cutlery. Remember to lay out all the proper flatware for the courses you plan to serve. Always place the utensil one will use first furthest from the plate, such as an appetizer fork or soup spoon. Lay the forks on the left side of the plate: first the appetizer fork, then the salad fork, and last the entrée fork, closest to the plate. The knife, with the

sharp edge facing towards the plate, fish knife, and soup spoon are set to the right of the plate, in that order from left to right. Dessert forks and spoons go at the top of the plate. And don't forget the butter knife, which lies atop the bread plate, blade facing the center of the bread plate, above the forks on the left. Drinks go above the knives to the right of the plate.

6. Place a nice folded linen napkin neatly to the left of the forks for formal occasions or on top of the plate for less formal gatherings.

APPLE JUICE *with* CRANBERRY *and* GINGER

*L*EMON BALM IS A PLANT FROM THE MINT FAMILY AND HAS A PLEASANT LEMON aroma. You can use either fresh or dried for this recipe. If you can, try pressing your own apple juice from either Pippin or Granny Smith apples—it really does make a difference in the flavor.

MAKES 4 TO 6 SERVINGS

1 Granny Smith apple

12 whole cloves

6 cups apple juice

1 (12-ounce) package fresh cranberries (about 3 cups)

$\frac{1}{2}$-inch piece fresh ginger, cut in half

$\frac{1}{4}$ cup maple syrup

1 teaspoon chopped fresh lemon balm, plus additional sprigs for garnish, or $\frac{1}{2}$ teaspoon dried, or 1 teaspoon grated lemon zest and 1 teaspoon finely chopped fresh mint

1 orange, sliced

2 lemons, 1 thinly sliced, 1 for garnish

STUD APPLE WITH THE CLOVES. In a large saucepan over high heat, combine all ingredients except garnishes and bring to a boil. Reduce the heat to low and simmer for 15 minutes. Pour the liquid through a fine-mesh sieve into a large pitcher. Serve hot in glass mugs garnished with a lemon twist and a sprig of lemon balm or mint.

HOT MULLED CIDER

A SIMPLE YET DELIGHTFULLY SPICED HOLIDAY DRINK. FOR EXTRA FESTIVE cheer, add your favorite brandy or rum.

6 cups apple cider

1 (16-ounce) package fresh cranberries (about 4 cups)

8 lemons, thinly sliced

8 oranges, thinly sliced

20 whole cloves

8 sticks cinnamon

1 cup granulated sugar

½ teaspoon vanilla extract (optional)

IN A LARGE SAUCEPAN OVER MEDIUM-HIGH HEAT, combine all of the ingredients except the vanilla and bring to a boil. Reduce the heat to medium low and simmer for 10 minutes. Turn off the heat and let the mixture steep until cooled to room temperature. Strain the mixture through a fine-mesh sieve; add the vanilla, if using. Serve warm.

SPARKLING PEAR PUNCH

THIS FESTIVE PUNCH WILL SET THE MOOD FOR EITHER A FORMAL OR casual holiday party. Red Bartlett pears add a stunning pink blush and champagne adds effervescence and elegance. Anjou pears or yellow Bartletts can be substituted for the red pears. Try adding a handful of crushed or whole pomegranate seeds or a couple of Clementine slices to the recipe as a variation for additional flavor or color.

SPICED SIMPLE SYRUP

3 whole cloves

2 star anise

$1/2$ teaspoon whole allspice berries

$1/2$ cup granulated sugar

$1/2$ vanilla bean, split and scraped, or $1/8$ teaspoon vanilla extract

PUNCH

2 (750-millileter) bottles Champagne or sparkling wine

5 Red Bartlett pears, 4 cut into 8 wedges, 1 sliced for garnish

2 blood oranges, cut into segments and chopped (about 1 cup)

2 lemons, sliced

3 Gala apples, cored and cut into 8 wedges

1 cup kumquats, washed and sliced

$1/2$ cup Spiced Simple Syrup (recipe above)

$1/2$ cup brandy

$1/4$ cup orange flavored liquor, such as Cointreau or triple sec

12 mint leaves, plus more for garnish

2-inch piece fresh ginger, peeled and thinly sliced

FOR THE SPICED SIMPLE SYRUP: In a small saucepan over medium-high heat, toast the cloves, star anise, and allspice until dark brown and fragrant. Add sugar, vanilla bean, and $1/2$ cup of water; bring to a boil. Reduce the heat and simmer for 8 minutes. Let the mixture cool to room temperature, then pass through a fine-mesh strainer. Set aside until needed; this syrup can be made ahead and refrigerated for up to one month.

FOR THE PUNCH: In a glass pitcher, combine all ingredients except garnishes; refrigerate for at least 1 hour or up to one day. Before serving, stir briskly to distribute the settled fruit and pulp and serve immediately over ice. Garnish with additional slices of pear and a mint sprig.

CHILLED APPLE SOUP *with* LOBSTER SALAD

*E*NJOY THIS ELEGANT, LIGHT, AND REFRESHING SOUP WITH A SLICE OF toasted brioche.

4 pounds Gravenstein or Granny Smith apples (about 8 large), cored and quartered

2 teaspoons chopped fresh ginger

1 tablespoon freshly squeezed lemon juice

$1/8$ teaspoon salt

1 recipe Lobster Salad (page 26)

$1/4$ cup finely chopped celery leaves, for garnish

PLACE HALF THE APPLES AND GINGER into a food processor and purée until very smooth. Pass mixture through a fine-mesh strainer into a bowl. Repeat with the remaining apples and ginger. Add the lemon juice and salt to the mixture. Cover with plastic wrap and place in the refrigerator until cold.

Place half a cup of lobster salad in the center of a soup bowl and pour $1/2$ cup of soup around the lobster. Sprinkle with 1 tablespoon of celery leaves.

Wine pairing: Chardonnay

SHELLFISH CHOWDER

*T*HIS CREAMY SOUP IS REMINISCENT OF MICHIGAN FISH BOILS. I'VE MADE this soup a bit lighter than the chowders of my childhood, which allows the shellfish and flavor to really shine. Serve with Dill Buttermilk Drop Biscuits (page 76).

MAKES 6 SERVINGS

3 tablespoons finely chopped salt pork, rind removed

2 strips bacon, finely chopped (about $1/4$ cup)

2 medium yellow onions, chopped (about 2 cups)

4 stalks celery, chopped (about $1^1/2$ cups)

2 teaspoons chopped fresh thyme

$1/2$ bay leaf

3 tablespoons all-purpose flour

4 cups lobster or crab stock (page 100), or bottled clam juice

$1^1/4$ cups heavy cream or half-and-half

$3/4$ cup whole milk

4 medium red potatoes, cooked, peeled, and diced (about 2 cups)

$1/8$ teaspoon cayenne pepper

1 teaspoon freshly ground black pepper

Kosher salt

1 teaspoon dry sherry

Tabasco, to taste

$1^1/2$ cups chopped cooked clams, crabmeat, and lobster

2 tablespoons chopped flat-leaf parsley, for garnish

4 teaspoons unsalted butter, cut into $1/2$ teaspoon portions, for garnish

IN A LARGE DUTCH OVEN OVER MEDIUM HEAT, cook the salt pork and bacon until golden brown and crisp, about 3 minutes. Add the onions, celery, thyme, and bay leaf. Cover and cook, stirring occasionally, for 4 minutes.

Add the flour and cook, stirring often, until the flour is lightly browned, about 3 minutes. Slowly add the stock, stirring constantly to avoid lumps, and simmer for 5 minutes. Add the cream and milk and cook for another 5 minutes.

Add the potatoes, cayenne pepper, and pepper. Taste the soup for seasoning; add the salt only if needed. (Chowder may be prepared in advance up to this point; if not serving immediately, cool and refrigerate.)

Add the sherry and Tabasco to taste. Add the shellfish and stir to combine. Ladle the soup into bowls and garnish each serving with chopped parsley and $1/2$ teaspoon of butter.

NOTE: For clam chowder, garnish with three steamed clams per serving. For lobster-corn chowder, use only one cup of potatoes and add $1^1/2$ cups grilled or blanched corn kernels to the soup.

Wine pairing: Chardonnay

ROASTED HARVEST SQUASH SOUP

*T*HIS VELVETY SOUP STRIKES THE PERFECT BALANCE BETWEEN NUTTINESS and sweetness. Roasting the squash before adding it to the soup creates an intensely sweet and rich squash flavor.

¹/₄ teaspoon freshly grated nutmeg

¹/₄ teaspoon freshly ground allspice

1 teaspoon kosher salt

1 teaspoon freshly ground black pepper

8 tablespoons (1 stick) unsalted butter, divided, 6 tablespoons melted, 2 tablespoons reserved

2 tablespoons honey

4 Granny Smith apples, cored and cut into ¹/₂-inch pieces

2 lemons, juiced

¹/₂ cup apple juice

3 pounds butternut, acorn, or delicata squash

2 medium leeks (white part only), chopped (about 2 cups)

2 medium yellow onions, chopped (about 2 cups)

5 cups vegetable stock (page 193)

1 teaspoon grated fresh ginger

¹/₃ cup crème fraîche, for garnish

ADJUST AN OVEN RACK TO THE MIDDLE POSITION and heat the oven to 400°F.

In a small bowl, combine the nutmeg, allspice, salt, pepper, melted butter, and honey; mix well. In a separate bowl, mix the apples, lemon juice, and apple juice; toss to coat.

Cut the squash in half; remove any seeds with a spoon. Coat each cavity with the reserved spice mixture and fill each cavity with half of the apple mixture. Transfer the squash to a roasting pan, skin-side down, and bake, basting occasionally with the cooking juices, until the squash are tender and a paring knife can be easily inserted, about 1 hour. (The squash should have patches of brown spots for the best flavor.) Remove from the oven and let cool enough to handle.

Using a metal spoon, scrape out the cooked squash into a bowl; set aside. Melt the reserved butter in a large saucepan over medium heat. Add the leeks, onions, and remaining apple mixture and cook, stirring occasionally, until the onions are tender and translucent, about 15 minutes. Add the squash, stock, and ginger; bring to a simmer, and cook for 25 minutes. Remove from the heat and let the soup cool slightly, about 10 minutes.

Using a food processor, purée the soup in batches until very smooth. (Pass the purée through a fine-mesh sieve if a smoother soup is desired.) Season with salt and pepper to taste. Ladle into soup bowls, dollop crème fraîche over the top, and serve.

NOTE: Soup can be made three days ahead or frozen for up to one month.

ENDIVE SALAD *with* TANGERINES *and* KUMQUATS

A WONDERFUL USE OF WINTER CITRUS FRUITS, THIS CRISPY, SWEET, AND TART salad is delectable and colorful. Be sure to use good olive oil for the unembellished dressing.

MAKES 6 SERVINGS

6 heads Belgian endive, outer wilted leaves removed

1 tablespoon freshly squeezed lemon juice

6 tablespoons extra-virgin olive oil

$1/2$ teaspoon kosher salt

$1/4$ teaspoon freshly ground black pepper

6 tangerines, peeled and cut into $1/4$-inch slices

18 kumquats, washed and cut into $1/8$-inch slices

TRIM THE ENDS OFF THE ENDIVE and separate the leaves.

In a medium bowl, mix the lemon juice, oil, salt, and pepper. Add the endive leaves and toss to coat. Arrange the leaves equally on six salad plates, top with tangerine slices, and sprinkle with the kumquats. Serve immediately.

LOBSTER SALAD

 THIS VERSATILE SALAD CAN BE SPREAD OVER TOASTED BRIOCHE FOR A sandwich, placed atop mixed greens for a salad, or added to the Chilled Apple Soup with Lobster Salad (page 22). Shrimp, crawfish, or Dungeness crab can be substituted for the lobster.

MAKES 1$1/2$ CUPS

8 ounces cooked lobster meat, cut into $1/2$-inch pieces

$1/4$ cup minced Granny Smith apple

$1/4$ cup finely chopped chives

$1/4$ cup crème fraîche or sour cream

1 lemon, zest grated and juiced

Freshly ground black pepper

Kosher salt

COMBINE ALL INGREDIENTS IN A LARGE BOWL. Gently mix together; season with salt and pepper to taste. Refrigerate until needed.

Wine Pairing: Chardonnay

GREEN BEAN *and* PERSIMMON SALAD

TENDER GREEN BEANS AND SWEET PERSIMMONS MAKE A DELICIOUS AND colorful salad to adorn your holiday table.

1 pound green beans, ends trimmed, cut into 1-inch pieces

$1/2$ pound yellow wax beans

1 tablespoon plus 1 teaspoon kosher salt, divided, plus more to taste

$1/4$ cup plus 2 tablespoons extra-virgin olive oil, divided

$1/4$ teaspoon freshly ground black pepper, plus more to taste

2 Fuyu persimmons, thinly sliced

2 medium tomatoes, peeled, seeded, and chopped (about 1 cup)

1 small cucumber, chopped (about 1 cup)

1 small red onion, finely chopped (about $1/2$ cup)

1 small garlic clove, finely chopped (about $1/2$ teaspoon)

$1/4$ cup chopped fresh basil

3 tablespoons balsamic vinegar

2 tablespoons freshly squeezed lemon juice

BRING 10 CUPS OF WATER TO A BOIL in a medium saucepan over high heat; add 1 tablespoon of salt and the beans, return to a boil and cook until the green beans are bright green and both beans are both crisp-tender, 2 to 3 minutes. Drain the beans and transfer them immediately to a large bowl filled with ice water. When the beans have cooled to room temperature, drain again and dry thoroughly with paper towels. Place in a large bowl; toss with 2 tablespoons of the oil, and salt and pepper, to taste; set aside.

Combine the persimmon, tomato, cucumber, onion, garlic, and basil in a medium bowl. Add the remaining $1/4$ cup of oil, vinegar, lemon juice, salt, and pepper. Toss to coat. Set aside for 10 minutes.

To serve, arrange a serving of the beans on a plate; spoon $1/2$ cup of the persimmon mixture over the top.

ROASTED PEAR *and* GOAT CHEESE SALAD

A WONDERFULLY ELEGANT HOLIDAY SALAD. YOU CAN SUBSTITUTE BLUE cheese for the goat cheese or add dried cranberries and toasted pine nuts to the stuffing for a more robust flavor.

CRANBERRY-ORANGE VINAIGRETTE

$1\frac{1}{2}$ cups fresh cranberries

$\frac{1}{4}$ cup granulated sugar

2 tablespoons cider vinegar

$\frac{1}{8}$ teaspoon kosher salt

1 large orange, segmented and chopped (about $\frac{1}{2}$ cup)

ROASTED PEAR AND GOAT CHEESE SALAD

2 ounces goat cheese (about 4 tablespoons)

1 ounce mascarpone cheese (about 2 tablespoons)

$\frac{1}{2}$ teaspoon white balsamic vinegar

$3\frac{1}{2}$ teaspoons freshly squeezed lemon juice, divided

$\frac{1}{2}$ teaspoon kosher salt, divided

2 Anjou pears, halved, stemmed, and cored

1 tablespoon melted butter

1 tablespoon granulated sugar

1 tablespoon honey, melted

$\frac{1}{2}$ teaspoon kosher salt

$\frac{1}{4}$ teaspoon freshly ground black pepper

2 tablespoons extra-virgin olive oil

4 small heads Bibb lettuce

24 Crunchy Honey Lavender Almonds (page 35)

FOR THE VINAIGRETTE: Place all vinaigrette ingredients, except the orange segments, plus $\frac{3}{4}$ cup of water, in a medium saucepan over medium heat. Cover and cook, stirring occasionally, until the cranberries pop, about 10 minutes. Lightly crush the cranberries with the back of a fork so the vinaigrette is thin and has small bits of cranberries throughout. Let cool to room temperature. Add the orange segments and set aside.

FOR THE SALAD: Adjust an oven rack to the middle position and preheat the oven to 350°F.

In a small bowl, mix together the goat cheese, mascarpone, vinegar, $\frac{1}{2}$ teaspoon of lemon juice, and $\frac{1}{4}$ teaspoon of salt until well combined; set aside.

Place the pears in a small baking dish with the remaining 3 teaspoons of lemon juice, sugar, honey, butter, cracked pepper, and $\frac{1}{4}$ teaspoon of salt; toss to coat. Bake pears, turning them often, until slightly tender and a knife can be inserted with slight resistance. Remove from the oven.

Preheat the broiler. Place 1 tablespoon of the cheese mixture into the cavity of the pears. Lay the pears cheese-side up in the baking dish; sprinkle with the ground pepper and drizzle with the olive oil. Broil until cheese begins to melt, about 1 minute. Remove from broiler and set aside.

For each serving, place the leaves from one head of lettuce on a salad plate in a blooming flower formation, drizzle with $\frac{1}{4}$ cup of the dressing, top with a pear half, and sprinkle with 6 almonds. Repeat with the remaining lettuce.

YANKEE SALAD *with* APPLE, WALNUTS, *and* BLUE CHEESE

*I*ABSOLUTELY LOVE THE COMBINATION OF SWEET, CRISP APPLES, TART, crunchy walnuts, and salty, creamy blue cheese. You will certainly love this combination in this salad too.

5 ounces Maytag blue cheese (about 1 cup), crumbled

1 large head romaine lettuce, sliced

1 small head radicchio, sliced

2 medium Granny Smith or Fuji apples, cored and cut into ½-inch dice

1 tablespoon freshly squeezed lemon juice

1 cup Spicy Glazed Walnuts (page 95)

½ cup Lemon-Basil Vinaigrette (page 96)

Freshly ground black pepper

Kosher salt

IN A LARGE BOWL, combine the cheese, romaine, radicchio, apples, lemon juice, and walnuts. Drizzle about ½ cup of the dressing over the salad and gently toss to coat evenly. Adjust seasonings to taste. Serve immediately.

CORN *and* SHRIMP FRITTERS

*T*HESE CORN FRITTERS ARE LIGHT AND CREAMY INSIDE AND CRISP ON THE outside. The Louis Dressing is a great recipe to dress up a plain shrimp cocktail.

MAKES 2 DOZEN FRITTERS • MAKES ABOUT 3 CUPS OF LOUIS DRESSING

FRITTERS

10 ounces shrimp

3 ears corn, cleaned

2 tablespoons cornstarch

2 tablespoons all-purpose flour

1 teaspoon baking powder

1/2 teaspoon kosher salt

1/4 teaspoon freshly ground black pepper

1/8 teaspoon cayenne pepper

1/4 cup beer

1 large egg yolk

1 tablespoon finely chopped serrano chile

1/4 cup finely chopped chives

1/4 cup sliced scallions (mostly white parts)

1/4 cup vegetable oil

LOUIS DRESSING

1 cup cocktail sauce

1 cup mayonnaise

1/2 cup finely chopped celery hearts and leaves

1/4 cup finely chopped cornichons

1/4 cup finely sliced scallions

2 tablespoons finely chopped chives

2 tablespoons finely chopped flat-leaf parsley

1 1/2 teaspoons freshly squeezed lemon juice

1/8 teaspoon cayenne pepper

PEEL AND DEVEIN THE SHRIMP and cut into 1/2-inch pieces. You should have about one cup set aside. Stand the corn upright inside a large bowl and, using a paring knife, carefully cut the kernels from the cob, then use the back of a butter knife to scrape off any pulp remaining on the cobs; you should have about 1 1/2 cups of corn and pulp. Set aside. In a medium bowl, sift together the cornstarch, flour, baking powder, salt, pepper, and cayenne. In a separate large bowl, whisk together the beer, egg yolk, and chile; stir in the corn, shrimp, chives, and scallions. Fold the flour mixture into the beer mixture, just until a thick batter has formed.

Add 1/4-inch of vegetable oil to a large skillet over medium heat. When the oil is almost smoking, drop heaping tablespoons of the batter into the oil. Fry until golden brown on one side, about 1 minute; flip the fritters and fry on the second side until golden brown, about 1 minute longer. Transfer the fritters to a paper towel–lined plate; sprinkle with salt and pepper to taste. Repeat with the remaining batter, adding more oil to the skillet if necessary. Serve immediately.

FOR THE DRESSING: Combine all of the ingredients in a medium bowl; mix well. Season with salt and pepper to taste.

Wine pairing: Gewürztraminer, Sauvignon Blanc

TWICE-BAKED BLUE CHEESE SOUFFLÉS
with CITRUS-FENNEL SALAD

THESE ARE A FAVORITE APPETIZER AT THE RESTAURANT I WORK AT IN Solvang, California. Use a good-quality blue cheese like Maytag. To save time in the kitchen, prepare the soufflés several days in advance; on the day of, all you will need to do is finish them in the oven when you are ready to serve. To round out the flavor, serve with the Citrus-Cranberry Glaze (page 90) drizzled over the top of the soufflés.

MAKES 6 INDIVIDUAL SOUFFLÉS

CITRUS-FENNEL SALAD

1 ½ cup fresh squeezed tangelo juice

¼ cup balsamic vinegar

¼ teaspoon kosher salt

¼ teaspoon freshly ground black pepper

2 tangelos, zested, peeled and sliced into segments

1 blood orange, peeled and sliced into segments

1 cup very thinly sliced fennel

1 cup watercress

BLUE CHEESE SOUFFLÉS

3 tablespoons unsalted butter, softened, divided

3 tablespoons all-purpose flour

1 cup whole milk

6 ounces blue cheese, crumbled, at room temperature

3 large eggs, yolks and whites separated

1 teaspoon kosher salt

½ teaspoon freshly ground black pepper

¾ cup heavy cream

FOR THE SALAD: Combine the zest, tangelo juice, and balsamic vinegar in a non-corrosive saucepan. Place over high heat and reduce until it coats the back of the spoon. Season with the salt and pepper and place in the refrigerator to chill. In a bowl combine the tangelo and orange segments, fennel, and watercress. Season with salt and pepper to taste and set aside. (When ready to serve drizzle the dressing on the side of the bowl and gently toss the salad until the greens are lightly coated.)

FOR THE SOUFFLÉS: Adjust an oven rack to the middle position and heat the oven to 280°F. If using a convection oven, preheat to 250°F. Line a baking sheet with parchment paper; set aside.

Grease 6 4-ounce soufflé ramekins with 1 tablespoon of the butter. Melt the remaining 2 tablespoons of butter in a small saucepan over medium-low heat. Add the flour, stirring constantly with a wooden spoon until mixture is light gold, about 3 minutes. Slowly add the milk while whisking; reduce the heat to low and simmer for 8 minutes.

Transfer the sauce to a stand mixer; add the blue cheese. Using the whisk attachment on low speed, beat the mixture until combined. With mixer off, let the mixture cool for 10 minutes (so you don't cook the eggs when they are added).

(continued)

With the mixer on high, add the salt and pepper and then the egg yolks, one at a time, until incorporated. Transfer the mixture to a medium bowl, cover, and cool to room temperature.

In the stand mixer fitted with the whisk attachment, whip the egg whites on high speed until soft peaks form. Using a rubber spatula, immediately stir one-quarter of the beaten whites into the reserved cheese mixture until almost no white streaks remain. Gently fold in the remaining whites until the mixture is just combined.

Pour the mixture into the prepared ramekins, filling them all the way to the top. Place the ramekins in a larger pan lined with a kitchen towel. Carefully place the pan on the oven rack and fill the pan with enough hot water to reach two-thirds of the way up the side of the ramekins, taking care not to splash water into the soufflés. Bake until the center is set, 35 to 40 minutes. Remove the soufflés from the oven; let cool to room temperature.

Gently unmold the soufflés and place them onto buttered parchment paper, top side up. Cover loosely and refrigerate until needed. (Soufflés can be held in the refrigerator at this point for up to three days.)

Adjust an oven rack to the middle position and heat the oven to 400°F.

Pour the heavy cream into a medium, ovenproof saucepan; add the soufflés, right side up, and place over high heat. Bring cream to a boil; transfer the pan into the oven. Bake until the soufflés have risen and absorbed most of the cream, about 8 minutes. Remove from the oven. Gently remove the soufflés from the pan. Arrange on a plate with the Citrus-Fennel Salad. Serve immediately.

CRUNCHY HONEY LAVENDER ALMONDS

*H*ONEY AND LAVENDER ARE AN EXCELLENT FLAVOR COMBINATION. THESE sweet and aromatic nuts are great served as a snack or on a cheese platter. Sprinkle them over the Roasted Pear and Goat Cheese Salad (page 28) for an unforgettable and flavorful holiday salad or give them as a thoughtful hostess gift.

MAKES 1 CUP

$\frac{1}{2}$ cup granulated sugar

$\frac{1}{4}$ teaspoon kosher salt

$\frac{1}{4}$ teaspoon freshly ground black pepper

3 tablespoons honey

2 tablespoons unsalted butter

$\frac{1}{8}$ teaspoon cayenne pepper

1 cup whole almonds

2 tablespoons finely chopped fresh lavender

ADJUST AN OVEN RACK TO THE MIDDLE POSITION and heat the oven to 350°F. Line a rimmed baking sheet with parchment paper.

Bring the sugar, 1/4 cup of water, salt, pepper, honey, butter, and cayenne to a boil in a medium saucepan over medium-high heat. Stir in the almonds and lavender and cook, stirring constantly with a wooden spoon, until the almonds are completely coated and the sugar has begun to lightly caramelize, about 3 minutes. Transfer the glazed almonds to the baking sheet and bake in the oven until fragrant and lightly browned, about 10 minutes. Transfer the pan to a cooling rack and let the nuts cool completely, in the pan, before serving, or place them in a tightly sealed container until needed.

NOTE: Nuts will keep for two weeks at room temperature.

CHEFS' FOOLPROOF TECHNIQUES:
USING A DOUBLE BOILER AND BAIN-MARIE

THERE ARE TWO COOKING TECHNIQUES I USE OFTEN IN THIS BOOK: A DOUBLE boiler and bain-marie. Here is an in-depth explanation of each technique and its function, explained as simply as possible.

DOUBLE BOILER

While double boilers are sometimes marketed as specialized equipment in stores, no fancy equipment is necessary to assemble a double boiler at home. To create one, just place a thick glass bowl over a pot of simmering water. This ubiquitous chefs' technique is used to prevent the scorching of certain foods since the items in the glass bowl, such as chocolate or custards, are exposed to hot steam rather than direct flames. Gentle heat from the steam will ensure your custards and chocolate do not curdle, scorch, or burn. The key is to not let the bottom of the glass bowl touch the water—the hot steam heats the bowl, not the boiling water. The bottom of the bowl should barely fit inside the pot and form a seal around the pot's rim. This creates a lid so the steam remains in the pot and gently heats the bowl. Take care when touching the bowl, as it does get very hot. I like to use a glass bowl as opposed to metal, since glass heats more evenly. If you must use a metal bowl, be sure to stir constantly to avoid hot spots.

BAIN-MARIE

The other chefs' technique is the use of a bain-marie, or water bath. To create a water bath, carefully place your baking dish or ramekins inside a larger pan lined with a kitchen towel. Move the pan into the oven and fill the larger pan with enough hot water to reach two-thirds of the way up the side of interior dishes. This method prevents food from burning and also creates a moist cooking environment with the steam that rises from the water during baking. This ensures your puddings, custards, or breads come out evenly cooked and very moist. Placing a kitchen towel in the large pan prevents the baking dish or ramekins from sliding about as you move the water bath from the counter to the oven. Also, be sure to fill the water bath after you have placed your items in the pan; doing the opposite order could result in your water bath being too deep and overflowing into your ramekins.

GRILLED CHICKEN *and* CARAMELIZED PEAR SALAD

THIS SALAD IS BOTH LIGHT AND RICH, WITH A TANTALIZING ZING. SALTY AND creamy chunks of cheese complement the sweetness of the pears and cool snap of the grapes. This appetizing salad can served without the chicken for vegetarians.

MAKES 4 SERVINGS

---

4 chicken breasts with wing bone attached (about 7 ounces each)

1 lemon, zest grated

¼ cup extra-virgin olive oil, divided

2 teaspoons kosher salt

1 teaspoon freshly ground black pepper

½ cup dried cranberries

3 tablespoons finely chopped fresh basil

2 tablespoons freshly squeezed lemon juice

2 tablespoons unsalted butter

2 Bartlett pears, halved, cored, and cut lengthwise into ½-inch-thick slices

¾ cup champagne or red grapes, halved and seeded

4 ounces feta or pecorino cheese, coarsely chopped

4 ounces baby spinach, arugula, red leaf lettuce, or mustard greens

Edible flowers, such as nasturtium or borage, for garnish (optional)

PREPARE AN OUTDOOR GRILL. Rub the chicken breasts with lemon zest, 2 tablespoons of the olive oil, the salt and pepper; set aside. In a small bowl, combine the cranberries, basil, lemon juice, and the remaining 2 tablespoons of olive oil; adjust seasonings to taste. Set aside.

Grill the chicken until golden brown and thickest part of the chicken registers 140°F on an instant-read thermometer, 7 to 8 minutes on each side. Remove from the grill, cover with foil, and let rest for 10 minutes.

While the chicken is resting, melt the butter in a large skillet over a high heat. Add the pears; cook, stirring occasionally, until golden brown and slightly softened, about 3 minutes. Transfer the pears to a large bowl. Add the grapes, feta, spinach, and reserved dressing to the bowl; toss to combine. Divide equally between four plates. Remove the chicken breast from the bones and cut the meat into three slices. Arrange over the salad, garnish with flowers if using, and serve.

Wine pairing: Sauvignon Blanc

SPICED HONEY-BAKED HAM

WARM SPICES PERFUME THIS ULTRA-FLAVORFUL AND MOIST HOLIDAY HAM, which was featured on *The Best Thing I Ever Ate*. The wonderfully sweet and aromatic pan drippings make a perfect spiced sauce for the Mashed Red Potatoes with Garlic (page 67). Make sure to serve the Onion-Bourbon-Horseradish Mustard as an accompaniment (page 98).

MAKES 6 TO 8 SERVINGS

6 star anise

6 cardamom pods

3 sticks cinnamon

2 teaspoons whole allspice berries

2 teaspoons whole cloves

1 cup Dijon mustard

1 cup lightly packed golden brown sugar

1 cup honey

1 tablespoon grated fresh ginger

1 tablespoon kosher salt

1 tablespoon freshly ground black pepper

$\frac{1}{4}$ teaspoon cayenne pepper

1 (8-pound) pork butt, skinless

4 cups citrus-flavored soda

4 cups apple cider

$\frac{1}{2}$ pineapple, rind removed, cored, and cut into $\frac{1}{2}$-inch-thick rings

ADJUST AN OVEN RACK TO THE MIDDLE POSITION and heat the oven to 275°F.

Place the star anise, cinnamon, cardamom, allspice, and cloves in a small saucepan over medium heat. Cook until lightly toasted and fragrant, about 5 minutes. Set aside.

In a medium bowl combine the mustard, brown sugar, honey, ginger, salt, pepper, and cayenne. Mix until a smooth paste forms; set aside.

With a serrated knife, carefully slice through the skin and fat of the ham, scoring it to make a 1-inch diamond pattern. Be careful not to cut into the meat. Place the ham skin-side up into a large roasting pan. Pour the soda and cider over the ham. Rub the prepared sugar paste on top of the ham and into the grooves of the scored fat and skin. Sprinkle the toasted spices over the ham and place pineapple slices on top and around the pork; place in the oven.

Bake the ham, basting every 15 minutes, until the center registers 150°F on an instant-read thermometer, $2\frac{1}{2}$ to 3 hours. Remove from the oven and tent the ham loosely with foil; let stand until the center of the ham registers 155°F, about 10 minutes.

To serve, slice the meat against the grain. The grain can be difficult to determine since the pork butt consists of different muscles groups—do your best to find a direction that yields the most attractive slices, even if it means turning the meat and trying again.

Wine pairing: brut sparkling wine

SAGE-BUTTER-ROASTED TURKEY

COOKING A TURKEY BREAST-SIDE DOWN MAY SEEM ODD, BUT IT ALLOWS THE dark meat to get a head start in the cooking process. This method also ensures the breast meat will not overcook. Placing a flavorful herbed butter under the skin permeates the meat with earthy sage flavor and helps keep it moist.

MAKES 12 SERVINGS

- 8 ounces (2 sticks) unsalted butter, softened, plus 6 tablespoons, melted, divided
- 3 tablespoons finely chopped fresh sage
- 2 tablespoons Dijon mustard
- 2 lemons, zest grated and juiced
- 2 teaspoons kosher salt, divided
- 2 teaspoons freshly ground black pepper, divided
- 1 (12- to 14-pound) young turkey, giblets, neck, and tail-piece removed and reserved for gravy (page 97)
- 2 medium yellow onions, chopped (about 2 cups)
- 3 medium carrots, chopped (about 2 cups)

ADJUST AN OVEN RACK TO THE LOWEST POSITION and heat the oven to 500°F.

In a medium bowl, mix together the 2 sticks of softened butter, sage, mustard, lemon juice, lemon zest, 1 teaspoon of salt, and 1 teaspoon of pepper; set aside. Rinse the turkey under cold water and thoroughly pat dry. Carefully separate the turkey skin from the meat on the breast, legs, and thighs; avoid breaking the skin. Rub half of the sage butter inside the cavity of the turkey and sprinkle with the remaining teaspoon of the salt and pepper. Evenly spread the rest of the sage butter under the skin of each breast half and under the skin of each leg. Tuck the tips of the drumsticks into the skin at the tail to secure; tuck the wings under the bird. Brush the turkey breast with 2 tablespoons of the melted butter. Scatter the vegetables into the roasting pan and pour 1 cup of water over them. Place a V-shaped roasting rack over the vegetables and put the turkey, breast-side down, onto the rack. Brush the back of the turkey with 2 tablespoons of the melted butter.

Roast the turkey for 25 minutes. Remove the pan from the oven, close the oven door to retain the heat, and reduce the oven temperature to 275°F. With a dish towel protecting each hand, rotate the turkey and place on rack breast-side up. Return to oven and continue to roast, basting every 30 minutes with the remaining 2 tablespoons of melted butter and the juices from the bottom of the pan (add more water if necessary), until the thickest part of the breast registers 160°F to 165°F and the thickest part of the thigh registers 175°F on an instant-read thermometer, about $2\frac{1}{2}$ to 3 hours longer. Transfer the turkey to a carving board and let rest, uncovered, for 30 minutes. See sidebar on how to carve a turkey (page 50).

A SPECIAL NOTE ON TURKEY

*T*HERE ARE MANY VARIETIES OF AVAILABLE TURKEYS AT THE MARKET THESE DAYS; some have labels declaring the turkeys are basted, kosher, or natural. "Basted" simply means the turkeys have been injected with a solution intended to make them more flavorful and tender. It could be a salty turkey stock or something as dubious as artificial flavors and fillers. It would be best not to purchase these turkeys.

Kosher turkeys are minimally processed but, in my experience, tend to be tough and a little dry. Avoid these birds too.

"Natural" turkeys are untreated fresh turkeys. This broad category includes free-range birds on small organic farms as well as birds raised in large commercial enterprises that are neither organic nor free-range. I recommend fresh natural, organic, free-range turkeys, from small regional producers, as they will have the best texture and flavor.

Now that you have purchased the best turkey, follow these five rules to ensure the best flavor and texture:

1. Use a V-shaped roasting rack. It's important for two reasons. First, the rack holds the turkey in position during roasting and keeps it from rolling on one side or the other. Second, it elevates the meat above the roasting pan, allowing air to circulate and promoting even cooking and browning.

2. Cook the turkey breast-side down for the first half of the cooking time, and flip it breast-side up for the remainder. This protects the breast meat and keeps it from overcooking, resulting in breast meat that is more moist. Use a towel or potholder in each hand when flipping the turkey and be very careful to protect your hands from the hot juices that can run out of the turkey.

3. Basting the turkey contributes to even browning, juicy meat, and intense flavoring. However, to ensure crispy skin, do not baste in the last hour of cooking, as that will turn the skin moist and flabby.

4. Use an instant-read thermometer to check the temperature of the turkey, which allows you to remove the bird from the oven at the exact moment of doneness, 170°F at the thickest part of the thigh. If you do not own a temperature gauge—and I highly recommend you invest in one—you can check for doneness by roasting the turkey until the legs move freely in their sockets and the juices run clear when the flesh is pierced with a knife.

5. The final and most important step is allowing the turkey to rest after you pull it from the oven. Resting allows for the redistribution and reabsorption of the juices in the meat. This makes for ultra-moist, flavorful meat while also giving the bird a chance to cool for easier carving.

Finally, a note on the size of the turkey. Do not buy turkeys that weigh over 16 pounds. If you have a large party, purchase two smaller turkeys instead of one larger turkey. You are paying for extra bone and cartilage with the larger birds. Also, they require extra cooking time, which can dry out the meat, and are more difficult to handle.

PAN-ROASTED TURKEY BREAST
with SWEET SQUASH MATCHSTICKS

T HERE IS NO NEED TO ROAST A WHOLE TURKEY, ESPECIALLY IF EVERYONE likes just the breast meat. Have your butcher remove the breast meat from the bone and chop the bones into two-inch pieces. Use a vegetable slicer or mandoline to get perfectly shaped matchsticks from your sweet squash. Serve with Celery Root and Pear Purée (page 61).

MAKES 4 SERVINGS

1 (2-pound) skin-on turkey breast half, boned, bones reserved for sauce

9 fresh sage leaves, plus 1 tablespoon chopped fresh sage

1 teaspoon kosher salt, divided

$3/4$ teaspoon freshly ground black pepper, divided

1 tablespoon vegetable oil

1 medium onion, chopped (about 1 cup)

6 sprigs thyme

1 cup turkey or chicken stock (page 101)

3 tablespoons unsalted butter

1 pound squash, such as banana, acorn, or butternut, peeled and cut into $1/4$-inch matchsticks

1 tablespoon firmly packed brown sugar

$1/2$ teaspoon freshly squeezed lemon juice

2 tablespoons heavy cream

1 tablespoon unsalted butter (optional)

WITH THE RACK IN THE MIDDLE, pre-heat the oven to 375°F.

Slightly loosen the skin from the turkey meat to form a pocket; place 6 of the sage leaves evenly under the skin. Turn the breast over and place 3 sage leaves under the tenderloin piece of the breast. Secure the tenderloin piece to the rest of the breast with butchers twine. Sprinkle breast evenly with $3/4$ teaspoon of salt and $1/2$ teaspoon of pepper.

Heat the oil in a large ovenproof skillet over medium heat until shimmering. Add the breast, skin-side down. Cook until the skin is well browned and crispy. Transfer breast to a plate; set aside.

Place the reserved bones and onion into the skillet and cook until onions are soft and golden brown. Add the thyme and stock. Reduce the heat and simmer for 5 minutes. Place the turkey breast on top of the bones and onion, skin-side up. Transfer the skillet to the oven and roast until the thickest part of the breast registers 160°F on an instant-read thermometer; remove from oven and keep warm.

Melt the butter in a large skillet over medium heat. Add the squash, brown sugar, and chopped sage. Sprinkle with $1/4$ teaspoon salt and $1/4$ teaspoon pepper. Cook, stirring frequently, until squash is tender and lightly browned, about 10 minutes. Set aside and keep warm.

Strain the juices from the skillet into a small saucepan set over high heat. Boil until the liquid has reduced by half, about 5 minutes. Add the lemon juice and cream; season with salt and pepper to taste. Swirl in the butter off the heat, if using.

To serve, slice turkey breast, spoon sauce over it, and place squash on top.

WOOD-GRILLED TURKEY CHOP
with WILD MUSHROOM GRAVY

TRY THIS INTERESTING COOKING AND SERVING TECHNIQUE FOR YOUR NEXT holiday turkey. The wood-grilled flavor really can't be beat and a chop cut is certainly an unexpected way to serve a turkey breast. See note for directions on how to prepare the turkey chop; your butcher can likely do it for you. The gravy can be made in 20 minutes. Serve with Winter Panzanella (page 70) for a complete meal.

MAKES 4 SERVINGS

TURKEY CHOP

3 to 4 cups small hickory or applewood chips

2 bay leaves

4 tablespoons juniper berries

1 tablespoon mustard seeds

1 stick cinnamon

4 cups apple cider

$1/2$ cup olive oil

$1/3$ cup Chardonnay vinegar or white wine vinegar

$1/4$ cup honey

12 garlic cloves

1 tablespoon kosher salt

2 teaspoons freshly ground black pepper

1 breast half of a 12- to 14-pound turkey, breastbone attached (see note)

1 recipe Lemon-Thyme-Mustard Butter (page 96)

WILD MUSHROOM GRAVY

2 tablespoons unsalted butter

12 ounces mushrooms (cremini, chanterelle, matsutake, portobello, or shiitake), stems removed and cut into bite-sized pieces (about 4 cups)

FOR THE TURKEY: Place the bay leaves, juniper berries, mustard seeds, and stick cinnamon in a small nonstick skillet over medium low heat. Cook until lightly toasted and fragrant, about 3 minutes. Place into a spice grinder and grind until smooth. Transfer spices to a large, glass baking dish. Add the apple cider, oil, vinegar, honey, garlic, salt, and pepper; mix to combine. Add the turkey chops, rolling them in the marinade. Cover with plastic wrap and refrigerate for 8 hours or overnight.

Prepare an outdoor grill. Place hickory or applewood chips on the hot coals. Remove the turkey from the marinade, pat dry with paper towels; rub the turkey with additional olive oil and season liberally with salt and pepper. Grill over medium-hot coals, 8 to 10 minutes on each side; basting occasionally with Lemon-Thyme-Mustard Butter. While the turkey is cooking, prepare the gravy as directed below. Cook the turkey until it is golden brown and the internal temperature reads 165°F on an instant-read thermometer.

FOR THE GRAVY: Melt the butter in a large saucepan over medium heat. Add the shallots. Cover and cook for 1 minute, stirring occasionally. Add the mushrooms, and cover and cook for another 5 minutes. Add the garlic and cook uncovered, stirring occasionally, until mushrooms are golden and tender, about 3 minutes longer. Add the sherry, vinegar, and stock. Reduce the heat to maintain a simmer and cook until the liquid has reduced by two thirds. Add the cream. Simmer until sauce has reduced by half. Adjust seasonings to taste, if necessary.

(continued)

6 medium shallots, sliced
(about 2 cups)

3 medium garlic cloves, finely
chopped (about 1 table-
spoon)

1 cup sherry

$\frac{1}{4}$ cup sherry vinegar

2 cups vegetable stock
(page 193) or chicken
stock (page 101)

1 cup heavy cream

Kosher salt

Freshly ground black pepper

$\frac{1}{4}$ cup finely chopped chives

8 anchovy fillets, for garnish

1 recipe Winter Panzanella
(page 70)

Sprinkle with the chives; set aside and keep warm.

To serve, place $\frac{1}{2}$ cup of the gravy on the bottom of a plate, add 1 cup of the panzanella, and place turkey chop on top; garnish with two anchovy fillets.

NOTE: Have your butcher slice the breast, with bone attached, from top to bottom into four equally thick pieces. Turn the innermost three pieces on their sides and tie butchers twine around the outside of the meat (it should resemble a pork chop). The bottom piece of the breast will be shaped in a triangle. Without turning the piece on its side, just tie the butchers' twine around it to make it appear circular.

RED CURRY TURKEY SCALOPPINI

*T*HIS IS A WONDERFULLY SIMPLE, LIGHT, AND REFRESHING MEAL FOR THOSE who want to avoid a heavy holiday dinner and the fuss of a whole bird. The curry paste and blood orange impart a delightfully exotic sweet, sour, and spicy flavor. Serve with Braised Napa Cabbage with Apple and Bacon (page 57) and Butternut Squash Gratin (page 60) to round out your avant-garde holiday meal.

2 tablespoons Thai red curry paste

4 tablespoons olive oil

2 teaspoons kosher salt, plus more for seasoning

1$\frac{1}{2}$ teaspoons freshly ground black pepper, plus more for seasoning

8 (4-ounce) turkey cutlets (about 3 pounds)

2$\frac{1}{2}$ cups blood orange juice or other orange juice

1 small jicama, chopped into $\frac{1}{2}$-inch pieces (about 1 cup)

3 blood oranges, peeled, sectioned, and cut into $\frac{1}{2}$-inch pieces

1 large Fuji apple, cut into $\frac{1}{2}$-inch pieces

$\frac{1}{4}$ cup chopped cilantro

2 small bunches radish sprouts, for garnish

IN A LARGE GLASS BAKING DISH, mix together the curry paste, olive oil, salt, and pepper. Rub the marinade into the turkey cutlets. Cover the dish with plastic wrap and marinate 4 to 6 hours in the refrigerator.

Place the blood orange juice in a small saucepan over medium heat. Simmer until the juice has reduced to $\frac{1}{2}$ cup. Pass the sauce through a fine-mesh strainer and let cool completely.

In a medium bowl, place the jicama, apple, and orange pieces. Pour in enough reduced juice to lightly coat the ingredients. Add the cilantro and adjust seasonings to taste. Set aside or refrigerate until ready to use.

In a large cast-iron skillet, add enough oil to coat the bottom of the pan. Place over high heat until the oil is shimmering. Add the turkey and cook until lightly golden brown and no longer pink in the center, 1 to 2 minutes per side. Transfer cooked cutlets to a paper towel–lined plate and tent with foil to keep warm.

On four large dinner plates, arrange the jicama salad at the top of the plate and place the turkey cutlet slightly off the salad. Finish by placing a bunch of radish sprouts in the center of the salad and serve.

Wine pairing: Sauvignon Blanc, Viognier, Gewürztraminer

HOW TO CARVE A TURKEY

*F*OLLOWING THESE ESSENTIAL CARVING TECHNIQUES WILL ENSURE NEAT portions and the best texture of your perfectly roasted turkey while keeping its beautiful presentation.

1. Allow the turkey to rest at least 30 minutes after you have removed it from the oven. This allows for the juices to be reabsorbed into the meat. It also lets the meat to firm up, making carving easier.

2. A proper knife is imperative. Choose a very sharp thin-bladed carving knife or an electric serrated knife.

3. With the turkey breast-side up, begin with the legs. Press the whole leg, including the thigh, away from the body with the flat side of the knife or your hand, exposing the joint where the thighbone meets the body. Place your knife at the joint and slice through the joint towards the backbone, separating the whole leg from the body. Place the leg on a serving platter. Repeat on the other side.

2. Separate the drumstick from the thigh by cutting through the joint. The knife should effortlessly slip between the joint. You should not be cutting through bone.

3. Next, using your hands or the back of the knife, press the whole wing away from the body to expose the joint. Place your knife where the wing and body connect and slice thought the joint towards the backbone, separating the wing from the body. Place the wing on the serving platter. Repeat on the other side.

4. For the breast meat, first remove the wishbone by cutting away a little bit of skin from the base of the turkey's breast to expose the wishbone. Carve around the top of the wishbone. Without damaging the breast meat, carefully pull out the wishbone with your fingers. Next, remove the breasts by cutting along the side of the breastbone. Then angle the knife and cut along the contour of the body and through the wing joint. The breast should easily come away from the body. Repeat with the other side. Slice the breast meat by first cutting off the wings and slicing the remaining meat against the grain. Transfer to a serving platter.

If you prefer to carve the breast meat directly from the turkey, first make a deep horizontal cut parallel and close to the wing into the bottom of the breast, all the way to the ribcage. (The breast will still be attached to the center breastbone.) Then make vertical slices parallel to the breastbone, starting closest to the wing, slicing through to the horizontal cut. The slices will fall away from the turkey. Continue carving until enough meat has been carved for first servings.

LEFTOVER TURKEY HASH

THIS IS A GREAT DISH USING LEFTOVER TURKEY; DELICIOUS FOR BREAKFAST, lunch, dinner, or a late-night snack. The variety of bell peppers makes for a colorful presentation; cut all the vegetables the same size for even cooking and a tidy appearance. Serve with crusty bread or toast. Add a poached egg and hollandaise for a nice brunch option or scramble with an egg and wrap in a tortilla for a quick meal.

MAKES 8 SERVINGS

2 small russet potatoes (about 11 ounces)

6 tablespoons unsalted butter

1 medium red bell pepper, chopped (about 1 cup)

1 medium yellow bell pepper, chopped (about 1 cup)

1 medium green bell peppers, chopped (about 1 cup)

1 medium yellow onion, chopped (about 1 cup)

1 stalk celery, chopped (about $1/2$ cup)

$1/2$ teaspoon kosher salt

$1/2$ teaspoon freshly ground pepper

$1/4$ teaspoon cayenne pepper

8 cups cooked turkey breast, cut into $1/2$-inch cubes

5 tablespoons chopped flat-leaf parsley

PLACE THE POTATOES IN A SMALL SAUCEPAN and add enough cold water to cover by 1 inch. Bring to a boil over high heat. Add 1 teaspoon of salt; reduce the heat to medium low and simmer gently until the potatoes are barely tender and a paring knife can be inserted with some resistance, about 15 minutes. Drain and cool to room temperature; peel and cut into $1/2$-inch pieces. Set aside.

Melt 2 tablespoons of the butter in a large cast-iron skillet over medium-low heat. Add the peppers, onion, and celery; cover and cook, stirring occasionally, for 3 to 4 minutes. Add the salt, pepper, and cayenne. Continue cooking, uncovered, until vegetables are lightly golden and tender, about 3 minutes longer. Remove the vegetables from the skillet. Increase the heat to high; melt the remaining 4 tablespoons of butter in the skillet. Add the potatoes and cook until golden brown. Reduce heat to medium; add the turkey and the reserved vegetables. Cook until turkey is heated through; sprinkle with the parsley and serve.

BRAISED SHORT RIBS *with* ONIONS *and* SUGAR PUMPKIN

*N*OT ONLY ARE SUGAR PUMPKINS GREAT FOR HOLIDAY DECORATIONS BUT also for cooking; in this dish they add underlying complexity, richness, and unique earthy sweetness. Roast the pumpkin seeds for a nice garnish.

MAKES 4 SERVINGS

4 pounds bone-in beef short ribs, trimmed of excess fat, cut into 8 pieces

2 tablespoons Spicy BBQ Dry Rub (page 268)

2 tablespoons olive oil

10 garlic cloves

1 (1-pound) sugar pumpkin, peeled, seeded, and cut into 2-inch pieces (about 2 cups)

2 large Vidalia onions, cut into 1-inch-thick slices

1 Anaheim chile, seeded and chopped

2 large beefsteak tomatoes, cored and chopped

1 cup corn stock (page 99) or vegetable stock (page 193)

1 cup Spiced Plum Barbecue Sauce (page 265) or any fruity barbecue sauce

SPRINKLE THE RIBS WITH THE RUB. Heat the oil in a large Dutch oven over medium-high heat until smoking. Add the beef and cook without stirring until well browned on one side, 4 to 6 minutes. Turn the beef and cook on the second side until well browned, 4 to 6 minutes longer, reducing the heat if the fat begins to smoke. Transfer the beef to a medium bowl; set aside.

Reduce the heat to medium low; add the garlic, pumpkin, onions, and chili. Cover and cook, stirring occasionally, until the vegetables have softened and begin to brown, about 20 minutes. Add the ribs and any accumulated juices, tomatoes, stock, and BBQ sauce. Cover and bring to a simmer. Cook over low heat until a fork slips easily in and out of the meat, 2 to $2\frac{1}{2}$ hours, using tongs to turn the meat twice during the cooking.

Transfer the ribs, pumpkin, and onions to a serving platter and keep warm. Use a spoon to skim the fat off the surface of the liquid. Add a $\frac{1}{2}$ cup of the liquid to the reserved meat to keep it moist. Simmer the remaining liquid over medium heat until it has reduced enough to coat the back of a spoon, about 25 minutes. Serve reduced sauce, ribs, and vegetables over soft polenta or grits.

Wine pairing: Amarone or Valpolicella

WOOD-GRILLED BUTTERFLIED LEG *of* LAMB

A BEAUTIFULLY GRILLED LEG OF LAMB IS DELICIOUS ALTERNATIVE TO turkey. Served with a sauce of fresh herbs and garlic, it can be a dish fit for the finest occasion. Be sure to press the herb marinade into the folds in the meat, allowing the flavor to permeate the lamb. Have the butcher remove the bone if you cannot find a boneless leg. Serve with chimichurri (page 91).

MAKES 8 SERVINGS

$\frac{1}{4}$ cup olive oil

12 garlic cloves

$\frac{1}{2}$ cup chopped fresh mint

$\frac{1}{4}$ cup chopped flat-leaf parsley

3 tablespoons chopped fresh rosemary

2 tablespoons fresh thyme

3 tablespoons Dijon mustard

2 tablespoons freshly ground black pepper

1 tablespoon kosher salt

1 (2-pound) boneless leg of lamb, trimmed of excess fat

Chimichurri (page 91)

COMBINE ALL THE INGREDIENTS except the lamb and chimichurri in a food processor; purée until smooth paste forms.

Apply the paste liberally to all sides of the meat. Wrap the lamb tightly in plastic wrap and refrigerate for at least 4 hours, or overnight. (For stronger flavor, refrigerate overnight.)

About an hour prior to cooking, remove the lamb from the refrigerator, unwrap, and let it come up to room temperature. Prepare an outdoor grill using a hardwood such as applewood or oak.

For medium rare, grill the lamb over a medium fire until the internal temperature reaches 135°F on an instant-read thermometer, 6 to 8 minutes on each side; or, for medium, grill until thermometer reads 155°F, 8 to 10 minutes on each side.

Transfer the lamb to a platter, tent loosely with foil, and let rest for 15 minutes. Cut into $\frac{1}{2}$-inch-thick slices, and serve with chimichurri.

Wine pairing: Riesling, Chardonnay, Pinot Noir

GRILLED SPICY SOLE FILLETS

*L*ET THIS SPICY DISH WARM YOU UP DURING THE COLD WINTER MONTHS. Serve with Spicy Creamy Yellow Grits with Shrimp (page 227). You can substitute flounder for the sole; likewise, you can use an indoor grill pan or frying pan instead of an outdoor grill.

MAKES 4 SERVINGS

6 sprigs thyme

2 lemons, zest grated and juiced

2 teaspoons ground ancho chile powder

2 tablespoons stone-ground mustard

$\frac{1}{2}$ cup peanut oil

2 teaspoons kosher salt

2 teaspoons finely ground black pepper

8 sole fillets, skin removed

1 recipe Red Onion and Tomato Relish (page 94)

1 recipe Spicy Creamy Yellow Grits with Shrimp (page 227)

CRUSH THE THYME SPRIGS with the back of a chef's knife. Place crushed thyme in a large bowl with the lemon zest and juice, chile powder, mustard, oil, salt, and pepper; set aside. Place the fish in a single layer in a large baking dish; coat one side with half of the spice mixture, pressing it into the fish; flip fish over and coat with the remaining spice mixture. Cover with plastic wrap and place in the refrigerator for 1 hour.

Prepare the grill.

Grill the fillets with the grill lid down, 4 minutes on the first side and 1 to 2 minutes on the second side. (Be sure to use a fish spatula to flip the fillets.)

To serve, mound $1\frac{1}{2}$ cups of the grits in the center of an individual plate, top with two fillets, and sprinkle $\frac{1}{2}$ cup of the relish over. Serve immediately.

Wine pairing: Riesling

BRAISED NAPA CABBAGE
with APPLE *and* BACON

THE CABBAGE PICKS UP A WONDERFUL SWEET AND SALTY FLAVOR FROM the apples and bacon.

1 tablespoon caraway seeds

6 strips bacon, finely chopped (about 1 cup)

1 medium yellow onion, thinly sliced

1 Granny Smith apple, peeled and cored, cut into $\frac{1}{2}$-inch dice

4 garlic cloves, finely chopped

1 small red cabbage, thinly sliced (about 4 cups)

1 medium Napa cabbage, thinly sliced (about 5 cups)

1 cup apple juice

$\frac{1}{2}$ cup red wine

2 tablespoons red wine vinegar

2 tablespoons brown sugar

2 bay leaves

1 tablespoon chopped fresh thyme

$\frac{1}{2}$ teaspoon kosher salt

$\frac{1}{4}$ teaspoon freshly ground black pepper

PLACE THE CARAWAY SEEDS IN A SMALL SAUCEPAN over medium heat. Cook until seeds are lightly toasted and fragrant, about 5 minutes. Set aside.

Place the bacon in a large pot over medium heat and cook until crispy, about 5 minutes. Drain all but 2 tablespoons of the fat. Add the onions, apple, and garlic. Cover and cook, stirring occasionally, until onions are slightly tender, 3 to 5 minutes. Add the rest of the ingredients; cover and reduce the heat to medium low. Simmer until the cabbage is tender and the braising liquid has reduced by two thirds, 25 to 30 minutes. Remove the bay leaves and discard. Serve immediately.

BUTTERED BRUSSELS SPROUTS *and* CHESTNUTS

QUICKLY PARBOILING THE BRUSSELS SPROUTS UNTIL JUST TENDER AND shocking them in cold water keeps them from developing the unappealing sulfur odor and flavor that intimidates many away from this lovely vegetable.

MAKES 6 SERVINGS

$1\frac{1}{2}$ pounds Brussels sprouts, ends trimmed, any yellow outer leaves removed, and cut in half from top to bottom

$\frac{3}{4}$ cup of water

$1\frac{1}{2}$ teaspoon kosher salt, divided

24 whole chestnuts, roasted and peeled (see note)

3 tablespoons unsalted butter

$\frac{1}{2}$ teaspoon freshly ground black pepper

FILL A LARGE BOWL HALF FULL OF ICE AND WATER; set aside.

Place the Brussels sprouts, $\frac{3}{4}$ cup of water, and $\frac{3}{4}$ teaspoon of salt in a large saucepan over high heat. Cover, and cook until the Brussels sprouts are tender and a knife can easily be inserted, about 5 minutes. Remove the Brussels sprouts from the heat, drain, and immediately transfer into the bowl of ice water. When the Brussels sprouts are cool to the touch, about 2 minutes, remove them from the water, drain thoroughly, and set aside.

In a large skillet over medium heat, place the butter, chestnuts, and $\frac{1}{4}$ cup of water; cook for 3 minutes. Add the Brussels sprouts, remaining $\frac{3}{4}$ teaspoon of salt, and pepper; continue to cook until they are heated through.

NOTE: To roast the chestnuts, preheat the oven to 425°F. Cut an "X" through the flat side of each chestnut shell with a sharp knife; do not skip this step as this allows steam to escape while the chestnuts are cooking, preventing them from exploding in the oven. Spread the chestnuts X-side up on a rimmed baking pan; add $\frac{1}{4}$ cup of water to the pan and bake until the shells peel back and the flesh is golden, about 20 minutes; stirring once. Remove the chestnuts from oven; shell and peel them while they are still warm.

BUTTERNUT SQUASH GRATIN

*A*LMOST ANY WINTER SQUASH CAN BE USED IN THIS RECIPE. THIS SLIGHTLY rustic side dish goes well with ham or turkey.

1½ cups fresh breadcrumbs

1 tablespoon finely chopped flat-leaf parsley

⅓ cup melted butter

1 medium butternut squash (about 2 pounds), peeled, seeded, and cut into ⅛-inch slices

3 medium yellow onions, thinly sliced (about 3 cups)

¾ cup grated Parmesan cheese

2 teaspoons fresh thyme

2 teaspoons chopped fresh sage

1 teaspoon kosher salt

½ teaspoon freshly ground black pepper

3½ cups heavy cream

ADJUST AN OVEN RACK TO THE MIDDLE POSITION and heat the oven to 350°F.

In a medium bowl, combine the breadcrumbs, parsley, and melted butter.

Toss the squash, onions, cheese, thyme, sage, salt, and pepper together in a medium casserole dish or cast-iron skillet. Add enough cream to almost cover the squash (do not use entire amount if not needed), pouring along the side of the baking dish to avoid washing off the herbs. Sprinkle the breadcrumb mixture evenly on top of the squash; cover with foil.

Bake for 45 minutes. Remove the foil and continue to bake until the top is golden brown, about 10 minutes longer. Cool for 5 minutes before serving.

CELERY ROOT *and* PEAR PURÉE

I LOVE CELERY ROOT. THIS UNDERUSED VEGETABLE HAS TREMENDOUS versatility since its flavor is so mellow. Here, the addition of pear makes this purée an unexpected, light, and sweet substitute for regular mashed potatoes. Feel free to add any herb—such as parsley, basil, or sage—or toasted pine nuts for extra flavor and texture. Serve with Pan-Roasted Turkey Breast with Sweet Squash Matchsticks (page 44).

MAKES 4 SERVINGS

1 (1 pound) celery root, peeled and cut into 1-inch pieces

2 Bartlett pears, stemmed, cored, and cut into 1-inch pieces

2 tablespoons unsalted butter

1 teaspoon kosher salt

½ teaspoon freshly ground black pepper

1 cup apple cider

ADJUST AN OVEN RACK TO THE MIDDLE POSITION and heat the oven to 350°F.

Place all of the ingredients in a baking dish with a tight-fitting lid. Bake until celery root is tender and a fork can easily be inserted with no resistance, about 1 hour. Transfer the contents into a blender; purée until smooth. Pass the mixture through a fine-mesh sieve for a smother consistency, if desired. Adjust seasonings to taste.

CHESTNUT *and* OYSTER GRATIN

THE SWEETNESS OF THE OYSTERS AND CHESTNUTS ADDS A NICE TOUCH TO THIS otherwise traditional savory potato gratin. Have your fishmonger shuck the oysters and reserve the liquor for you. Try to use fresh chestnuts; however, canned chestnuts will also work in this dish.

MAKES 8 SERVINGS

6 tablespoons unsalted butter, divided

3 large red potatoes, thinly sliced (about 3 cups)

2 cups shucked oysters, liquor reserved

1 cup heavy cream

1¼ teaspoons kosher salt

½ teaspoon freshly ground black pepper

1 medium yellow onion, chopped (about 1 cup)

2 pounds whole chestnuts, roasted, peeled, and roughly chopped (about 4 cups) (see note on page 58)

¼ cup chopped fresh dill

¼ teaspoon ground nutmeg

¼ teaspoon cayenne pepper

1 cup grated Parmesan cheese

ADJUST AN OVEN RACK TO THE MIDDLE POSITION and heat the oven to 450°F. Grease a medium baking dish with 2 tablespoons of the butter.

In a large saucepan over medium-low heat, combine the potatoes, reserved oyster liquor, cream, salt, and pepper; bring to a simmer. Cook, adjusting the heat as necessary to maintain a light simmer, until the potatoes are almost tender (when a knife can be inserted into the center with some resistance), about 15 minutes. Set aside.

In a small skillet over medium-low heat, add 2 tablespoons of the butter and the onion; cook, stirring occasionally, until the onions are translucent, about 5 minutes. (The recipe can be made up to three days ahead at this point.)

Place the potato mixture, oysters, onion, chopped chestnuts, dill, nutmeg, and cayenne in a large bowl; stir to combine. Transfer the mixture into the prepared baking dish and sprinkle with the cheese. Dot the top with the remaining 2 tablespoons of butter.

Bake until the cream is thickened and bubbling on the sides, and the top is golden brown, about 10 minutes. Cool for 10 minutes before serving.

GRILLED CORN *with* ROASTED PEPPER BUTTER

THIS IS A PERFECT FLAVORFUL SIDE DISH TO THROW ON THE GRILL. YOU CAN also roast in the oven at 450°F.

4 ears corn, husk attached but peeled back and silk removed

2 tablespoons olive oil

1 red bell pepper, stemmed, seeded and chopped

3 garlic cloves, crushed

8 tablespoons (1 stick) unsalted butter, softened

1 tablespoon tarragon vinegar

1 teaspoon kosher salt

1/2 teaspoon freshly ground black pepper

PREPARE AN OUTDOOR GRILL.

Heat the oil in medium skillet over medium-high heat until shimmering. Add the pepper; cook, stirring occasionally, until just beginning to soften, about 3 minutes. Reduce the heat to low; add the garlic. Cover and cook until the peppers are very soft and lightly browned, about 10 minutes. Transfer to a small bowl; let cool to room temperature.

Place the cooled pepper and garlic in a food processor and purée until smooth. Add the butter, vinegar, salt, and pepper; pulse to thoroughly combine. Spread 2 tablespoons of the butter on each ear of corn; wrap the husk around each ear. Wrap each ear in aluminum foil, pouring 2 tablespoons of water in each package before sealing completely.

Grill the corn over the hot coals until tender and aromatic, about 10 minutes.

CORN *and* SAGE STUFFING

*W*ITH LITTLE ADDITIONAL EFFORT, MAKING YOUR OWN BREAD CUBES yields delicious results. For even cooking, chop the vegetables uniformly, into about ¼-inch pieces.

8 tablespoons (1 stick) unsalted butter plus 2 tablespoons

1½ cups turkey stock (page 101), divided

3 ears corn, husks and silk removed

3 large eggs

2 medium yellow onions, chopped (about 2 cups)

2 stalks celery, chopped (about 1 cup)

1 small green bell pepper, chopped (about ¼ cup)

1 small poblano chile, finely chopped (about 2 tablespoons)

1 tablespoon kosher salt

2 teaspoons freshly ground black pepper

2½ cups crusty day-old French bread, cut into 1-inch pieces (see note)

2½ cups cornbread (page 74), cut into 1-inch pieces

⅓ cup chopped flat-leaf parsley

3 tablespoons finely chopped sage

2 teaspoons finely chopped fresh thyme

¼ cup finely chopped chives

ADJUST AN OVEN RACK TO SECOND LOWEST POSITION and heat the oven to 375°F. Grease a large baking dish with the 2 tablespoons of butter and add ½ cup of the turkey stock; set aside.

Stand the corn upright inside a large bowl and, using a paring knife, carefully cut the kernels from the corn cob, then use the back of a butter knife to scrape off any pulp remaining on the cobs; you should have about 1½ cups of corn. Set aside.

In a small bowl, combine the eggs and the remaining cup of turkey stock; mix well. Set aside.

Melt the butter in a medium saucepan over medium heat. Add the onions, celery, green peppers, chiles, salt, and pepper; cover. Cook, stirring occasionally, until the onions are tender and translucent, 5 to 8 minutes.

Transfer the vegetable mixture into a large bowl; add the French bread, cornbread, parsley, sage, thyme, chives, corn, and egg mixture; toss gently until moistened and combined. Place the stuffing into the prepared baking dish and cover; if you don't have a cover for the baking dish, you can cover the dish with parchment paper and aluminum foil. (Recipe can be made up to a day ahead at this point and stored in the refrigerator until needed.)

Place the baking dish onto a sheet pan. Bake for 45 minutes; uncover and bake another 45 minutes, or until the crust is golden brown.

NOTE: If you only have fresh bread available, adjust an oven rack to the middle position and heat the oven to 250°F. Spread the bread cubes in a single layer on a rimmed baking sheet. Bake until thoroughly dried but not browned, about 30 minutes, stirring halfway through the baking time.

KUMAMOTO OYSTER *and* SAUSAGE STUFFING

SUBSTITUTE DUCK OR CHICKEN SAUSAGE IF YOU PREFER. HAVE YOUR FISH-monger shuck the oysters and reserve the liquor.

10 tablespoons unsalted butter, divided

2 cups corn stock (page 99) or vegetable stock (page 193), divided

2 teaspoons olive oil

1 pound andouille sausage, cut into 1-inch pieces

3 cups bread, any combination of French, Parmesan cheese loaf, or ciabatta, cut into $^1/_2$-inch pieces

$^1/_3$ cup chopped flat-leaf parsley

2 teaspoons finely chopped thyme leaves

1 teaspoon kosher salt, plus more for seasoning

1 teaspoon freshly ground black pepper, plus more for seasoning

$^1/_8$ teaspoon cayenne pepper

2 stalks celery, chopped (about 1 cup)

1 medium yellow onion, chopped (about 1 cup)

4 garlic cloves, finely chopped

1 lemon, zest grated

3 ounces brown mushrooms, quartered (about 1 cup)

3 large eggs

$^1/_2$ cup dried cranberries or cherries

16 to 24 Kumamoto oysters, shucked, liquor reserved

$^1/_2$ cup grated Parmesan cheese

ADJUST AN OVEN RACK TO THE SECOND LOWEST POSITION and heat the oven to 375°F. Grease a 13 x 9-inch baking dish with 2 tablespoons of the butter and pour in $^1/_2$ cup of the corn stock.

Heat the olive oil in a medium saucepan until shimmering; add the sausage. Cook until sausage is lightly browned, about 5 minutes.

Place the bread, parsley, thyme, salt, pepper, and cayenne in a large bowl and toss to combine.

Melt 6 tablespoons of the butter in a large skillet over medium-low heat. Add the onions and celery; sprinkle with salt and pepper. Cover and cook until the vegetables have softened, 3 to 5 minutes. Add the garlic, lemon zest, and mushrooms. Cover and cook, stirring occasionally, until the mushrooms have softened, 5 minutes. Pour the mixture into the bread mixture and stir to combine.

In a small bowl whisk together the eggs and the remaining 1$^1/_2$ cups of corn stock; add to the bread mixture. Fold in the sausage, dried berries, and oysters. Evenly spread the stuffing into the prepared baking dish; sprinkle with the cheese; dot the top with the remaining 2 tablespoons of butter.

Place the baking dish on a sheet pan. Bake until the top is golden brown and crispy, 35 to 45 minutes. Serve.

MASHED RED POTATOES *with* GARLIC

S ILKY SMOOTH MASHED POTATOES ARE USUALLY AT THEIR BEST WHEN topped with rich holiday gravy; however, these potatoes are bold enough to stand on their own. Garlic adds a savory bite, though the potatoes would still be creamy and flavorful without it. For those who valiantly attempt to control their holiday indulgences, an excellent nonfat version is noted below.

MAKES 6 SERVINGS

1$\frac{1}{2}$ pounds red potatoes (about 9 small), scrubbed

1 head garlic, cloves separated and peeled

1 cup heavy cream or half-and-half

4 tablespoons unsalted butter

$\frac{1}{2}$ cup crème fraîche

3 tablespoons chopped fresh chives

Kosher salt

Freshly ground black pepper

$\frac{1}{4}$ cup whole milk, if necessary

ADJUST AN OVEN RACK TO THE MIDDLE POSITION and heat the oven to 375°F.

Place the potatoes in a large saucepan and add cold water to cover by 1 inch. Bring to a boil over high heat. Add 1 teaspoon of salt; reduce the heat to medium low. Simmer gently until the potatoes are tender and a paring knife can be inserted into the potatoes with little resistance, 20 to 25 minutes. Drain the potatoes; transfer to a rimmed sheet pan, spread in an even layer, and place in the oven. Bake until the potatoes are dry and easily split when pierced with a fork, about 10 minutes.

While the potatoes are cooking, simmer the garlic, cream, and butter in a small saucepan over medium-low heat until the garlic is very tender, about 10 minutes. Set aside.

Working in batches, pulse the potatoes and the garlic mixture in a food processor until just smooth, filling the food processor only half way for each batch; do not overprocess. Transfer puréed potatoes to a large bowl. Fold in the crème fraîche, chives, and adjust seasonings to taste. Thin with the milk, if necessary. Keep warm until ready to serve.

NOTE: For a nonfat alternative, substitute nonfat milk for the heavy cream and whole milk and nonfat sour cream for the crème fraîche; omit the butter completely. You can also increase the chives to $\frac{1}{4}$ cup for more flavor. Adjust the consistency with more nonfat milk, if necessary.

SWEET POTATO GRATIN

I BELIEVE SWEET POTATOES ARE A MUST AT ANY HOLIDAY TABLE. THIS GRATIN is sweet and savory and a perfect complement to any holiday turkey, ham, or beef dish. Sprinkle toasted, chopped pecans over top for extra texture and color.

MAKES 6 SERVINGS

$^1\!/_4$ cup finely ground fresh breadcrumbs

$^1\!/_4$ cup grated Parmesan cheese

$1^1\!/_2$ cups half-and-half

2 teaspoons kosher salt

$^1\!/_2$ teaspoon freshly ground black pepper

$^1\!/_8$ teaspoon ground cinnamon

3 sprigs thyme, leaves removed, or $^1\!/_2$ teaspoon dried thyme

3 tablespoons unsalted butter

1 small yellow onion, cut in half, then into $^1\!/_4$-inch slices (about 1 cup)

1 medium garlic clove, finely chopped (about 1 teaspoon)

3 pounds sweet potatoes (3 to 4 medium), peeled and cut into $^1\!/_8$-inch-thick slices (about 4 cups)

ADJUST AN OVEN RACK TO THE MIDDLE POSITION and heat the oven to 325°F. Grease a 2-quart baking dish.

In a small bowl, stir the breadcrumbs and cheese together until combined. Set aside.

Whisk together the half-and-half, salt, pepper, cinnamon, and thyme in a medium bowl; set aside.

Melt the butter in a large skillet over medium-low heat. Add the onions. Cook, stirring occasionally, until softened and well browned, about 10 minutes. Add the garlic and cook until fragrant, about 30 seconds. Spread the cooked onions evenly in the prepared baking dish. Layer the sweet potatoes over the onions. Pour the half-and-half mixture over the potatoes. (This can be covered and refrigerated at this point, up to two days ahead.)

Sprinkle the breadcrumb mixture evenly over the top. Bake until the sauce is thick and bubbling around the sides, and the top is golden brown, about 45 minutes. Cool for 5 minutes before serving.

Note: Gratin can be made up to two days ahead. Cover and store cooled, finished gratin in the refrigerator. Reheat at 350°F, covered, for twenty minutes, or until heated through. Finish the dish under the broiler to re-crisp the topping.

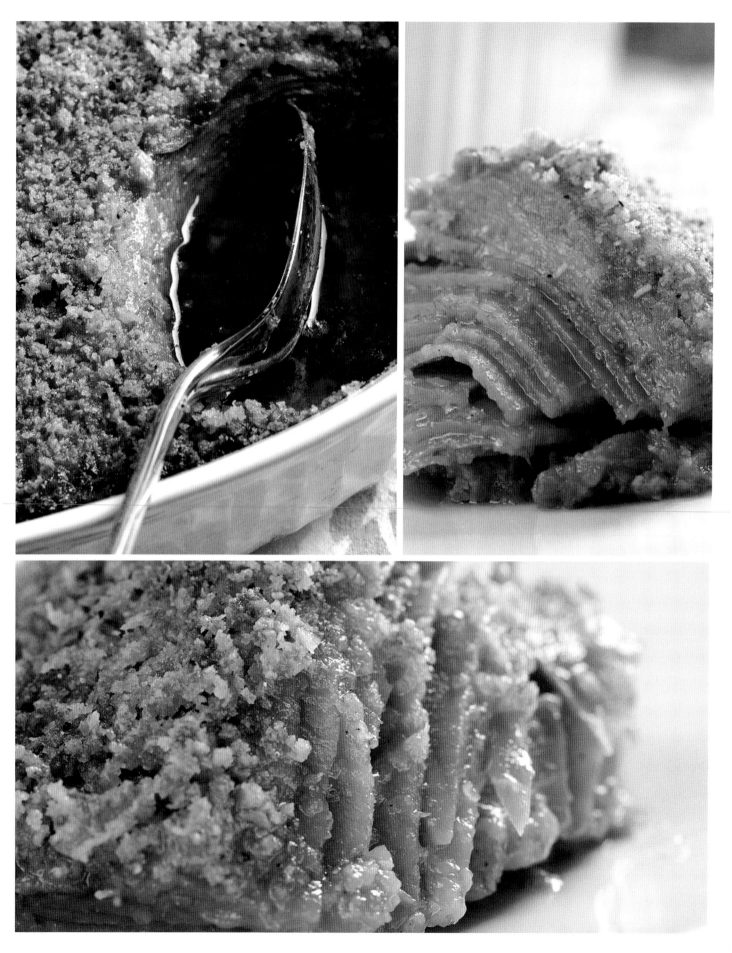

WINTER PANZANELLA

*J*UST THE THOUGHT OF COMBINING EARTHY SWEET SQUASH AND HEARTY crusty bread warms my soul. This is a comforting winter dish that makes excellent use of the abundant squash varieties available during this time of year. Use a combination of squash for the best flavor. Serve with the Wood-Grilled Turkey Chop with Wild Mushroom Gravy (page 47).

MAKES 4 TO 6 SERVINGS

Assorted winter squash, such as butternut, acorn, hubbard, or kabocha, peeled and cut into $^{1}/_{2}$-inch pieces (about 2 cups altogether)

$^{1}/_{2}$ cup olive oil, divided

4 tablespoons unsalted butter, melted, divided

$^{1}/_{2}$ teaspoon kosher salt, plus more for seasoning

$^{1}/_{2}$ teaspoon freshly ground black pepper, plus more for seasoning

1 yellow onion, finely chopped

2 cups ciabatta or French bread, cut into $^{1}/_{2}$-inch pieces

1 small red bell pepper, cored, seeded, and chopped (about $^{1}/_{4}$ cup)

1 small poblano pepper, seeded and chopped (about $^{1}/_{4}$ cup)

2 medium garlic cloves, finely chopped (about 2 teaspoons)

1 red Bartlett pear, cored and finely chopped

$^{1}/_{3}$ cup chopped flat-leaf parsley

2 tablespoons capers, rinsed

2 tablespoons white balsamic vinegar

1 tablespoon finely chopped fresh sage

8 pickled white anchovy fillets, for garnish

ADJUST AN OVEN RACK TO THE MIDDLE POSITION and heat the oven to 350°F.

In a large bowl, mix the squash with $^{1}/_{4}$ cup of oil, 3 tablespoons of butter, salt, and pepper. Transfer to a baking sheet and roast in oven until squash is golden brown and tender, about 1 hour.

While the squash is roasting, heat $^{1}/_{4}$ cup of the oil in a large skillet over medium heat. Add the onions and cook for 1 minute. Add the remaining butter, bread, red pepper, poblano, and garlic; toss to combine and transfer to a baking sheet. Place in the oven and bake until the bread is lightly toasted, stirring occasionally, about 10 minutes.

In a large bowl, combine the squash mixture, bread mixture, pear, parsley, capers, vinegar, and sage; toss to combine. Adjust seasoning with salt and pepper, if necessary. Transfer to a serving platter and lay the anchovies over the top. Serve immediately.

A SPECIAL NOTE ON WINTER SQUASH

A S THE SEASONS CHANGE AND COLD WEATHER COMES, SOME SQUASH DO not die on the vine; hearty varieties just put on colorful winter coats and become ripe for picking. Winter squash are certainly beautiful enough to adorn your home and holiday table. However, they have far more to offer than being an effortless table decoration. To select the most flavorful squash, follow these guidelines:

- Choose solid, heavy squash with stems that are firm, full, and corky. If you can easily scrape off the skin or press your nail into it, the squash is not mature and thus not good to eat. The skin should be fairly hard and dull without any soft areas or cracks. The heavier the squash feels, the sweeter and more moist it will be.
- Squash do not have to be refrigerated. Store them in a dry place at room temperature and they will keep for several weeks. However, if you do cut them, wrap them in plastic and store in the refrigerator for up to two weeks.
- Almost all winter squash are interchangeable in my recipes; the only exception to this is the spaghetti squash. Here are my favorite varieties:

ACORN: This dark green, hard, round squash has orange flesh and is mild and creamy.

BUTTERNUT: The orange flesh of this variety is sweet and fruity, and tastes somewhat like sweet potatoes. Look for large squash with evenly beige skin that have a long, thick neck and are slightly rounded at the bottom.

HUBBARD: A large, bumpy, thick-skinned squash with a fairly sweet flavor. The exterior skin can range in color from dark green to bright orange.

KABOCHA: Developed in Japan, this medium-sized squash has a flattened round shape and rough edible skin that ranges in color from green to tan. It has an unusually rich, sweet flesh. It can be used instead of sweet potatoes.

SPAGHETTI SQUASH: Yellow, cream, or tan in color, this oblong, medium-sized squash is named as such because its flesh is stringy and turns into strands that resemble spaghetti when cooked. The strands have a mild, crisp, and lightly sweet flavor.

SUGAR OR PIE PUMPKIN: This name applies to small, round pumpkins, about 1 to 2 pounds each. They range from dull and stringy to meaty and sweet.

CORNBREAD

A COMBINATION OF FLOURS LENDS TO THE LIGHT AND AIRY TEXTURE AND great corn flavor of this bread.

MAKES 6 TO 8 SERVINGS

6 tablespoons unsalted butter, 2 tablespoons softened, 4 tablespoons melted and cooled slightly

2 large eggs

1 cup buttermilk

$^{1}/_{4}$ cup granulated sugar or maple sugar

2 tablespoons honey, melted

$^{1}/_{2}$ cup cornmeal

$^{1}/_{2}$ cup corn flour

$^{1}/_{2}$ cup cake flour

2$^{1}/_{2}$ teaspoons baking powder

1 teaspoon freshly ground black pepper

$^{1}/_{2}$ teaspoon salt

ADJUST AN OVEN RACK TO THE MIDDLE POSITION and heat the oven to 350°F. Grease an 8-inch square baking dish with the softened butter.

Whisk the eggs, buttermilk, sugar, and honey in a medium bowl until combined. Set aside.

In a large bowl, sift together the cornmeal, corn flour, cake flour, baking powder, pepper, and salt. Using a rubber spatula, make a well in the center of the flour mixture; pour the egg mixture into the well. Gently fold the mixture together to barely combine; add the melted butter and continue folding until the butter is just incorporated; do not overmix. Pour the batter into the prepared baking dish; smooth the surface with a rubber spatula.

Bake until light brown and a toothpick inserted in the center comes out clean, 25 to 30 minutes. Cool pan on a cooling rack for 10 minutes. Invert the cornbread onto the cooling rack, turn right side up, and continue to cool about 10 minutes longer, or until just warm. Cut into pieces and serve.

CRANBERRY SCONES *with* ORANGE GLAZE

HOMEMADE SCONES ARE A PERFECT WAY TO START THE DAY. THE CRANberries and orange zest will fill your kitchen with a heavenly holiday aroma as the scones bake.

MAKES 16 SCONES

CRANBERRY SCONES

3 cups cake flour, plus more for dusting

1 cup whole wheat flour

$\frac{1}{4}$ cup granulated sugar

2 tablespoons ground almond flour

2 tablespoons baking powder

1$\frac{1}{2}$ teaspoons salt

3 tablespoons whole oats

8 tablespoons (1 stick) unsalted butter, frozen

2 cups heavy cream or half-and-half

1 tablespoon grated orange zest

2 teaspoons vanilla extract

1$\frac{1}{4}$ cups fresh cranberries, chopped, or dried cranberries

ORANGE GLAZE

1 cup confectioners' sugar

1 orange, 2 tablespoons juice, $\frac{1}{2}$ teaspoon grated zest

ADJUST OVEN RACK TO MIDDLE POSITION and heat the oven to 400°F.

FOR THE SCONES: In a large bowl, sift together the cake flour, whole wheat flour, sugar, almond flour, baking powder, and salt. Stir in the oats; set aside.

Grate the frozen butter on the large holes of a box grater. Add the grated butter to the flour mixture and cut the mixture together using the back of a fork or pastry cutter until the butter is slightly incorporated and a few lumps remain.

In a small bowl, stir the cream, orange zest, and vanilla together; add the cream mixture to the flour mixture. Fold with a spatula until just combined; gently fold in the cranberries. Transfer the dough to a lightly floured board and pat the dough into a $^3/_4$-inch-thick rectangle. Cut the dough into rounds using a 3-inch biscuit cutter or into 8 wedges using a knife. Place the rounds or wedges onto a baking sheet, 1 inch apart.

Bake the scones until puffed and lightly browned, 20 minutes. Cool the scones on the baking sheet set on a cooling rack for 5 minutes, then transfer the scones to the cooling rack.

TO MAKE THE GLAZE, mix the sugar, juice, and zest in a small bowl until smooth. Drizzle over the scones.

Serve warm or cool to room temperature.

DILL BUTTERMILK DROP BISCUITS

*T*HESE SAVORY BISCUITS HAVE A CRISP, OUTER CRUST AND TENDER, FLAKY interior. The versatile dough can also make a sweet biscuit. Simply swap the dill and pepper for an additional tablespoon sugar and a pinch of grated lemon zest.

MAKES 20 TABLESPOON-SIZE BISCUITS

$\frac{1}{3}$ cup buttermilk

$\frac{1}{2}$ cup sour cream

1 cup all-purpose flour

1 tablespoon granulated sugar

1$\frac{1}{2}$ teaspoon baking powder

$\frac{1}{2}$ teaspoon table salt

6 tablespoons unsalted butter, 4 tablespoons chilled and cut into $\frac{1}{2}$-inch pieces, 2 tablespoons melted

2 tablespoons chopped fresh dill

$\frac{1}{4}$ teaspoon freshly ground black pepper

ADJUST AN OVEN RACK TO THE MIDDLE POSITION and heat the oven to 475°F. Line a rimmed baking sheet with parchment paper. In medium bowl, mix the buttermilk and sour cream together; set aside.

Pulse the flour, sugar, baking powder, and salt together in food processor to combine. Scatter the chilled butter over the top and pulse the mixture until it resembles coarse oatmeal. Transfer the mixture to a large bowl. Make a well in the center of the flour mixture and pour in the buttermilk mixture; stir with a rubber spatula until just incorporated. Sprinkle in the dill and pepper and stir gently to combine; do not overmix. Using a tablespoon, scoop a level amount of batter and drop onto the prepared baking sheet. Repeat with the remaining batter. Brush the tops with the melted butter.

Bake until the tops are golden brown and crisp, 10 to 12 minutes. Transfer biscuits to a cooling rack and cool 5 minutes before serving.

NOTE: To make larger biscuits just use a $\frac{1}{4}$-cup measuring cup to scoop the dough and bake for twelve to fourteen minutes. Also, to refresh day-old biscuits just heat them in a 300°F oven for five to eight minutes.

PERSIMMON BREAD

*U*NFORTUNATELY, MOST AMERICANS HAVE NEVER TASTED A PERSIMMON. They are missing out on its unique creamy texture and sublime sweet flavor combination of pumpkin, plum, and honey. This quick bread is unusual enough to be memorable and encompass all the flavors of the holidays. You can bake several loaves at once since they freeze wonderfully. Take one out to enjoy with unexpected holiday guests for brunch or wrap it decoratively for a lovely hostess or holiday gift.

MAKES 2 (8-INCH) LOAVES

2 1/4 cups Hachiya persimmon pulp (about 8 very ripe persimmons)

4 eggs, room temperature, lightly beaten

8 ounces (2 sticks) unsalted butter, melted and cooled to room temperature

2/3 cup brandy, cognac, bourbon, or whiskey

2 tablespoons honey

1 tablespoon vanilla extract

1 lemon, 2 tablespoons juice, 1 teaspoon grated zest

1 orange, 2 tablespoons juice, 1 teaspoon grated zest

2 teaspoons grated fresh ginger

1 1/2 teaspoons salt

3 3/4 cups all-purpose flour

2 1/2 cups granulated sugar

2 teaspoons baking soda

2 teaspoons ground cinnamon

2 teaspoons ground nutmeg

1/2 teaspoon ground allspice

2 cups walnuts or pecans, chopped and toasted

2 cups raisins or diced dried fruit such as apricots, cranberries, or dates

ADJUST AND OVEN RACK TO THE MIDDLE POSITION and heat the oven to 350°F. Butter the bottom and sides of two 8-inch loaf pans and dust with flour; tap out any excess flour. Line the bottom of each pan with a piece of parchment paper.

Remove the skin from the persimmons and seed the fruit. Place the pulp in a blender and blend until smooth. Set aside.

In a medium bowl, mix together the persimmon pulp, eggs, butter, brandy, honey, vanilla, lemon juice and zest, orange juice and zest, ginger, and salt; set aside.

Sift together the flour, sugar, baking soda, cinnamon, nutmeg, and allspice into a large bowl. Using a rubber spatula, gently fold the persimmon mixture into the flour mixture until just combined; add the nuts and the raisins (the batter will be thick and heavy); do not overmix. Scrape the batter evenly into the prepared loaf pans; smooth the surface with a rubber spatula.

Bake for 30 minutes, then switch and rotate the pans; reduce the oven temperature to 325°F. Continue to bake until deep golden brown and a toothpick inserted in the center comes out clean, an additional 20 to 30 minutes. Cool pans on a cooling rack for 5 minutes; then invert the loaves onto the cooling rack, remove parchment, then turn right-side up and continue to cool until warm, about 25 minutes. Cut into slices and serve.

NOTE: The persimmon bread can be made up to five days in advance.

PREPARING FOR A DINNER PARTY

*B*EING THOROUGHLY PREPARED AND GIVING AMPLE FORETHOUGHT TO your event will help ensure a successful and unstressful dinner. The key is to do as much work as possible ahead of time so that you, too, can enjoy the special day.

1. Decide how many guests will be attending and assess how much space you have in your home and at the table.

2. Set the proper atmosphere with appropriate lighting and soft music. Have everything in place, the table set, and ready for your guests before they arrive.

3. Prepare all the food for the party ahead of time; keep hot items warm in an oven set at 200°F.

4. Use small white Christmas lights for a sparkling backdrop. Candles add instant drama and intimate lighting, so place small votives around your table. Do not use scented candles; you don't want other odors competing with the enticing aromas of your well-prepared entrées.

5. Decorate your table with a simple flower arrangement or sliced seasonal fruit set in clear bowls of water. Have name cards out so guests know where to sit.

6. Chill and open wine; set out wine glasses with wine charms (so people can find their drink if they set it down) and plenty of cocktail napkins.

7. Always have some food out for extra-hungry guests. A nice platter with sliced cheeses, dried fruit, sliced Prosciutto or salami, and fresh olives works perfectly. Don't forget plenty of fresh bread or crackers.

8. To prevent running back and forth to the kitchen, I like to have a staging area near the dining table to easily retrieve courses. All items that don't need to stay hot should be placed there. For instance, the salad can wait in the staging area; with the salad dressing in the bottom of the serving bowl and the lettuce and garnishes on top, you can toss it together just before serving. Place the dessert there as well (unless it must remain chilled) with serving utensils and appropriate dessert plates. Keep coffee in a thermal container to stay hot, with cream and sugar on the side. Drinks, side dishes, condiments, and sauces, plus extra napkins and flatware, can also stay in this area.

APPLE CRUMB PIE

A WONDERFULLY DELICIOUS APPLE PIE IS GRACED WITH A SIMPLE YET flavorful crunchy crumb topping. Use Granny Smith or Pippin apples for this recipe and top with Buttermilk Ice Cream (page 81).

MAKES 1 (9-INCH) PIE, SERVING 8

Sour Cream Piecrust (page 89), only one crust used

FILLING

$3^{1}/_{2}$ pounds (about 7 large) firm tart apples, such as Granny Smith or Pippin, peeled, cored, and cut into $^{1}/_{4}$-inch-thick slices (about 9 cups)

1 tablespoon lemon juice

2 tablespoons all-purpose flour

$^{1}/_{2}$ cup granulated sugar

$^{1}/_{4}$ teaspoon freshly grated cinnamon

CRUMB TOPPING

$^{3}/_{4}$ cup all-purpose flour

$^{1}/_{2}$ cup granulated sugar

$^{1}/_{2}$ cup packed light brown sugar

1 teaspoon ground cinnamon

$^{1}/_{4}$ teaspoon ground ginger

$^{1}/_{4}$ teaspoon ground nutmeg

$^{1}/_{8}$ teaspoon salt

6 tablespoons unsalted butter, cut into $^{1}/_{4}$-inch cubes and chilled

ADJUST AN OVEN RACK TO THE MIDDLE POSITION and heat the oven to 375°F.

FOR THE CRUST: Lay the prepared dough on a lightly floured work surface and roll the dough outward from its center into a 12-inch circle, about $^{1}/_{8}$-inch thick. Loosely fold into quarters and transfer to a 9-inch glass pie plate and delicately unfold and press it into the pie plate letting the excess hang over the pie plate. Trim off the excess dough to about $^{1}/_{2}$-inch larger than the edge of the pie plate. Tuck the excess $^{1}/_{2}$-inch of dough underneath itself to form a neat, even edge that sits on the top the pie plate and press a decorative trim with your thumb and forefinger. Place the crust in the refrigerator until needed.

FOR THE FILLING: In a large bowl, toss the apples with the lemon juice. Add the flour, sugar, and cinnamon; stir to combine and set aside.

FOR THE CRUMB TOPPING: In a food processor, pulse the flour, white sugar, brown sugar, cinnamon, ginger, nutmeg, salt, and lemon zest to combine. Scatter the butter pieces over the top and pulse until the mixture resembles coarse oatmeal. Transfer the mixture to a medium bowl and refrigerate until you are ready to assemble the pie. (This step can be completed one day ahead.)

Place the reserved apples in the prepared pie dough, piling them higher in the center. Sprinkle half of the crumb topping on top of the apples and place the remaining crumb topping back in the refrigerator until needed. Bake pie for 20 minutes, then add the additional topping to the apples and rotate the pie plate. Continue baking for another 40 minutes, or until the apples are tender when poked with a knife and topping is deep golden brown. Let the pie cool on a cooling rack until filling has set, about 2 hours; serve slightly warm or at room temperature.

BUTTERMILK ICE CREAM

BUTTERMILK MAKES THIS ICE CREAM TANGY AND RICH; A PERFECT companion for the sweet Persimmon Walnut Upside-Down Cake (page 87) or Apple Crumb Pie (page 80).

MAKES 4 CUPS

1 $2/3$ cup whole milk

1 $1/4$ granulated sugar

1 cup heavy cream

1 tablespoon honey

$1/8$ teaspoon kosher salt

1 vanilla bean, split and seeds scraped

8 large egg yolks

1 cup buttermilk

IN A MEDIUM SAUCEPAN OVER MEDIUM HEAT, bring the milk, sugar, cream, honey, salt, and vanilla seeds to a simmer.

As the milk mixture begins to simmer, whisk the yolks in a large bowl until broken up and combined. Then temper the egg yolks: while whisking the yolks vigorously, slowly pour 1 cup of the hot milk mixture into the yolks; then, while whisking the milk mixture, slowly add the yolk mixture into the pot with the simmering milk mixture. Reduce the heat to low; cook, stirring constantly, until the custard has reached 180°F on an instant-read thermometer, or has thickened and coats the back of a spoon. Remove from the heat; stir in the buttermilk. Pour the custard through a fine-mesh strainer into a medium bowl, cover, and place in the refrigerator for at least 4 hours or overnight.

Pour the custard into an ice-cream maker and process according to the manufacturer's directions.

CLASSIC PUMPKIN PIE

I ABSOLUTELY LOVE PUMPKIN PIE AND NO DESSERT SYMBOLIZES THANKSGIVING better. I've perfected this ubiquitous pie to tantalize your senses: it has velvety smooth texture, amazing pumpkin flavor, and just enough fragrant spices. Use the extra spice mixture over ice cream, in your morning oatmeal, or even in your coffee.

MAKES 1 (9-INCH) PIE, SERVING 8

Sour Cream Piecrust (page 89), only one crust used

SPICE MIXTURE
$^3/_4$ teaspoon ground allspice

$1^3/_4$ teaspoons ground cinnamon

$^3/_4$ teaspoon ground ginger

$^1/_2$ teaspoon salt

$^1/_4$ teaspoon ground cloves

PUMPKIN CUSTARD
$1^1/_2$ cups heavy cream

3 large eggs, beaten

2 tablespoons brandy

2 teaspoons Spice Mixture

1 cup canned unsweetened pumpkin purée

$^3/_4$ cup lightly packed brown sugar

1 tablespoon granulated sugar

ADJUST OVEN RACK TO THE MIDDLE POSITION and heat the oven to 350°F.

FOR THE CRUST: Lay the prepared dough on a lightly floured work surface and roll the dough outward from its center into a 12-inch circle, about $^1/_8$-inch thick. Loosely fold into quarters and transfer to a 9-inch glass pie plate and delicately unfold and press it into the pie plate letting the excess hang over the pie plate. Trim off the excess dough to about $^1/_2$-inch larger than the edge of the pie plate. Tuck the excess $^1/_2$-inch of dough underneath itself to form a neat, even edge that sits on the top the pie plate and press a decorative trim with your thumb and forefinger. Line the pie shell with a double layer of foil and fill with pie weights, old dried beans, or pennies.

Bake the piecrust for 15 minutes. Remove the weights and foil and continue to bake the crust until light golden brown and crisp, about 5 minutes longer. Place pie plate on cooling rack while assembling pumpkin custard. Keep oven on.

FOR THE SPICE MIXTURE: In a small bowl, combine all of the ingredients for the spice mixture; set aside.

FOR THE PUMPKIN CUSTARD: While piecrust is baking, whisk the cream, eggs, brandy, and 2 teaspoons of the spice mixture in a medium bowl until combined. Add the pumpkin, brown sugar, and sugar; whisk to combine. Pour the pumpkin custard into the warm pre-baked piecrust. Bake until the edges of the pie are set and the center registers 175°F on an instant-read thermometer, about 45 minutes. Cool the pie to room temperature on a cooling rack, 2 to 3 hours, before serving.

THREE-LAYER PUMPKIN PIE

A FAMILY FAVORITE, THIS THREE-LAYER CONFECTION IS TALKED ABOUT WELL before the holidays approach. Not only is this a visually appealing pie but also a symphony of marvelous pumpkin flavors and textures. This pie contains uncooked egg whites; because of the slight risk of salmonella, raw eggs should not be served to the very young, the ill or elderly, or to pregnant women. Use pasteurized liquid egg whites if you are uncomfortable using raw egg whites or see the note for a variation with cooked egg whites.

MAKES 1 (9-INCH) PIE, SERVING 8

Sour Cream Piecrust (page 89), only one crust used

SPICE MIXTURE

$3/4$ teaspoon ground allspice

$1^3/4$ teaspoons ground cinnamon

$3/4$ teaspoon ground ginger

$1/2$ teaspoon salt

$1/4$ teaspoon ground cloves

PUMPKIN CUSTARD

$3/4$ cup heavy cream

2 large eggs, beaten

1 tablespoon brandy

1 teaspoon Spice Mixture

$1/2$ cup canned unsweetened pumpkin purée

$1/3$ cup lightly packed brown sugar

$1^1/2$ teaspoons granulated sugar

PUMPKIN CHIFFON

1 envelope (1 tablespoon) unflavored granulated gelatin

$1^1/2$ cups canned unsweetened pumpkin purée

ADJUST OVEN RACK TO THE MIDDLE POSITION and heat the oven to 350°F.

FOR THE CRUST: Lay the prepared dough on a lightly floured work surface and roll the dough outward from its center into a 12-inch circle, about $1/8$-inch thick. Loosely fold into quarters and transfer to a 9-inch glass pie plate and delicately unfold and press it into the pie plate, letting the excess hang over the pie plate. Trim off the excess dough to about $1/2$-inch larger than the edge of the pie plate. Tuck the excess $1/2$-inch of dough underneath itself to form a neat, even edge that sits on the top the pie plate and press a decorative trim with your thumb and forefinger. Line the pie shell with a double layer of foil and fill with pie weights, old beans, or pennies.

Bake the piecrust for 15 minutes. Remove the weights and foil and continue to bake the crust until light golden brown and crisp, about 5 minutes longer. Place pie plate on cooling rack while assembling pumpkin custard. Keep oven on.

FOR THE SPICE MIXTURE: In a small bowl, combine all of the ingredients for the spice mixture; set aside.

FOR THE PUMPKIN CUSTARD: While the pie shell is baking, whisk the cream, eggs, brandy, and 2 teaspoons of the spice mixture in a medium bowl until combined. Add the pumpkin, brown sugar, and white sugar; whisk to combine. Pour the pumpkin custard into the warm pre-baked piecrust. Bake until the edges of the pie are set and the center registers 175°F on an instant-read thermometer, about 30

(continued)

¾ cup lightly packed
   brown sugar

4 large egg yolks

2 teaspoons Spice Mixture

3 large egg whites

1 tablespoon granulated sugar

WHIPPED CREAM

1½ cups heavy cream

3 tablespoons granulated
   sugar

minutes. Cool the pie to room temperature on a cooling rack, 1 to 2 hours, then refrigerate.

FOR THE CHIFFON LAYER: In a small saucepan, combine the gelatin and ¼ cup cold water and soak for 5 minutes. Meanwhile, in a medium saucepan over medium-low heat, whisk together the pumpkin purée, brown sugar, yolks, and 2 teaspoons of the spice mixture. While stirring constantly, bring to a simmer, then remove from the heat and transfer to a medium bowl; set aside. Place saucepan with the gelatin over low heat until completely melted, 1 to 2 minutes. Remove from the heat. Add the gelatin to the chiffon mixture; stir until thoroughly combined. Cover the bowl and place in the refrigerator until mixture is just set and the center jiggles slightly when shaken, 15 to 20 minutes.

In medium bowl, using an electric mixer, whip the heavy cream on medium speed until small bubbles form, about 30 seconds. Increase the speed to medium high and sprinkle in the sugar; continue to whip the cream until it thickens and forms stiff peaks, about 2 minutes. Reserve ¼ cup; cover and place in refrigerator until needed.

TO ASSEMBLE PIE: Using an electric mixer, whip the egg whites at medium-low speed until frothy, 1 to 2 minutes. While the mixer is running sprinkle in the sugar, increase the mixer speed to medium high, and whip until stiff peaks form, 1 to 2 minutes. Using a whisk, stir about one-quarter of the whipped egg whites into the chiffon mixture to lighten it; using a rubber spatula, gently fold in the remaining egg whites and reserved ¼ cup heavy cream until no white streaks remain. Spread the chiffon mixture onto the prepared pumpkin pie, mounding it slightly in the middle. Spread the whipped cream attractively over the top of the pie. Serve immediately or refrigerate until needed.

NOTE: If you prefer to cook your egg-white meringue, place a medium bowl over a saucepan of barely simmering water and add the egg whites and sugar. (See double boiler explanation on page 36.) Lightly whisk until the egg whites register 140°F on an instant-read thermometer or they are hot to the touch. Pour the hot whites into a room-temperature bowl and whip with an electric mixer on medium-high speed until doubled in volume and stiff peaks form, 1 to 2 minutes. Resume recipe, using these cooked whipped whites in place of the uncooked whipped whites.

PERSIMMON WALNUT UPSIDE-DOWN CAKE

A SEASONAL VERSION OF THE CLASSIC UPSIDE-DOWN CAKE. FRESH SWEET persimmons and slightly tart, crunchy walnuts create a balanced favor and impressive-looking results. For an extra treat, serve with Buttermilk Ice Cream (page 81).

MAKES 1 (9-INCH) ROUND CAKE, SERVING 8

TOPPING

4 tablespoons unsalted butter

1/2 cup firmly packed brown sugar

1 pound Fuyu persimmons, peeled, pitted, and cut into 1/2-thick slices

1/2 cup chopped walnuts, toasted

CAKE

1 1/4 cups all-purpose flour

1 1/2 teaspoons baking powder

1 teaspoon baking soda

4 large eggs, separated

8 tablespoons (1 stick) unsalted butter, softened

1 cup granulated sugar

1/2 teaspoon salt

1 teaspoon vanilla extract

1 1/2 teaspoons lemon zest

ADJUST THE OVEN RACK TO THE LOWEST POSITION and heat the oven to 350°F.

FOR THE TOPPING: Place a cast-iron skillet over medium heat and melt the butter and brown sugar in the bottom of the pan until it begins to bubble. Remove from the heat and sprinkle walnuts over mixture; overlap the persimmon slices on top; set aside.

FOR THE CAKE: In a medium bowl, sift together the flour, baking powder, and baking soda; set aside.

In a separate medium bowl, using an electric mixer, beat the egg whites at a medium-high speed until stiff peaks form, about 3 minutes; set aside.

In a large bowl, using an electric mixer, beat the butter, sugar, and salt together at medium-low speed until the sugar is moistened, about 30 seconds. Increase the speed to medium high and beat until the mixture is light and fluffy, about 2 to 3 minutes, scraping down the bowl with a spatula halfway through. With the mixer running at medium speed, add the egg yolks one at a time, beating well after each addition and scraping down the bowl halfway though. Beat in the vanilla and lemon zest. Turn the mixer to low speed and slowly add the flour mixture and beat until smooth and fully incorporated, about 10 seconds.

Using a rubber spatula, stir 1/3 of the beaten egg whites into the batter to lighten it. Gently fold the remaining whites into the batter until no white streaks remain, do not overmix. Pour the batter into the pan and spread evenly over the fruit. Lightly tap the pan against the countertop two times to settle the batter.

Bake until the cake is golden brown and a toothpick inserted into the center comes out clean, 30 to 35 minutes, rotating the pan halfway through the baking time.

(continued)

Cool the pan on a cooling rack for 20 minutes. Run a small knife around the sides of the cake to loosen. Place an upside-down serving platter tightly over the top of the cake pan; using a potholder to protect your hands, invert the cake pan and serving plate together. Lift off the cake pan so that the cake is now sitting fruit-side up on the serving plate. If any fruit sticks to the pan bottom, remove it and position it back on top of the cake. Serve warm.

NOTE: For a Strawberry Rhubarb Upside-Down Cake variation, butter the bottom and sides of a 9-inch non-stick round cake pan that is at least 2 inches high; set aside. Adjust the oven rack to the lowest position and heat the oven to 350°F.

In a medium bowl, combine 2 cups halved strawberries (8 ounces), 2 cups rough chopped rhubarb pieces (about 2 cups), 1 tablespoon freshly squeezed lemon juice, $\frac{1}{2}$ cup sugar, and 1 teaspoon vanilla; toss to coat and let sit for 15 minutes. Melt 2 tablespoons unsalted butter in a medium saucepan over high heat; add the berry mixture and bring to a boil. Reduce heat to medium low; simmer until mixture has thickened and become glossy, about 20 minutes. Pour the fruit mixture into the prepared pan and lightly smooth it into an even layer. Set aside. Proceed with the rest of the cake preparation as directed.

SOUR CREAM PIECRUST

*T*HIS IS THE ULTIMATE TENDER AND FLAKY PIECRUST RECIPE. THE ENZYMES IN the sour cream make the crust exceptionally tender and the butter ensures its flakiness. You can also use this crust for pot pies or little turnovers, savory or sweet. If you need only one crust for a recipe, freeze the other half of the dough for up to one month.

MAKES 2 PIECRUSTS

3 cups all-purpose flour

$\frac{1}{4}$ teaspoon salt

12 ounces (3 sticks) unsalted butter, cut into $\frac{1}{4}$-inch pieces and frozen

$1\frac{1}{4}$ cups sour cream

PULSE THE FLOUR AND SALT TOGETHER in a food processor until combined. Scatter the pieces of butter over the top of the flour mixture; pulse until the butter is the size of large peas, about 20 pulses. Add sour cream and pulse until the dough forms one large ball.

Divide the dough into two even pieces. Turn each piece of dough onto a sheet of plastic wrap and flatten each into a 4-inch disk. Wrap each piece tightly in plastic wrap and refrigerate for 1 hour to let the dough rest. Before rolling the dough out, let it sit on the counter to soften slightly, about 10 minutes.

NOTE: The dough can be refrigerated for up to two days or frozen for up to one month. If frozen, let the dough thaw completely on the counter before rolling out.

CITRUS-CRANBERRY GLAZE

*T*HIS GLAZE WILL ADD WONDERFUL SWEET-SOUR CHARACTER WHEN SERVED with baked ham or turkey. It's also delicious as an accompaniment to an appetizing cheese board with crackers. I'm particularly fond of serving this bright, tart glaze with the Twice-Baked Blue Cheese Soufflés (page 33).

(page 33)

MAKES 2 CUPS

2 cups freshly squeezed tangerine juice

1 cup freshly squeezed Meyer lemon juice

1 cup freshly squeezed orange juice

1 cup white wine

$\frac{1}{4}$ cup Champagne vinegar

1 small white onion, chopped (about $\frac{1}{2}$ cup)

1 tablespoon finely chopped lemongrass

$\frac{1}{4}$ teaspoon red pepper flakes

1 star anise

$\frac{1}{4}$ bay leaf

1 teaspoon coriander seeds, lightly toasted

$\frac{2}{3}$ cup cranberries

IN A MEDIUM SAUCEPAN OVER MEDIUM-LOW HEAT, combine all the ingredients except the cranberries. Simmer the sauce until it has reduced by two thirds, or until it lightly coats the back of a wooden spoon, about 15 minutes.

Strain the sauce through a fine-mesh sieve and then return the sauce back into the pot. Add the cranberries. Simmer over medium-low heat until the cranberries start to pop open. Remove the sauce from the heat; let cool 30 minutes before serving.

CHIMICHURRI

THIS FAMOUS PIQUANT SAUCE HAILS FROM ARGENTINA AND IS EXCELLENT as a marinade or sauce to accompany grilled meats. Try it on the Wood-Grilled Butterflied Leg of Lamb (page 54).

MAKES 1 CUP

4 garlic cloves, finely chopped

1 teaspoon kosher salt

$\frac{1}{2}$ teaspoon freshly ground black pepper

1 teaspoon freshly squeezed lemon juice

2 tablespoons red wine vinegar

2 teaspoons finely chopped fresh oregano

1 teaspoon red pepper flakes

$\frac{1}{4}$ cup extra-virgin olive oil

1 small red onion, finely chopped (about $\frac{1}{4}$ cup)

$\frac{1}{4}$ cup finely chopped flat-leaf parsley

2 tablespoons finely chopped fresh mint

IN A MORTAR AND PESTLE, or cutting board with the side of a knife, mash the garlic, salt, and pepper together until a paste is formed. Transfer the paste to a medium bowl; add the lemon juice, vinegar, oregano, and red pepper. Whisk in the olive oil, onion, parsley, and mint.

JELLIED CRANBERRY SAUCE

I ABSOLUTELY LOVE CRANBERRY SAUCE AND IT IS SO SIMPLE TO MAKE. FOREGO the canned version and make your own this year; the cranberry flavor is so clean, crisp, sweet, and tart you will never eat the canned product again. If only frozen cranberries are available, do not defrost them before use; just pick through them and add two minutes to the simmering time.

MAKES 3 CUPS

2 (12-ounce) bags cranberries, washed and picked over

1 cup granulated sugar

¼ cup packed dark brown sugar

2 tablespoons freshly squeezed lemon juice

2 tablespoons vanilla extract

⅛ teaspoon ground cinnamon

⅛ teaspoon kosher salt

IN LARGE SAUCEPAN OVER MEDIUM HEAT, combine all of the ingredients; cover, and bring to a simmer. Reduce the heat to low; uncover, and simmer, stirring occasionally until the sauce has slightly thickened and most of the berries have popped open, 10 to 15 minutes. Pass the sauce through a food mill or fine-mesh sieve for a finer consistency; for a chunkier texture, just use as is. Cool to room temperature, and serve.

NOTE: The cranberry sauce can be covered and refrigerated for up to seven days; let it stand at room temperature for thirty minutes before serving.

RED ONION AND TOMATO RELISH

THIS LIGHT AND BRIGHT RELISH CAN ACCOMPANY ANY MEAT, POULTRY, OR FISH. I am particuarly fond of it with the Grilled Spicy Sole Fillets (page 55).

MAKES 2 CUPS

1 small red onion, finely chopped (about 1 cup)

1 large tomato, seeded and finely chopped (about 1 cup)

$\frac{1}{2}$ cup finely chopped chives

$\frac{1}{4}$ cup extra-virgin olive oil

1 tablespoon sherry vinegar

2 teaspoons freshly squeezed lemon juice

2 teaspoons freshly squeezed lime juice

1 teaspoon kosher salt

$\frac{1}{2}$ teaspoon freshly ground black pepper

$\frac{1}{8}$ teaspoon dry mustard

COMBINE ALL OF THE INGREDIENTS in a medium bowl; stir to combine. Let mixture stand at room temperature for at least 30 minutes before serving. Adjust seasoning with salt and pepper, if necessary. Serve or refrigerate until needed.

SPICY GLAZED WALNUTS

SERVE THESE SWEET AND SAVORY NUTS WITH THE YANKEE SALAD WITH APPLE, Walnuts, and Blue Cheese (page 30) or the Twice-Baked Blue Cheese Soufflés (page 33). They also make a nice garnish on a cheese platter or a thoughtful hostess gift or office present.

$2/3$ cup honey

$2/3$ cup granulated sugar

8 tablespoons unsalted butter

2 teaspoons kosher salt

2 teaspoons freshly ground black pepper

$1/2$ teaspoon cayenne pepper

4 cups walnuts

ADJUST AN OVEN RACK TO THE MIDDLE POSITION and heat the oven to 350°F. Line a rimmed baking sheet with parchment paper. In a medium saucepan over medium-high heat, combine the honey, sugar, $1/2$ cup of water, butter, salt, pepper, and cayenne. Bring to a boil, whisking constantly. Stir in the walnuts and cook, stirring constantly with a wooden spoon, until almost all the liquid has evaporated and the nuts are completely coated and shiny, about 3 minutes. Transfer the glazed walnuts into the parchment paper–lined baking sheet. Bake until toasted and fragrant, about 10 minutes. Remove from the oven and let the nuts cool completely; do not refrigerate.

NOTE: Nuts can be stored in a tightly sealed container for up to three weeks.

LEMON-THYME-MUSTARD BUTTER

SERVE THIS AROMATIC BUTTER ON POULTRY, FISH, POTATOES, OR VEGETABLES. It is especially good with the Wood-Grilled Turkey Chop with Wild Mushroom Gravy (page 47).

MAKES ½ CUP

6 tablespoons unsalted butter, softened

1 tablespoon chopped fresh thyme

3 tablespoons Dijon mustard

½ teaspoon kosher salt

¼ teaspoon freshly ground black pepper

½ lemon, juiced

COMBINE ALL THE INGREDIENTS IN A SMALL BOWL; mix well. Cover and refrigerate. Serve at room temperature.

LEMON-BASIL VINAIGRETTE

CHARDONNAY VINEGAR HAS A SMOOTH YET CRISP FRUITY FLAVOR AND A fresh lemon citrus fragrance. It invariably enhances the lemon flavor in this dressing. It can be found at upscale grocer's or specialty kitchen stores. If you're unable to find it, just substitute Champagne vinegar or white wine vinegar. Store in the refrigerator for up to two weeks.

MAKES 2 CUPS

3 lemons, zest grated from 2 lemons, ½ cup freshly squeezed lemon juice

1 cup extra-virgin olive oil

¼ cup Chardonnay vinegar

1³/₄ tablespoons Dijon mustard

½ tablespoon dry mustard

½ cup chopped fresh basil

1 small red onion, finely chopped (about ½ cup)

½ teaspoon kosher salt

½ teaspoon freshly ground black pepper

IN A LARGE BOWL, whisk together all of the ingredients. Let vinaigrette sit at room temperature for at least ½ hour. Adjust seasonings to taste. Serve at room temperature.

NOTE: For an emulsified dressing, place mustard and dry mustard in a blender; purée while alternately adding the lemon juice, vinegar, and oil. Transfer the contents to a medium bowl and stir in the remaining ingredients.

TURKEY GRAVY

I'VE BEEN MAKING THIS GRAVY FOR YEARS. IT NEVER FAILS TO PLEASE AND your family will definitely enjoy it. The sherry vinegar is my secret ingredient that gives the gravy a rich balanced flavor. Store-bought stock will work fine in a pinch.

MAKES 4 CUPS

4 tablespoons unsalted butter

1 medium yellow onion, chopped

$\frac{1}{2}$ cup all-purpose flour

8 cups cold turkey stock (page 101), or organic, free-range, low-sodium chicken stock

8 sprigs flat-leaf parsley

3 sprigs thyme

2 sprigs sage

$\frac{1}{2}$ bay leaf

1 tablespoon sherry vinegar

$\frac{1}{2}$ teaspoon kosher salt

$\frac{1}{2}$ teaspoon freshly ground black pepper

MELT THE BUTTER IN A LARGE SAUCEPAN over medium heat. Add the onions, cover, and cook until they have softened, stirring occasionally, about 5 minutes. Remove the cover and turn the heat to low. Stir in the flour and cook, stirring occasionally, until the flour has turned slightly brown, about 7 minutes. Slowly whisk in the cold turkey stock and add the parsley, thyme, sage, bay leaf, and vinegar; increase the heat to medium high and bring to a boil. Then, reduce heat to low and simmer, stirring often, until the gravy has reduced by half, about 1 hour.

Pass the gravy through a fine-mesh sieve into a large bowl. Season with salt and pepper to taste.

NOTE: The gravy can be made up to four days ahead.

ONION-BOURBON-HORSERADISH MUSTARD

*U*SE FRESH HORSERADISH IF YOU CAN FIND IT. THIS PREPARED MUSTARD makes an excellent hostess gift or stocking stuffer. Serve with Spiced Honey-Baked Ham (page 39) and Dill Buttermilk Drop Biscuits (page 76).

MAKES 2 CUPS

3 tablespoons olive oil

1 large Vidalia onion, or other sweet onion, finely chopped (about 1¼ cup)

⅓ cup bourbon

1 cup Dijon mustard

5 tablespoons grated fresh horseradish

4 tablespoons mustard seeds, toasted and ground

3 tablespoons freshly squeezed lemon juice

1 teaspoon kosher salt

1 teaspoon freshly ground black pepper

HEAT THE OLIVE OIL IN A SMALL SAUCEPAN over medium heat. Add the onions; cook, stirring occasionally, until onions are tender and light brown, about 10 minutes. Remove the pan from the heat and add the bourbon. Place the pan back over the heat. Simmer the sauce, stirring occasionally, until it is thick and has reduced by a third, about 5 minutes. Remove the pan from the heat; cool the onion mixture to room temperature.

In a medium bowl, combine the onion mixture, mustard, horseradish, mustard seeds, lemon juice, salt, and pepper. Refrigerate until needed.

NOTE: Mustard will keep for one month in the refrigerator.

CORN STOCK

ORN IS A STAPLE IN THE MIDWEST, WHERE I AM FROM, AND WE USE EVERY last part of it. I wouldn't consider myself an American chef without using it. Use this versatile stock in place of vegetable stock and in other recipes in the book, as it really adds an subtle, sweet, and nutty flavor.

10 ears corn, husks and silk removed, chopped into 2-inch pieces

3 medium carrots, chopped

1 white onion, chopped

2 stalks celery, chopped

6 garlic cloves

$\frac{1}{4}$ cup finely sliced lemon grass

$\frac{1}{2}$ bay leaf

12 sprigs flat-leaf parsley

1 tablespoon black peppercorns

COMBINE ALL THE INGREDIENTS in a large Dutch oven. Add enough water to just cover the ingredients; bring to a boil over medium-high heat. Reduce the heat to low and simmer for 45 minutes. Remove from the heat. Strain the stock through a fine-mesh strainer into a large bowl; discard solids. Cool stock to room temperature. Transfer the stock to an airtight container and refrigerate until needed. Stock can be made up to 4 days ahead.

NOTE: The stock can be frozen in one-cup portions for up to three months.

LOBSTER STOCK

USE FOR SHELLFISH CHOWDER (PAGE 23) OR ADD YOUR FAVORITE VEGETABLES, noodles, and shrimp for an easy soup. Crab shells can be easily substituted to make a crab stock.

MAKES 8 CUPS

2 tablespoons olive oil

1 medium yellow onion, thinly sliced (about 1 cup)

2 stalks celery, coarsely chopped (about 1 cup)

2 medium carrots, coarsely chopped (about 1 cup)

1 leek, white part only, thinly sliced

3 large cooked lobster shells, or crab shells

4 plum tomatoes, fresh or canned, halved

4 cups vegetable stock (page 193)

1 cup sherry

1 cup dry white wine

PLACE THE OLIVE OIL IN A LARGE POT over high heat. Add the onions, celery, carrots, and leeks. Cover and reduce the heat to low. Cook the vegetables, stirring often, until tender and the onions are translucent, about 8 minutes. Increase the heat to high, add the shells, tomatoes, stock, 6 cups of water, sherry, and wine and bring to a boil. Reduce the heat to maintain a simmer. Cook, uncovered, for 1 hour.

Remove from the heat and pass stock through cheesecloth or a fine-mesh sieve. Refrigerate until needed or divide among 1-pint containers and freeze for up to three months.

TURKEY *or* CHICKEN STOCK

A GREAT GRAVY STARTS WITH FLAVORFUL TURKEY STOCK. THIS SIMPLE seasoned stock takes little time to prepare and is well worth the slight effort. Ask your butcher for a turkey carcass as they usually have them during the holidays. For a richer tasting stock, try roasting the turkey bones, as described below.

5½ pounds uncooked turkey parts, such as carcass, neck, backbone, and wings, chopped into 3-inch pieces (or similar uncooked chicken parts)

4 medium leeks (white part only), sliced thinly (about 2 cups)

2 medium yellow onions, quartered

5 medium carrots, cut into 1-inch pieces

4 stalks celery

3 bay leaves

16 stalks flat-leaf parsley

2 cups white wine

2 tablespoons sherry vinegar

1 tablespoon freshly ground black pepper

PLACE ALL OF THE INGREDIENTS in a large stockpot. Add 5 quarts cold water and bring to a boil. Reduce the heat to medium low and simmer uncovered for 2 hours. Occasionally skim the solids that accumulate on the surface, as this will ensure a clear stock.

Strain the stock through a fine-mesh sieve into a large bowl. Refrigerate or freeze until needed. Stock can be frozen for up to four months.

NOTE: For a darker and more complex stock, you can roast the turkey bones and parts before adding them to the stockpot. Adjust an oven rack to the middle position and heat the oven to 400°F. Place the turkey bones, giblets, and neck in a large roasting pan. Roast until golden brown, about 25 minutes. Transfer the roasted bones and any accumulated juices to the stockpot and begin recipe.

THANKSGIVING DINNER MENUS

A TRADITIONAL THANKSGIVING MENU

Drink:
Apple Juice with Cranberry and Ginger *(page 18)*

Appetizers:
Twice-Baked Blue Cheese Soufflés *(page 33)*;
Citrus-Cranberry Glaze *(page 90)*

Soup:
Shellfish Chowder *(page 23)*

Salad:
Yankee Salad with Apple,
Walnuts, and Blue Cheese with
Lemon-Basil Vinaigrette *(page 30)*

Entrée:
Sage-Butter-Roasted Turkey *(page 40)*

Sides:
Turkey Gravy *(page 97)*; Mashed Red Potatoes
with Garlic *(page 67)*; Buttered Brussels Sprouts
and Chestnuts *(page 58)*; Corn and Sage
Stuffing *(page 65)*; Sweet Potato Gratin *(page 68)*;
Jellied Cranberry Sauce *(page 93)*

Bread:
Persimmon Bread *(page 77)*

Dessert:
Three-Layer Pumpkin Pie with
Sour Cream Piecrust *(page 84)*

"SOMETHING DIFFERENT" THANKSGIVING MENU

Drink:
Sparkling Pear Punch *(page 21)*

Appetizer:
Corn and Shrimp Fritters *(page 31)*

Soup:
Roasted Harvest Squash Soup *(page 25)*

Salad:
Endive Salad with Tangerines
and Kumquats *(page 26)*

Entrée:
Spiced Honey-Baked Ham *(page 39)*

Sides:
Braised Napa Cabbage with
Apple and Bacon *(page 57)*;
Butternut Squash Gratin *(page 60)*

Bread:
Dill Buttermilk Drop Biscuits *(page 76)*

Dessert:
Apple Crumb Pie with
Sour Cream Piecrust *(page 80)*

QUIET DINNER FOR TWO MENU

Salad:
Endive Salad with Tangerines
and Kumquats *(page 26)*

Entrée:
Pan-Roasted Turkey Breast with
Sweet Squash Matchsticks *(page 44)*

Sides:
Celery Root and Pear Purée *(page 61)*;
Roasted Broccoli Rabe with
Fennel and Orange *(page 158)*

Dessert:
Persimmon Walnut
Upside-Down Cake *(page 87)*

THANKSGIVING DINNER FROM THE GRILL MENU

Appetizer:
Broiled Oysters with
Mignonette Sauce *(page 130)*

Salad:
Roasted Pear and Goat Cheese Salad *(page 28)*

Entrée:
Wood-Grilled Turkey Chop with
Wild Mushroom Gravy *(page 47)*

Sides:
Winter Panzanella *(page 70)*;
Grilled Corn with Roasted
Red Pepper Butter *(page 63)*; Wine-
Braised Artichokes *(page 153)*

Dessert:
Apple Crumb Pie with
Sour Cream Piecrust *(page 80)*

THANKSGIVING PREPARATION SCHEDULE

COOKING FOR A LARGE GATHERING CAN BE A DAUNTING UNDERTAKING BUT if you stay focused and stick to a well-planned agenda, you will be surprised just how easy and fulfilling the task can be. Here is a simple plan to help you stay on track for your special holiday meal. Use this template for other holiday menus in this book.

UP TO THREE WEEKS AHEAD:

Call grocer and order fresh turkey.

Prepare and freeze Lobster Stock for the Shellfish Chowder
   (or omit this step if using bottled clam juice).

Prepare and freeze the Turkey Stock.

Prepare and freeze the Persimmon Bread.

UP TO ONE WEEK AHEAD:

Make and freeze Sour Cream Piecrust in pie plates.

Make the Citrus-Cranberry Glaze. Refrigerate in glass jars.

Make the Spicy Glazed Walnuts.

Make the Jellied Cranberry Sauce.

UP TO FOUR DAYS AHEAD:

Prepare the Turkey Gravy.

UP TO THREE DAYS AHEAD:

Prepare the Apple Juice with Cranberry and Ginger.

Prepare the Twice-Baked Blue Cheese Soufflés up to make-ahead point.

UP TO TWO DAYS AHEAD:

Pick up fresh turkey.

Prepare the Shellfish Chowder up to make-ahead point.

Prepare the Sage Butter for turkey.

Prepare the Sweet Potato Gratin up to make-ahead point.

Bake the Three-Layer Pumpkin Pie.

Prepare the Corn and Sage Stuffing to make-ahead point.

Prepare the Lemon-Basil Vinaigrette.

THANKSGIVING MORNING:

Finish the Corn and Sage Stuffing.

Make the Mashed Red Potatoes with Garlic.

Assemble ingredients for the Buttered Brussels Sprouts and Chestnuts.

Assemble the Yankee Salad with Apple, Walnuts, and Blue Cheese.

> Toss the diced apples in the lemon juice to prevent browning. Place apples on the bottom of a salad bowl and with lettuces on top, followed by the blue cheese and the nuts. Do not add dressing. Cover tightly and refrigerate.

A FEW HOURS BEFORE DINNER:

Place the turkey in the oven.

Finish the Shellfish Chowder.

Cook the Sweet Potato Gratin.

Boil Brussels sprouts for Buttered Brussels Sprouts and Chestnuts.

AT THE LAST MINUTE:

Reheat the Corn and Sage Stuffing and Mashed Red Potatoes and Garlic together in the oven.

Finish Buttered Brussels Sprouts and Chestnuts.

Heat the Turkey Gravy.

Finish the Twice-Baked Blue Cheese Soufflés.

Add dressing to Yankee Salad with Apple, Walnuts, and Blue Cheese; toss.

Christmas Dinner

$\mathcal{A}$SK ME OR ANYONE ABOUT THEIR FAVORITE HOLIDAY MEMORIES, AND THEY almost never seem to be about the opening of elaborate or expensive gifts. I believe in the truly intangible gift of gathering together, when everyone makes what can— nowadays—be an enormous effort to congregate in one place at the same time. It is truly the best present to receive, and the memories last a lifetime. I'm not alone in that belief. If there is any doubt that the holidays are about presence, not presents, just check the airports and roadways.

The opportunity to prepare an exceptional feast for my family and friends is my biggest gift to bestow. It's a personal gesture that requires some time and a lot of forethought, but it is always graciously remembered and definitely savored.

Christmas dinners have always been big productions for my family and me. Decorating the home and Christmas tree absolutely helps set the holiday mood. It seems as though you can't walk down the street without passing a smile; everyone is happy during this holiday, and for me, it's because I'm looking forward to sharing a great meal and being with family. I'm certain that children's eagerness and excitement for presents help fuel the momentous energy flowing through the air. It definitely was in my home with so many sisters and brothers. I'm so thankful that my parents always took the time to make a delicious and impressive meal that really solidified the importance and significance of the holiday. It may have been freezing outside but the warmth inside and the aroma of roasting beef and candied yams always made us look forward to winter.

I have thought of new ideas and recipes that will remind you of the dinners of Christmas past. The Black Mustard Beef Tenderloin with Red Wine Sauce (page 140) with Roasted Cauliflower Florets (page 160) is so simple yet incredibly flavorful, and reminds me of Christmas dinners of my youth. My Chicken Liver Pâté with Pear and Currants (page 134) or Roasted Spiced Duck with Kumquat and Pomegranate Glaze (page 146) are great recipes for this time of year because they utilize the best of the seasonal winter fruits. These special meals and menus represent some of my most creative and delicious recipes. There are your traditional favorites—like rib roast and roasted pork—but with wonderful spices, cooking techniques, and presentation ideas that will ensure extra flavorful and juicy entrées with a lot of "wow" factor. Happy holidays!

EGGNOG, 114

HOT CHOCOLATE WITH CHAMPAGNE SABAYON, 115

WINTER CITRUS PUNCH WITH SPICED POMEGRANATE ICE, 117

BEET AND APPLE BORSCHT, 118

ELEPHANT GARLIC SOUP WITH DUNGENESS CRAB SALAD, 121

CRAB CAKE AND CITRUS SALAD, 122

CRISPY SHRIMP SALAD WITH CRANBERRIES AND GOAT CHEESE, 123

GREEN GODDESS SALAD WITH SHRIMP, 124

SHAVED FENNEL AND MUSHROOM SALAD, 125

SPINACH SALAD WITH POMEGRANATES AND BLUE CHEESE, 126

WINTER VEGETABLE SALAD, 129

BROILED OYSTERS, 130

CAVIAR POTATO PUFFS, 131

CHICKEN LIVER PÂTÉ WITH PEAR AND CURRANTS, 134

FOIE GRAS POPPERS, 135

BRAISED LAMB SHOULDER WITH BUTTER BEANS, 136

COFFEE-SPICED PRIME RIB ROAST, 139

BLACK MUSTARD BEEF TENDERLOIN WITH RED WINE SAUCE, 140

HONEY- AND CIDER-VINEGAR-BASTED RACK OF PORK, 143

GRILLED CORNISH GAME HENS WITH SPICED CHERRY RUB, 144

ROASTED SPICED DUCK WITH KUMQUAT AND POMEGRANATE GLAZE, 146

CRISPY FLOUNDER WITH CARA CARA ORANGE SAUCE AND LUMP CRAB, 149

BASIL GNOCCHI, 151

ARTICHOKE AND ELEPHANT GARLIC SOUFFLÉ SPOONBREAD, 152

WINE-BRAISED ARTICHOKES, 153

CANDIED YAMS, 154

DOUBLE-STUFFED BAKED POTATOES, 157

ROASTED BROCCOLI RABE WITH FENNEL AND ORANGE, 158

ROASTED CAULIFLOWER FLORETS, 160

ROASTED SPAGHETTI SQUASH NOODLES, 161

WHIPPED SWEET POTATOES, 162

BOSTON BROWN BREAD, 163

CINNAMON BREAD WITH BROWN-SUGAR SWIRL, 164

CHIVE-ONION POPOVERS WITH TOASTED CARDAMOM, 166

SOFT ROLLS, 168

RED ONION AND PARMESAN CRACKERS, 169

CHOCOLATE BRIOCHE PUDDING, 171

CHOCOLATE CREAM PUFFS, 172

CHOCOLATE WHIPPED CREAM, 174

DEVIL'S FOOD CHOCOLATE CUPCAKES, 175

ESPRESSO DOUBLE-CHOCOLATE SOUFFLÉ BROWNIES, 176

CHRISTMAS ORANGE SHORTBREAD, 177

GINGER SNAP COOKIES WITH LEMON THYME, 178

PARSNIP COOKIES WITH MAPLE GLAZE, 179

HOLIDAY TANGERINE BARS, 180

PUMPKIN COOKIES WITH LEMON CREAM CHEESE FROSTING, 183

MILK CHOCOLATE AND DRUNKEN PRUNE ICE CREAM, 184

HOT FUDGE SAUCE, 185

HORSERADISH CRÈME FRAÎCHE, 186

MIGNONETTE SAUCE, 186

PERSIMMON DRESSING, 187

GREEN APPLE AND PUMPKIN BUTTER, 188

CHAMPAGNE SABAYON, 189

KAHLUA SABAYON, 190

BEER BATTER, 191

SEASONED FLOUR, 191

QUINCE COMPOTE, 192

VEGETABLE STOCK, 193

A SPECIAL NOTE ON HOLIDAY TRADITIONS

*H*OLIDAY TRADITIONS ARE AN ESSENTIAL PART OF THE FAMILY GATHERING, no matter what your beliefs are or how you celebrate the season. Whether you observe a spiritual, cultural, or commercial holiday, your family traditions make the seasonal celebration uniquely personal.

Popular *Thanksgiving traditions* include the presidential pardon of a lucky turkey, football games, and department store parades. Try making your own family tradition by volunteering at a soup kitchen, preparing a special dish, or doing something unusual with pumpkin each year. My family's favorite Thanksgiving custom is our Jenga tournament.

Christmas is definitely the most celebrated holiday around the world. Traditions vary but often include decorating the Christmas tree, attending church, exchanging presents, roasting chestnuts, exchanging cookies, even leaving some treats out for Santa. To start your own tradition, try creating a family ornament each year, exchanging one handmade gift, playing a special card game, or, my favorite, watching a classic movie—complete with buttered popcorn and candy.

The New Year holiday has, by far, the most interesting food traditions. Every culture carries some belief that eating certain foods on *New Year's Day* will ensure a prosperous, healthy, and happy path. The foods that promise such luck are leafy greens that resemble folded money and beans that look like coins when cooked, which signify wealth and good fortune. Pork symbolizes progress because pigs move forward while foraging. Unlucky foods are lobster and chicken since they both move backwards. Also, you should never eat anything with wings at this time, as it's believed your fortune will fly away.

Other less delicious New Year traditions include watching your favorite football game or the Rose Parade. A thoughtful family tradition is to write each family member a letter stating your memories of the past year and what you are hoping for in the next. Seal the letters with wax and open them on New Year's Day the following year. It's a fun way to see what you were thinking exactly one year ago and find out how many wishes came true.

EGGNOG

*E*GGNOG GETS ITS NAME FROM THE WORD *NOGGIN,* WHICH IS A SMALL MUG OR cup in which eggnog was served in earlier times. These days, eggnog is still a wonderful and anticipated treat during the holidays. In this recipe, the ice cream adds a velvety smooth vanilla flavor to the beverage. Greater or lesser amounts of liquors may be added depending on taste. This recipe contains directions for both the traditional version with raw eggs and a cooked-egg version; because of the slight risk of salmonella, raw eggs should not be served to the very young, the ill or elderly, or to pregnant women.

MAKES 6 SERVINGS

6 large eggs, separated

³/₄ cup granulated sugar, divided

¹/₂ cup brandy

¹/₂ cup dark rum

1 tablespoon vanilla extract

1 pint vanilla ice cream, softened

4 cups heavy cream

Freshly grated nutmeg, to taste

FOR TRADITIONAL EGGNOG (with raw eggs): In a large bowl, beat the egg yolks with an electric mixer on medium-high speed until they lighten in color. Gradually add ¹/₂ cup of the sugar and continue to beat until the mixture is light yellow and fluffy, about 3 minutes. Add the brandy, rum, vanilla extract, and ice cream; stir to combine. (This can be made two days in advance and refrigerated.)

In a separate bowl, beat the egg whites with an electric mixer on high speed until soft peaks form; with the mixer still running, gradually add the remaining ¹/₄ cup sugar and beat until stiff peaks form. Gently fold egg whites into egg yolk mixture. Stir in 1 cup of heavy cream; gently fold in remaining the remaining 3 cups. Cover and chill for at least 3 hours. Dust with freshly grated nutmeg before serving.

FOR COOKED-EGG EGGNOG: In a large bowl beat the egg yolks with an electric mixer on medium-high speed until they lighten in color. Gradually add ¹/₂ cup of the sugar and continue to beat until the mixture is pale yellow and fluffy, about 3 minutes; set aside.

In a medium saucepan, over medium heat, bring the heavy cream to a simmer, stirring occasionally. Remove the cream from the heat and slowly add it into the egg mixture, stirring constantly. Return cream and egg mixture back into the pot and cook over medium-low heat, stirring constantly, until the mixture registers 160°F on an instant-read thermometer, 8 to 10 minutes. (Do not let the custard overcook or simmer.) Remove from the heat, stir in the brandy, rum, and vanilla extract. Pour the mixture into a medium bowl, cover, and place in refrigerator to chill thoroughly. (This step can be done two days in advance.)

Place the egg whites and remaining sugar in a medium glass bowl set over a pot of barely simmering water. Whisk constantly until the sugar has dissolved and the egg whites have reached 140°F on an instant-read thermometer, or they are hot to the touch, 5 to 7 minutes. Carefully remove the bowl from the pot of simmering water and beat the egg whites on low speed until soft peaks form. Increase the mixer speed to high and beat the egg whites until stiff peaks form; set aside. Stir the vanilla ice cream into the chilled egg yolk mixture until thoroughly blended. Gently fold in the egg whites. Cover and chill for at least 3 hours. Dust with freshly grated nutmeg before serving.

HOT CHOCOLATE *with* CHAMPAGNE SABAYON

THE HOT CHOCOLATE CAN BE MADE SEVERAL DAYS AHEAD AND WARMED JUST before service. For a more adult beverage, add your favorite liquor and Champagne Sabayon (page 189) or Kahlua Sabayon (page 190). It's also good with the Chocolate Whipped Cream (page 174).

MAKES 4 SERVINGS

2 ounces bittersweet chocolate

2 ounces semisweet chocolate

$\frac{1}{3}$ cup firmly packed dark brown sugar

2 cups whole milk

2 cups heavy cream

1 teaspoon vanilla extract

1 recipe Champagne Sabayon (page 189) or Kahlua Sabayon (page 190)

MELT THE CHOCOLATES AND SUGAR together in a double boiler: a medium glass bowl set over a saucepan filled with 1 inch of simmering water. Add the milk and cream and cook, stirring occasionally, until the milk is hot and steaming. Turn off the heat; add the vanilla. Keep mixture warm until ready to serve. Dollop sabayon on top.

WINTER CITRUS PUNCH
with SPICED POMEGRANATE ICE

ALL COLORS, SEASONAL FRUITS, FRAGRANT SPICES, AND ROBUST FLAVORS are showcased in this memorable and festive punch. For extra holiday cheer, add rum or Cointreau.

2 cups fresh pomegranate juice

3 star anise, crushed

10 peppermint leaves, plus additional sprigs for garnish

2 cups freshly squeezed tangerine juice

2 cups freshly pressed pineapple juice

2 cups freshly squeezed blood orange juice

2 cups freshly squeezed orange juice

$\frac{1}{2}$ cup freshly squeezed Meyer lemon juice

1 tangerine, sliced $\frac{1}{2}$-inch thick, for garnish

1 blood orange, sliced $\frac{1}{2}$-inch thick, for garnish

1 Meyer lemon, sliced $\frac{1}{2}$-inch thick, for garnish

COMBINE THE POMEGRANATE JUICE, star anise, and peppermint leaves in a small pot over medium-high heat; bring to a boil. Turn off the heat and let the liquid steep for 15 minutes, then strain into a medium glass pitcher to cool to room temperature. Pour cooled liquid into empty ice cube trays and freeze completely.

In a large pitcher, combine the tangerine, pineapple, blood orange, orange, and lemon juices together and refrigerate until needed.

Place the juice and the frozen cubes in a large punch bowl; place the slices tangerine, orange, and lemon on the surface. Or, serve in individual glasses over the frozen cubes of pomegranate ice; garnish with sprigs of peppermint and sliced fruit.

BEET *and* APPLE BORSCHT

*T*HIS VIBRANT RUBY-RED-COLORED SOUP WILL MAKE A LOVELY PRESENTATION on your holiday table. The soup can be served hot or cold. Straining the soup gives the final product a velvety appearance and texture. Serve with Caviar Potato Puffs (page 131).

MAKES 6 SERVINGS

1 pound medium red beets, scrubbed and tops removed

4 sprigs thyme

10 sprigs dill, plus 2 tablespoons chopped, for garnish

12 garlic cloves

2 tablespoons olive oil

1$\frac{1}{2}$ teaspoon kosher salt, divided

1$\frac{1}{8}$ teaspoon freshly ground black pepper, divided

2 tablespoons unsalted butter

2 small yellow onions, chopped (about 2 cups)

2 medium carrots, chopped (about 1 cup)

$\frac{1}{4}$ head red cabbage, chopped (about 1 cup)

2 small Yukon gold potatoes, chopped (about 1 cup)

2 Granny Smith apples, cored, peeled and chopped

6 cups vegetable stock (page 193) or chicken stock (page 101)

2 tablespoons cider vinegar or Cabernet Sauvignon

$\frac{1}{2}$ cup crème fraîche, for garnish

Caviar Potato Puffs (page 131), for garnish

ADJUST AN OVEN RACK TO THE MIDDLE POSITION and heat the oven to 350°F.

Place the beets on a large piece of aluminum foil; add the thyme, sprigs of dill, and garlic; drizzle with the olive oil and sprinkle $\frac{1}{2}$ teaspoon of the salt and $\frac{1}{8}$ teaspoon of the pepper. Cover with another piece of aluminum foil and seal the edges. Place the foil packet on a baking sheet pan; bake until the beets are tender and a knife can be easily inserted into the beet, about 1 hour. When the beets are cool enough to handle, rub off the skins with a paper towel and roughly chop; set aside. Reserve the cooked garlic cloves.

Melt 2 tablespoons of the butter in a large pot over medium-low heat. Add the onions, carrots, and cabbage; cover and cook, stirring occasionally, until vegetables are lightly browned and tender, 15 minutes. Add the reserved garlic, beets, potatoes, apples, stock, vinegar, and remaining salt and pepper; simmer for 25 minutes.

Working in batches, purée the soup in a food processor until smooth. Serve hot or cold with a dollop of crème fraîche, three to four Caviar Potato Puffs, and a sprinkling of the dill.

Wine pairing: Riesling

ELEPHANT GARLIC SOUP *with* DUNGENESS CRAB SALAD

LEPHANT GARLIC IS NOT TRUE GARLIC; IN FACT, IT IS A MEMBER OF THE LEEK family. Its flavor is very mellow yet sweet and mildly garlicky. Most grocers carry elephant garlic next to the onions.

MAKES 4 SERVINGS

1 pound elephant garlic, peeled

6 cups vegetable stock (page 193)

4 tablespoons unsalted butter, divided

4 tablespoons extra-virgin olive oil, divided

$\frac{1}{2}$ teaspoon kosher salt, plus more for seasoning

$\frac{1}{2}$ teaspoon freshly ground black pepper, plus more for seasoning

2 leeks (white part only), roughly chopped (about 1$\frac{1}{2}$ cups)

1 medium yellow onion, chopped (about 1$\frac{1}{2}$ cups)

1 small fennel bulbs, chopped (about 1 cup)

1 bay leaf

1 small dried red chile or $\frac{1}{2}$ teaspoon red pepper flakes

2 tablespoons sherry vinegar

1 cup heavy cream

1 recipe Lobster Salad (page 26), substituting cooked Dungeness crab leg and body meat for the lobster

ADJUST AN OVEN RACK TO THE MIDDLE POSITION and heat the oven to 350°F.

In a glass baking dish, place the garlic, 1 cup of the vegetable stock, 2 tablespoons of the butter, 2 tablespoons of the oil, salt, and pepper. Cover with foil and bake until tender, about 1 hour.

Melt the remaining 2 tablespoons of butter and 2 tablespoons of olive oil in a medium skillet over medium heat. Add the leeks, onions, fennel, bay leaf, and chile; cover and cook, stirring occasionally, for 5 minutes. Add the remaining vegetable stock, vinegar, and the cooked garlic with its juices. Gently simmer, uncovered, for 20 minutes. Remove and discard the bay leaf and chile (if using flakes, leave them in the soup). Purée the soup in a blender or food processor, then pour through a fine-mesh strainer into a large bowl. Stir in the cream; adjust seasonings to taste.

To serve, pour $\frac{3}{4}$ cup of the soup into a bowl and top with $\frac{1}{4}$ cup of the crab salad.

NOTE: For a sophisticated presentation, use your cappuccino machine's steamer or a small blender to froth the soup before serving.

CRAB CAKE *and* CITRUS SALAD

I DON'T KNOW ANYONE WHO DOESN'T LIKE MY CRAB CAKES. I LOVE THIS SALAD and make it often for myself and guests. It reminds me of my time in Northern California when I used to pick up fresh crab from Fisherman's Wharf in San Francisco. The lump crabmeat sold at the fish counter will work just as well for this fresh and zesty crab cake.

MAKES 4 SERVINGS

1 1/2 cups freshly squeezed tangerine juice

1/2 cup freshly squeezed Meyer lemon juice

1/2 cup balsamic vinegar

1/2 teaspoon kosher salt

1 teaspoon freshly ground pepper

10 ounces fresh lump crabmeat (about 2 cups)

1/2 cup fresh white breadcrumbs

2 teaspoons freshly squeezed lemon juice

1 tablespoon finely chopped pasilla chile

1 tablespoon finely chopped yellow bell pepper

1 tablespoon finely chopped red bell pepper

1 tablespoon finely chopped red onion

1 tablespoon finely chopped celery

1 tablespoon finely chopped flat-leaf parsley

1/2 cup mayonnaise

1/8 teaspoon cayenne pepper

2 tangerines, peeled and sliced into 1/2-inch slices

2 Meyer lemons, peeled and sliced into 1/2-inch slices

2 1/2 cups mixed baby greens

Vegetable oil, for frying

Butter, for frying (optional)

IN A SMALL SAUCEPAN OVER HIGH HEAT bring the tangerine juice, lemon juice, and vinegar to a boil. Reduce the heat to medium low; simmer until the sauce lightly coats the back of a spoon, about 15 minutes. Remove the dressing from the heat and adjust seasoning to taste. Set aside.

In a large bowl, mix the crab, breadcrumbs, lemon juice, chile, peppers, onion, celery, parsley, mayonnaise, salt, pepper, and cayenne until thoroughly combined. Form the crab mixture into eight cakes.

In a large nonstick skillet over medium-high heat add equal parts of oil and butter to evenly coat the bottom of the pan. Add the crab cakes and cook until heated through and golden brown on each side, about 3 minutes per side. Place cooked crab cakes on a paper towel–lined plate to drain.

In a large bowl, toss the tangerine slices, lemon slices, watercress, frisée, and mizuna with enough dressing to lightly coat the salad. Divide the salad equally among four plates and top with two crab cakes. Drizzle additional dressing over the top and serve immediately.

CRISPY SHRIMP SALAD *with* CRANBERRIES *and* GOAT CHEESE

A LIGHT AND REFRESHING SALAD THAT CAN BE SERVED AS A STARTER OR meal. Have your fishmonger prepare the shrimp for you.

MAKES 4 SERVINGS

1 lemon, juice freshly squeezed and zest grated

1 red onion, finely chopped (about ½ cup)

3 garlic cloves, finely chopped

2 tablespoons extra-virgin olive oil

4 strips bacon

16 jumbo shrimp, peeled with tails attached, deveined, and butterflied

2 ounces arugula (about 2 cups)

2 ounces Bibb lettuce (about 2 cups)

½ cup chopped roasted red bell pepper

1 medium tomato, chopped (about ½ cup)

½ cup dried cranberries

½ cup hazelnuts, toasted and chopped

½ cup crumbled goat cheese

Kosher salt

Freshly ground black pepper

Peanut oil, for frying

1 recipe Beer Batter (page 191)

1 recipe Seasoned Flour (page 191)

IN A SMALL BOWL, WHISK TOGETHER the lemon juice and zest, onion, garlic, and olive oil; set the dressing aside.

Adjust an oven rack to the middle position and heat the oven to 325°F.

Line the bottom of a rimmed baking tray with parchment paper. Place the bacon on top and cover the bacon with another sheet of parchment. Place a cast-iron pan on top of the parchment, over the bacon. Bake in the oven until the bacon is crispy, about 30 minutes. Transfer the bacon to a paper towel–lined plate to drain; set aside.

Heat a ⅛-inch of peanut oil in a large skillet over medium heat until thin wisps of smoke appear. Dredge the shrimp in the seasoned flour and dip in the beer batter and lay in the hot oil, repeat with the remaining shrimp. Fry the shrimp until they are golden brown and crispy, about 1 minute on each side. Transfer them to a paper towel–lined plate to drain.

Among four plates, divide the arugula, Bibb lettuce, tomatoes, red peppers, and cranberries; place four shrimp on top, drizzle with the reserved dressing; top with the bacon, hazelnuts, and goat cheese. Serve immediately.

GREEN GODDESS SALAD *with* SHRIMP

*T*HIS IS A GORGEOUS SALAD THAT COMBINES SWEET SHRIMP, CRISPY CUCumbers, and creamy chickpeas, and is topped with a fresh, bright, tangy homemade dressing.

MAKES 4 SERVINGS

GREEN GODDESS DRESSING

$\frac{1}{2}$ cup olive oil

4 anchovy fillets or 2 tablespoons anchovy paste

$\frac{3}{4}$ cup chopped fresh tarragon leaves

5 scallions, white and green parts, chopped (about $\frac{3}{4}$ cup)

$\frac{1}{3}$ cup chopped flat-leaf parsley

1 tablespoon capers, rinsed

1 tablespoon freshly squeezed lemon juice

2 teaspoons tarragon vinegar

$\frac{1}{2}$ cup sour cream

$\frac{1}{2}$ cup mayonnaise

Kosher salt

Freshly ground black pepper

GREEN GODDESS SALAD

8 ounces green leaf lettuce (about 8 cups), cut into bite-size pieces

1 cup sliced cucumber

1 cup cherry or grape tomatoes

1 cup cooked chickpeas

1 cup artichoke hearts (freshly cooked, marinated, frozen, or canned)

2 ribs celery, thinly sliced (about $\frac{1}{2}$ cup)

12 ounces shrimp, peeled, deveined, cooked, and chilled

1 avocado, chopped

FOR THE DRESSING: In a blender, process the oil, anchovies, tarragon, scallions, parsley, capers, lemon juice, and vinegar; purée until smooth. Transfer to a medium bowl; stir in the sour cream, mayonnaise, and adjust seasoning to taste. (The dressing can be refrigerated in an airtight container for up to one week.)

FOR THE SALAD: Divide the lettuce among four salad plates; top evenly with cucumber, tomatoes, chickpeas, artichoke hearts, and celery. Lay shrimp on top; drizzle with dressing; sprinkle with avocado. Serve immediately.

SHAVED FENNEL *and* MUSHROOM SALAD

U SE A VEGETABLE SLICER OR MANDOLINE ON THE THINNEST SETTING TO GET the most delicate and practically translucent slices from the fennel.

1 (1-pound) fennel bulb, very thinly sliced

$\frac{1}{2}$ pound button mushrooms, stems trimmed, wiped clean, and very thinly sliced

4 ribs celery, cut into $\frac{1}{4}$-inch slices (about 1 cup)

1 small red onion, finely chopped (about $\frac{1}{2}$ cup)

$\frac{1}{2}$ cup niçoise olives, pitted and sliced

2 tablespoons capers, rinsed

$\frac{1}{3}$ cup chopped flat-leaf parsley

$\frac{1}{3}$ cup chopped fresh basil

2 tablespoon chopped fresh tarragon

$\frac{1}{3}$ cup Lemon-Basil Vinaigrette (page 96)

4 ounces baby arugula (about 1 cup)

4 ounces aged Manchego or pecorino cheese, shaved

Freshly cracked pepper

Kosher salt

ADD THE FENNEL, MUSHROOMS, CELERY, ONIONS, olives, capers, parsley, basil, and tarragon to a medium bowl with the vinaigrette; toss to coat. Adjust seasoning if necessary. Add the arugula and toss gently to combine. Transfer the salad to a serving bowl or platter; sprinkle the salad with shaved Manchego, salt, and fresh cracked pepper. Serve immediately.

Substitute Kalamata olives if you cannot find niçoise.

SPINACH SALAD *with* POMEGRANATES *and* BLUE CHEESE

WITH LITTLE TIME AND MANY OTHER HOLIDAY PREPARATIONS, ENJOY THIS simple salad and let the special, festive dressing shine.

MAKES 4 TO 6 SERVINGS

6 ounces baby spinach
(about 6 cups)

2 ounces Maytag blue cheese,
crumbled

1/2 cup pomegranate seeds

1/3 cup Persimmon Dressing
(page 187)

24 Spicy Glazed Walnuts,
or to taste (page 95)

PLACE SPINACH AND BLUE CHEESE in a large bowl and toss with dressing. Place individual portions on salad plates, sprinkle with the pomegranate seeds and walnuts. Serve immediately.

WINTER VEGETABLE SALAD

*C*OLORFUL AND SWEET ROOT VEGETABLES, EARTHY MUSHROOMS, AND fragrant herbs will make everyone want to eat their vegetables.

MAKES 4 SERVINGS

8 pearl onions, peeled

¼ cup plus 1 tablespoon olive oil, divided

8 baby carrots

4 baby parsnips, peeled

12 baby asparagus spears

4 baby red beets

8 baby golden beets

10 ounces shiitake, chanterelle, morel, or cremini mushrooms, stems discarded, wiped clean, and sliced

2 garlic cloves, finely chopped (about 1 teaspoon)

1 small yellow onion, chopped (about ½ cup)

2 cups vegetable stock (page 193)

1 tablespoon sherry vinegar

¼ cup chopped flat-leaf parsley

2 tablespoons chopped fresh tarragon

½ cup baby arugula, for garnish

Kosher salt

Freshly ground black pepper

ADJUST AN OVEN RACK TO THE MIDDLE POSITION and heat the oven to 400°F. Fill a large bowl with ice water.

In a small roasting pan or baking dish, toss the onions with 1 tablespoon of the olive oil and add 4 tablespoons of water. Cover with aluminum foil and bake for 10 minutes; set aside.

Bring 3 cups of water to a boil in a medium saucepan over high heat. Add 1 teaspoon of salt and the carrots, return to a boil, and cook until the carrots are bright orange and crisp-tender, 1 to 2 minutes. Remove the carrots with a slotted spoon and immediately transfer them to the ice bath. When the carrots have cooled to room temperature, remove with a slotted spoon and drain on a paper towel–lined plate.

Repeat with this process with the parsnips, asparagus, and beets. Use a paper towel to rub off the skin from the beets; then cut into quarters and set aside.

Heat the remaining oil in a large skillet until thin wisps of smoke appear; add the mushrooms, cook for 1 minute; add the garlic and onion; cook for 1 minute longer. Add the stock and sherry vinegar; simmer until the mixture has thickened and lightly coats the back of a spoon. Transfer the mixture to a large bowl and add the pearl onions, cooked vegetables, parsley, tarragon, and arugula; toss to combine. Season with salt and pepper to taste. Serve.

BROILED OYSTERS

BROILING ENHANCES THE NATURAL SWEETNESS OF OYSTERS. YOUR GUESTS will love this easy and elegant appetizer. Another quick and tasty option is to grill the oysters. Follow the steps below, just place a grill pan on a very hot, pre-heated grill. Cook for five minutes or until oysters curl slightly.

MAKES 6 SERVINGS

18 small fresh oysters
Rock salt
1 recipe Mignonette Sauce
  (page 186)

ADJUST AN OVEN RACK TO THE TOP POSITION (about 3 inches from the heat source); set the oven to broil. Spread an even $1/4$-inch layer of rock salt on a rimmed baking sheet.

Shuck the oysters, leaving them with their juice and attached to their bottom shells.

Place oysters on the prepared baking sheet.

Broil the oysters until they are just heated through, about 2 minutes. Place a teaspoon of Mignonette sauce on each oyster. Serve.

NOTE: Shells will be hot out of the oven, so take care not to burn yourself. Transfer the oysters to a rock-salt-lined serving platter or appetizer plate with tongs.

Wine pairing: Sauvignon Blanc, Chardonnay, or sparkling wine

CAVIAR POTATO PUFFS

*I*F YOU DON'T WANT TO USE YOUR BEST CAVIAR, TRY PADDLEFISH CAVIAR, which comes from the American paddlefish and resembles the sevruga sturgeon grade from the Caspian Sea but at an affordable price. The caviar is smooth and silky with a rich flavor.

MAKES 24 (1-INCH) POTATO PUFFS

1 pound Russet potatoes (2 medium), scrubbed and dried

1 medium fennel bulb, chopped (about 1 cup)

1 small yellow onion, chopped (about 1 cup)

2 tablespoons unsalted butter

$\frac{1}{4}$ cup chopped chives

1 lemon, zest grated

1 teaspoon kosher salt, divided

$\frac{1}{2}$ teaspoon freshly ground black pepper, divided

2 large eggs plus 2 large egg yolks, divided

3 ounces caviar

2 tablespoons crème fraîche

2 cups potato starch or Seasoned Flour (page 191)

3 cups finely ground white breadcrumbs

$\frac{1}{2}$ cup whole milk

Grapeseed or vegetable oil, for frying

WITH THE RACK IN THE MIDDLE, heat the oven to 375°F. Rub the potatoes with vegetable oil and bake on a foil-lined baking sheet until crisp and brown and a knife can easily pierce the flesh, about 1 hour.

While the potatoes are baking, melt the butter in a large skillet over low heat. Add the fennel, onion, $\frac{1}{2}$ teaspoon of the salt, and $\frac{1}{4}$ teaspoon of the pepper; cook for 10 minutes, stirring often. Cover the pan; cook, stirring occasionally, until the vegetables have completely broken down and have turned into paste, another 15 minutes. Add a bit of water if the vegetables begin to stick to the bottom of the pan; set aside.

Peel the potatoes while they are still warm. Using a ricer or food mill with the largest die, press potatoes into a large bowl. Add the reserved fennel paste, egg yolks, chives, lemon zest, remaining salt, and pepper. Adjust seasoning to taste. (Recipe can be made to this point and held in the refrigerator for up to two days.) Gently fold in the caviar and crème fraîche.

Fill a pastry bag, or resealable plastic bag with a corner cut, with the filling and squeeze out into small cylindrical shaped pieces that are about $\frac{3}{4}$-inch wide and 1-inch long. Place the potato starch in a shallow dish; in a second shallow dish, mix the whole eggs and milk together; in a third shallow dish, spread the breadcrumbs. Working with one potato puff at a time, coat the potato puff in the starch, coat with a thin coating of the egg mixture, and coat evenly with the breadcrumbs. Place the breaded potato puffs in a single layer on a baking sheet.

Cover the bottom of a large frying pan with $\frac{1}{2}$ inch of oil and heat until shimmering. Add the potato puffs in a single layer and fry until golden brown on all sides. Transfer the potato puffs to a paper towel–lined plate. Repeat with the remaining potato puffs. Serve warm.

Wine pairing: sparkling wine

SELECTING THE RIGHT WINE

ELECTING THE RIGHT WINE CAN TURN A SIMPLE MEAL INTO A MEMORABLE and elegant feast. The good news is that great wines don't have to cost a small fortune. There are wonderful mid-range bottles from $15 to $30 that deliver balanced robust flavors to complement any meal. Finding the perfect wine can be confusing among the wide variety of regions, varietals, and producers. I like to keep things simple. When cooking for a crowd, stick with one versatile red wine and one light white wine to accompany all the courses. An inexpensive brut sparkling wine can be served alone or mixed with fruit juices for festive and elegant holiday drinks.

For the red option, a Pinot Noir is most versatile and will work perfectly with your holiday dishes. Since it is a light wine with savory, earthy notes, it complements many foods; its underlying acidity works well with a wide range of flavors. Pinot Noir pairs well with meats, poultry, and even fish.

A Pinot Grigio is the best option for a white wine. It has great fruity crispness that cleanses the palate for a wide variety of foods and flavors. Keep several bottles chilled for your gathering.

Sparkling wine elevates any meal to a special affair. Champagne is sparkling wine from the Champagne region in France; prosecco is sparkling wine from Italy. Many other countries make sparking wine as well. *Brut* is the term that describes a sparking wine's dryness. The more "brut" a wine, the less sweet and drier it is. The terms that are used to describe the sweetest sparkling wines to the driest sparkling wines are as follows, in order from the sweetest to least sweet: doux, demi-sec, sec, extra dry, brut, and extra brut. When making a sparkling wine cocktail with fruit juice or flavored liquor, use brut or extra brut sparkling wines to counteract the sweetness of the mixer. Purchase bottles of demi-sec, sec, or extra dry if drinking the sparkling wine without any sweet mixers.

CHICKEN LIVER PÂTÉ *with* PEAR *and* CURRANTS

*P*REPARE THIS PÂTÉ ONE OR TWO DAYS IN ADVANCE TO ALLOW THE FLAVORS to meld. Serve with Red Onion and Parmesan Crackers (page 169) and Jellied Cranberry Sauce (page 93). Pâté can be made up to five days in advance.

MAKES 8 SERVINGS

¹/₄ cup currants or raisins

¹/₄ cup port wine

Vegetable-oil spray

1 pound chicken livers

¹/₂ teaspoon kosher salt

¹/₂ teaspoon freshly ground pepper

4 tablespoons duck fat, vegetable oil, or clarified butter

1 small yellow onion, chopped (about ¹/₂ cup)

1 medium carrot, thinly sliced (about ¹/₃ cup)

2 ribs celery, chopped (about ¹/₃ cup)

2 shallots, thinly sliced

1 ounce whiskey (optional)

¹/₂ bay leaf

2 teaspoons malt vinegar

1 pear, peeled, cored, and chopped

SOAK THE CURRANTS IN THE WINE OVERNIGHT. Drain the currents; reserve the wine.

Lightly spray the inside of a small loaf pan with vegetable-oil spray and line the bottom with parchment paper.

Trim the sinews from the livers. Pat the livers dry with a paper towel and sprinkle with the salt and pepper.

In a large skillet over medium heat, melt 1 tablespoon of the duck fat. Add the onions, carrots, celery, and shallots. Cook, stirring often, until the vegetables are tender and deep golden brown. Transfer the vegetables to a food processor.

In the same skillet over high heat, combine the reserved port, whiskey, and bay leaf. Bring to a boil and reduce the liquid by half. Remove the bay leaf and pour the liquid into the food processor.

In the same skillet over high heat, melt 1¹/₂ tablespoons of the duck fat until sizzling. Add half of the chicken livers; cook on one side until crispy and golden brown, about 2 minutes, then flip the livers and cook until the second side is well browned, 1 or 2 minutes longer. Do not overcook; livers should remain light pink inside. Add the livers and fat to the food processor. Wipe the skillet clean with a paper towel and repeat the process with the remaining duck fat and livers.

Add the vinegar and pears to the food processor and purée contents until very smooth and creamy. Transfer to a bowl and generously season with salt and pepper to taste (seasonings will mellow as pâté is refrigerated). Fold in the currants. Spread the pâté onto the prepared small loaf pan. Cover with plastic wrap and refrigerate overnight.

Wine pairing: Sauternes

FOIE GRAS POPPERS

*T*HESE MAKE A GREAT APPETIZER OR ARE DELICIOUS SERVED WITH THE Black Mustard Beef Tenderloin with Red Wine Sauce (page 140). The creamy interior of the foie gras contrasts nicely with the crispy fried exterior. Use a very high quality, aged balsamic vinegar for the best results.

MAKES 12 POPPERS

1 lobe foie gras, cut into 1-inch pieces

Kosher salt

Freshly ground black pepper

2 tablespoons balsamic vinegar

1 large egg

½ cup whole milk

4 slices fresh bread, crusts removed and processed into fine crumbs

1 lemon, zest grated

1 cup Seasoned Flour (page 191)

Vegetable oil, for frying

COAT THE BOTTOM OF A LARGE SKILLET WITH OIL and place over high heat; season the foie gras with salt and pepper. When oil is shimmering, add the foie gras and sear on all sides, about 2 minutes. Transfer the foie gras to a plate and sprinkle with the vinegar. Cool to room temperature.

In a shallow bowl, mix the egg and milk; set aside. In another shallow bowl mix the breadcrumbs, lemon zest, and salt and pepper to taste. Place the flour in another bowl.

Coat each foie gras cube with the flour, then egg wash, then the seasoned flour; repeat with the remaining cubes. Place the breaded cubes on a plate lined with parchment paper; cover and freeze for 6 hours or overnight.

Cover the bottom of a large saucepan with 2 inches of oil and heat the oil to 350°F. Fry the poppers until golden brown. Transfer to a paper towel–lined plate to drain. Sprinkle with salt and pepper. Serve 3 per person.

BRAISED LAMB SHOULDER *with* BUTTER BEANS

*I*NDIAN LONG PEPPERS MAY BE DIFFICULT TO FIND, HOWEVER, MANY ASIAN, Indian, or Middle Eastern stores carry them as well as online specialty spice stores. Do order some as they impart a wonderful aroma and distinctive fruity and peppery flavor to this dish. You can also use them as a substitute for black pepper with other dishes as well, so don't be afraid to purchase some and try a new spice. Have your butcher bone out the lamb shoulder and tie it into a roll.

MAKES 6 SERVINGS

SPICE BAG

$^1/_2$ teaspoon red pepper flakes

1 teaspoon black peppercorns

2 bay leaves

4 thyme sprigs

2 Indian long peppers (optional)

STEW

$^1/_2$ cup dried butter beans, soaked overnight in cold water

$^1/_4$ cup vegetable oil plus 1 tablespoon, divided

3 slices thick-cut bacon (about 2 ounces)

1 (3- to 4-pound) boneless lamb shoulder, tied

Kosher salt

Freshly ground black pepper

2 stalks celery, cut into $^1/_4$-inch slices (about 1 cup)

2 medium carrots, cut into 1-inch bias-cut pieces (about $1^1/_4$ cups)

4 medium yellow onions, cut into $^1/_4$-inch dice, $^1/_4$ cup reserved for garnish

1 poblano chile, seeded and finely chopped (about $^1/_2$ cup)

12 garlic cloves, sliced

ADJUST OVEN RACK TO THE MIDDLE POSITION and heat the oven to 300°F.

FOR THE SPICE BAG: Place the items for the spice bag in cheesecloth. Wrap closed with butchers' twine.

FOR THE STEW: Drain the soaked beans and place them in a medium saucepan. Cover beans by 1 inch with cold water and 1 tablespoon of salt; bring to a boil. Turn off the heat and let the beans cool completely in the water; drain. (This helps remove indigestible sugars that can cause gas.)

Place $^1/_4$ cup of oil and bacon in a large Dutch oven over medium heat; cook until the bacon is crispy, about 5 minutes. Remove the bacon, crumble and set aside. Increase the heat to high; sprinkle all sides of the lamb with salt and pepper; add to the Dutch oven with the bacon fat. Sear the lamb on all sides until golden brown; transfer to a plate; set aside. Add the celery, carrots, onions, poblano, and garlic to the pot. Cook, stirring occasionally, until the vegetables are tender, about 10 minutes. Add the beans, stock, vinegars, fresh and canned tomatoes, 1 cup of water, and spice bag, simmer for 20 minutes. Place the lamb into pot; cover, and place in the oven.

Cook the lamb until a fork easily slips in and out of the meat, about $3^1/_2$ hours.

Transfer the lamb to a cutting board and cover with aluminum foil; let rest for 15 minutes. Using a spoon, remove and discard excess fat from the surface of the cooking liquid. Place the pot over high heat and bring the liquid to a boil. Lower the heat to medium; simmer the liquid

3 cups Tomato Ham Hock
Stock (page 255)

3 medium tomatoes, cut into
1-inch pieces

1 (28-ounce) can organic
whole tomatoes, chopped

2 tablespoons sherry vinegar

2 tablespoons red wine
vinegar

$\frac{1}{2}$ cup balsamic vinegar

6 ounces dandelion greens
(about 6 cups)

until reduced by half. Adjust the seasoning with salt and pepper, if necessary.

Heat the remaining tablespoon of oil in a large skillet over high heat until shimmering; add the $\frac{1}{4}$ cup of onions, cook for about 2 minutes. Add the dandelion greens and wilt lightly, season to taste, and add the reserved bacon. Remove from the heat.

Slice the lamb into 1-inch-thick pieces. For each serving, spoon the bean stew in the middle of a plate, place two slices of lamb on top, and top with greens. Serve.

Wine pairing: Riesling, Chardonnay, Pinot Noir

A SPECIAL NOTE ON FRESH HERBS

I LIKE TO FINISH A DISH WITH A LITTLE HIT OF FRESH HERBS FOR A SPARK OF color and freshness. The good news is that nowadays you can get fresh local basil and other warmer weather herbs year-round. When used as a main flavor or garnish, fresh herbs pull a recipe together by infusing the dish with unparalleled fresh aromas and flavors. Here are some useful tips on how to buy and store fresh herbs so you can readily have them to garnish all your dishes like a professional chef.

1. Pick fresh herbs that have hearty leaves and stems. The leaves should be fragrant and vibrant green with no brown spots.

2. Loosely wrap herbs in a damp paper towel; seal in a resealable plastic bag filled with air. Refrigerate for up five days. Check the herbs daily, as some of them loose their flavor after a couple of days.

3. When herbs are sold in bunches, place them stems down in a glass of water, the water level should cover the stems by one inch. Enclose in a large resealable plastic bag. Change the water every other day. Most herbs will last up to a week with this method.

4. To revive limp herbs, trim $\frac{1}{2}$-inch of stems and place the whole herb in ice water for an hour.

5. Wash herbs just before using; pat dry with a paper towel.

COFFEE-SPICED PRIME RIB ROAST

T̶HE COFFEE AND CHILI POWDER ADD A NICE EARTHY ASPECT THAT COMPLE-ments and enhances the bold, beef flavor of the rib roast. Have your butcher prepare the prime rib with the fat cap still attached. Have him cut under the fat cap as though it were going to be removed but leave it attached on one side.

MAKES 4 TO 6 SERVINGS

RUB

6 garlic cloves, chopped

2 tablespoons finely ground espresso beans

1 tablespoon chili powder

$\frac{1}{2}$ teaspoon ground cloves

2 tablespoons kosher salt

2 teaspoons freshly ground pepper

ROAST

7 pounds prime first-cut rib roast, with 3 full ribs

$\frac{1}{4}$ cup grapeseed oil or vegetable oil

Kosher salt

Freshly ground black pepper

ADJUST AN OVEN RACK TO THE LOWER middle position and heat the oven to 400°F.

FOR THE RUB: Combine the ingredients in small bowl; mix well. Set aside.

Peel back the fat cap and sprinkle the meat with the rub. Roll the fat layer back over the roast and truss with butchers' twine. (Roast can be made to this point up to two days ahead.)

Place the roast, rib-side down, in a large roasting pan and coat the roast with the oil; generously sprinkle with the salt and pepper.

Roast for 30 minutes; reduce the oven temperature to 275°F and roast for another 2 to 2$\frac{1}{2}$ hours or until internal temperature is 130°F for medium rare; 140°F for medium. Remove the roast from the oven and let it rest for 20 minutes before slicing.

NOTE: If you have a portion that is more rare than you guest would like, return that portion to the kitchen and place it in the pan with the roast's drippings. Cook on top of the stove for 30 seconds on both sides or until desired doneness.

Wine pairing: Cabernet Sauvignon

BLACK MUSTARD BEEF TENDERLOIN
with RED WINE SAUCE

A SPICY-SWEET COATING BRINGS OUT GREAT BEEFY FLAVOR. DO TRY TO USE fresh horseradish, as it really makes a difference in the flavor; store-bought horseradish can be used in a pinch, but decrease the amount by two tablespoons. For a complete holiday meal serve with Foie Gras Poppers (page 135) and Roasted Cauliflower Florets (page 160).

MAKES 4 SERVINGS

BEEF TENDERLOIN

2 tablespoons
  black mustard seeds

2 tablespoons black
  peppercorns

$1/2$ cup freshly grated
  horseradish

$1/4$ cup olive oil

2 tablespoons kosher salt

1 cup sherry vinegar

1 (2-pound) beef tenderloin,
  trimmed

RED WINE SAUCE

2 tablespoons olive oil

2 medium onions, chopped

2 Granny Smith apples, cored
  and cut into wedges

2 bottles of red wine, such as
  Pinot Noir or Syrah

1 teaspoon black peppercorns

ADJUST AN OVEN RACK TO THE MIDDLE POSITION and heat the oven to 250°F.

In a small skillet over medium heat toast the mustard seeds and peppercorns until fragrant, about 2 minutes. Transfer to a spice grinder and grind until smooth. Place spices in a small bowl; add the horseradish, 1 tablespoon of the oil, and salt; set aside. Place the vinegar in the same skillet over medium-high heat; simmer until liquid has reduced to $1/4$ cup. Cool to room temperature and add to spice mixture; stir to combine into a paste and set aside.

Place the remaining 3 tablespoons of oil in a large cast-iron skillet over medium-high heat; add the beef and brown on all sides. Transfer to a plate and let cool slightly; evenly coat with the reserved spice paste.

Place the beef on a cooling rack set over a sheet pan. For medium rare, roast in the oven until the internal temperature reaches 125°F on an instant-read thermometer, about 1 hour. Remove from the oven and let the beef rest 15 minutes before carving.

While beef is roasting, heat the oil in a large saucepan over medium-high heat. Add the onions and cook, stirring occasionally, until tender and light golden brown, about 8 minutes. Add the apples, wine, and peppercorns. Bring to a boil, reduce heat, and simmer until sauce has reduced by three quarters or until sauce coats the back of a spoon.

Pass the sauce through a fine-mesh strainer. Cool and refrigerate until needed, or serve immediately with the beef.

HONEY- AND CIDER-VINEGAR-BASTED RACK *of* PORK

I LOVE PAIRING SWEET AND SOUR FLAVORS WITH PORK. I CREATED THIS RECIPE at the Lark Creek Inn and it was always a holiday favorite. Impress your guests with this stunning rack of pork that's full of flavor and presents beautifully. Check with your butcher ahead of time to ensure they have a bone-in pork loin with the chine bone (backbone) removed; you may have to special order one. Also, ask the butcher to french the rib bones. A boneless pork loin can also work in this recipe. Serve with Whipped Sweet Potatoes (page 162) and Jellied Cranberry Sauce (page 93).

MAKES 7 TO 8 SERVINGS

4 tablespoons unsalted butter

2 large yellow onions, sliced (about 4 cups)

4 cups chicken stock (page 101)

4 cups cider vinegar

2 cups freshly pressed apple juice

8 parsley stems

2 thyme sprigs

1 bay leaf

2 teaspoons black peppercorns

1 teaspoon cumin seed

1 cup honey

¼ cup Dijon mustard

½ cup olive oil

4 teaspoons kosher salt, plus more for seasoning

3 teaspoons freshly ground black pepper, plus more for seasoning

1 (4- to 5-pound) rack of pork, about 7 or 8 ribs

ADJUST AN OVEN RACK TO THE MIDDLE POSITION and heat the oven to 350°F.

Place a V-shaped rack inside a rimmed baking pan. Cover the bottom with ½ cup of water.

Melt the butter in a large saucepan over medium-high heat. Add the onions; cook, stirring occasionally, until golden brown. Add the stock, vinegar, apple juice, parsley, thyme, bay leaf, and peppercorns. Bring the sauce to a boil; reduce the heat to maintain a simmer. Reduce the liquid until it coats the back of a spoon, 45 to 55 minutes. Pass the sauce through a fine-mesh strainer. (You should have 3 to 4 cups of sauce.) Adjust the seasoning with salt and pepper to taste. Reserve 2 cups for the finished dish; use the remaining sauce to baste the pork.

Place the cumin in a small nonstick skillet over medium-low heat. Cook until lightly toasted and fragrant, about 3 minutes. Place in a spice grinder and grind until smooth. Transfer to a small mixing bowl. Add the honey, mustard, oil, salt, and pepper; mix well. Rub half of the mixture over the pork and place the pork on the roasting rack.

Roast the pork until golden brown and the internal temperature reads 140°F on an instant-read thermometer; baste occasionally with the remaining honey spice sauce and pan drippings. If pork becomes too brown, cover with foil. Let the pork rest for 20 minutes before slicing. Serve with reserved honey spice sauce.

GRILLED CORNISH GAME HENS
with SPICED CHERRY RUB

*I*NDIAN LONG PEPPERS, ALSO KNOWN AS PIPPALI LONG PEPPERS, CAN BE FOUND at most Asian, Indian, or Middle Eastern grocers. Their spicy and pungent flavor complements the sweet cherries and the gaminess of the hens. Serve this succulent dish with Toasted Blood Orange Couscous (page 226).

MAKES 4 SERVINGS

1 1/2 cups organic black cherry juice

1/2 cup dried organic cherries

1 teaspoon coriander seed

1 teaspoon fennel seed

1 teaspoon mustard seeds

1/2 teaspoon red pepper flakes

4 Indian long peppers or 1 teaspoon black peppercorns

2 lemons, peeled and diced

1 teaspoon ground turmeric

1 teaspoon kosher salt

1/2 teaspoon freshly ground black pepper

1/4 cup olive oil

4 (1-pound) Cornish game hens, butterflied (see note)

IN A SMALL SAUCEPAN OVER MEDIUM-HIGH HEAT, simmer the juice and cherries until reduced by half. Purée until smooth and set aside.

In a small nonstick skillet over medium-low heat, toast the coriander seed, fennel seed, mustard seed, red pepper flakes, and Indian long peppers or peppercorns until lightly browned and fragrant, 2 to 3 minutes. Transfer the spices to a spice grinder and grind until smooth. Place the ground spices in a medium bowl, add the cherry purée, lemon, turmeric, salt, and pepper; set aside.

Rub the hens with the spiced cherry rub; place in a single layer in a glass dish; cover with plastic wrap; marinate in the refrigerator for at least 4 hours or up to overnight. Let the hens sit at room temperature for 30 minutes before grilling.

Prepare a gas or coal grill. Place the hens over a medium flame or moderately hot coals, basting occasionally with the marinade. Turn the hens twice while cooking. Cook the hens until golden brown and an instant-read thermometer inserted into the thickest part of the hen registers 165°F, 30 to 40 minutes. Remove the hens to a large plate and tent with foil to keep warm; let rest 5 minutes before serving.

Split the hen in half, down the middle through the breast bone; arrange the halves so they overlap in the center of the plate.

NOTE: To butterfly the hens, use poultry shears to remove the wing tips and cut out the backbone; with the breast-side up, press the rib cage down firmly to flatten. Turn the hen over and remove any excess fat and liver from inside cavity; rinse the bird thoroughly under cold water and pat dry with paper towels.

ROASTED SPICED DUCK *with* KUMQUAT *and* POMEGRANATE GLAZE

*R*OAST DUCK IS CERTAINLY A HOLIDAY TREAT. ENJOY THIS JUICY DUCK with its extra crisp and flavorful skin.

MAKES 4 SERVINGS

ROAST DUCK

1 stick cinnamon

1 teaspoon whole allspice berries

4 cardamom pods

1 dried ancho chile

1 tablespoon kosher salt

$^1/_2$ cup freshly ground black pepper

$^1/_4$ cup honey

$^1/_4$ cup green or jasmine tea leaves or 4 green or jasmine tea bags

1 cup apple cider or apple juice

2 (4- to 5-pound) ducks

2 medium Granny Smith apples, cut into wedges

KUMQUAT AND POMEGRANATE GLAZE

2 cups sliced kumquats

1 cup fresh pomegranate seeds

1 cup pomegranate juice

$^1/_4$ cup rice vinegar

$^1/_4$ cup mirin

1 teaspoon grated fresh ginger

$^1/_4$ cup lemongrass (white part only), thinly sliced

5 garlic cloves

2 tablespoons honey

IN A SMALL SAUCEPAN OVER MEDIUM HEAT, toast the cinnamon, allspice, cardamom, and chili until lightly toasted and fragrant, about 2 minutes. Remove the stem from the chile and grind the spices in spice grinder. Pass the ground spices through a fine-mesh sieve to remove any large pieces; mix in the salt and pepper. Set aside.

Bring the cider and honey to a boil in a small pot over high heat. Add the tea and steep for 3 minutes. Pass the liquid through a fine-mesh sieve to remove the tea leaves; cool for 10 minutes. Add the cooled liquid to the reserved spice mixture; stir to combine; set aside.

Rinse the duck under cold water; reserve the neck and giblets for the sauce. Cut off the wing tips and reserve. Pat the duck dry with paper towels and rub with the wet spice mixture with your hands, coating the entire surface evenly. Set the ducks on a cooling rack and stuff the apple in each cavity; transfer to the refrigerator, uncovered, for 36 hours. (This process ensures a crispy skin.)

Adjust an oven rack to the middle position and heat the oven to 350°F.

Place the ducks breast-side up on a V-shaped rack set in a roasting pan. Cover the bottom of the roasting pan with $^1/_4$-inch of water. Roast the ducks, basting occasionally with the drippings, until the thickest part of the breast reaches 140°F on an instant-read thermometer and the skin is crispy, about $1^3/_4$ hours. Transfer the duck to a carving board and let rest, uncovered, for 15 minutes.

While the duck roasts, combine the kumquats and pomegranate seeds in a small bowl; set aside. Place the remaining glaze ingredients in a small saucepan and bring to a boil; reduce the heat to maintain a simmer; cook until the liquid has reduced by two thirds. Remove from the heat and let the sauce cool for 5 minutes. Pass the sauce through a fine-mesh strainer into the bowl with the reserved kumquat and pomegranate seeds; stir to combine. Adjust the seasoning with salt and pepper, if necessary. Serve warm.

NOTE: For an even crispier skin, place the duck under the broiler until desired crispness is achieved.

Wine pairing: Pinot Noir

CRISPY FLOUNDER *with* CARA CARA ORANGE SAUCE *and* LUMP CRAB

C ARA CARA ORANGES ARE AVAILABLE FROM NOVEMBER TO JANUARY. THEY look similar to navel oranges, but their interior has a distinctive pinkish-red hue and an exceptionally sweet flavor with a tangy cranberry-like zing. Valencia oranges can be used as a substitute. Serve with Roasted Spaghetti Squash Noodles (page 161).

MAKES 4 SERVINGS

CARA CARA ORANGE SAUCE

2 large Cara Cara oranges, scrubbed

$^1/_4$ cup olive oil plus 1 teaspoon, divided

2 teaspoons kosher salt

1 teaspoon freshly ground black pepper

$^1/_4$ cup grapeseed oil or vegetable oil

2 tablespoons freshly squeezed lemon juice

2 tablespoons freshly squeezed orange juice

1 small red onion, finely chopped (about $^1/_4$ cup)

1 teaspoon Dijon mustard

2 tablespoons finely chopped chives

2 tablespoons chopped flat-leaf parsley

1 tablespoon chopped chervil

1 teaspoon unsalted butter

8 ounces lump crabmeat, cartilage and shells removed

CRISPY FLOUNDER

4 (8-ounce) flounder fillets, skin-on, boneless, scaled, and scored

1 $^1/_2$ teaspoons kosher salt

ADJUST AN OVEN RACK TO THE TOP POSITION (about 3 inches from the heat source); heat the oven to 500°F.

FOR THE SAUCE: On a large sheet of aluminum foil, place the whole oranges, $^1/_4$ cup of olive oil, $^1/_4$ teaspoon salt, and $^1/_4$ teaspoon pepper. Wrap the contents in the foil and seal the edges to ensure no leaks. Place the foil packet on a rimmed baking sheet and place under the broiler. Cook, turning the packet often, until the oranges are fragrant and soft, about 15 minutes. Remove the foil packet from the oven and let cool for 5 minutes.

Place the contents in the foil packet into a food processor and purée until smooth; transfer to a large bowl. Add the grapeseed oil, citrus juices, onion, mustard, chives, parsley, chervil, and remaining 1$^3/_4$ teaspoons salt and $^3/_4$ teaspoon pepper to the bowl; stir to combine; set aside.

Heat the butter and remaining olive oil in a skillet over high heat until the butter stops foaming; add the crab and cook for 20 seconds. Stir the crab into the reserved sauce. Serve or refrigerate until needed.

FOR THE FISH: Pat the flounder fillets dry with a paper towel. Sprinkle with the salt and pepper. Divide the oil evenly between 2 12-inch stainless steel or cast-iron skillets and heat over high heat until just beginning to smoke. Add the fillets skin-side down and cook, without moving, until the edges of the fillets are opaque and the bottoms are crisp and golden brown, about 4 minutes. Reduce the heat to low; using two spatulas, gently flip the fillets. Equally divide the 2 tablespoons of the butter, rosemary, lemon juice, and zest among each

(continued)

- 1 teaspoon freshly ground black pepper
- $\frac{1}{2}$ cup grapeseed oil
- 2 tablespoons unsalted butter
- 2 (2-inch) rosemary sprigs
- 2 lemons, juiced
- 1 orange, zest grated (about 1 tablespoon)
- 1 recipe Roasted Spaghetti Squash Noodles (page 161)

pan; spoon the sauce over the fillets while cooking another 2 to 3 minutes. Cook until the thickest part of the fillet easily separates into flakes when a toothpick is inserted. Transfer the fillets to a paper towel–lined plate to drain.

To serve, twirl the warm spaghetti squash with a fork like you would spaghetti; place in the center of each plate. Place a fillet over the squash. Spoon $\frac{1}{4}$ cup of the Cara Cara sauce over the fillet.

Wine pairing: Sauvignon Blanc

BASIL GNOCCHI

*F*RESH BASIL BOOSTS THE FLAVOR OF THESE LIGHTER-THAN-CLOUDS gnocchi. The secret is drying out the cooked potato and adding the flour a little at a time to the dough, stopping when the dough just comes together. Serve these clouds with a simple marinara sauce and shredded Parmesan cheese.

MAKES 50 (1-INCH) GNOCCHI

1 large Russet potato, unpeeled and scrubbed well

1 large egg plus 1 large egg yolk

15 large basil leaves, chopped

2 tablespoons chopped flat-leaf parsley

1 tablespoon chopped fresh chives

1 tablespoon grated Parmesan cheese

Kosher salt

Freshly ground black pepper

$\frac{1}{2}$ cup all-purpose flour, 3 tablespoons reserved for dusting

ADJUST AN OVEN RACK TO THE MIDDLE POSITION and heat the oven to 350°F.

Place the potato in a small saucepan, cover with 1 inch of cold water, and add 1 teaspoon of salt. Bring to a boil over medium-high heat then reduce the heat to low and simmer until potato is tender and a fork can be inserted with little resistance, about 35 minutes. Remove the potato from the water and cut in half, lengthwise. Place the potato on a baking sheet, cut-side up, and bake in the oven until dry and crumbly, about 10 minutes.

Remove the dried potato from the oven, cool slightly. Using a small spoon, scrape the potato flesh from the skin. Pass the pulp through a food mill into a medium bowl or press the warm potato through a sieve, using the back of a spoon.

In a food processor, combine the egg, egg yolk, basil, parsley, and chives; blend until smooth. Fold the egg mixture into the potato. Add the cheese and season with salt and pepper to taste.

Gradually add the flour into the potato mixture, a little at a time. Gently fold the mixture with a rubber spatula after each addition of flour until you have a smooth dough firm enough to roll; do not over-mix. Turn the dough out onto a lightly floured surface and separate into 6 equal portions. Lightly flour your hands and gently roll each piece into a log-shaped roll measuring $\frac{1}{2}$-inch around. Cut each log into 1-inch pieces.

Cook the gnocchi in boiling salted water until the gnocchi float to the surface, 3 to 4 minutes. Remove from water with a slotted spoon and drain. Serve immediately. (Uncooked gnocchi can be frozen for later use or prepared a day ahead and refrigerated.)

ARTICHOKE *and* ELEPHANT GARLIC
SOUFFLÉ SPOONBREAD

RTICHOKES AND GARLIC IS A CLASSIC FLAVOR COMBINATION, ROBUST yet delicate enough for this light and airy spoonbread. Elephant garlic is more closely related to a leek or scallion, and the flavor is much milder and sweeter than garlic, so substitute a leek or scallion if you cannot find it.

MAKES 6 SERVINGS

3 large eggs

1 cup whole milk

4 tablespoons unsalted butter

2 teaspoons finely chopped red or green jalapeño chiles

1 teaspoon kosher salt

$^1/_2$ teaspoon freshly ground black pepper

$^3/_4$ cup yellow cornmeal, such as Anson Mills

1 cup buttermilk

2 cups Wine-Braised Artichokes (page 153), sliced $^1/_8$-inch thick, or store-bought marinated artichokes, rinsed and patted dry

1 large head elephant garlic, chopped (about $^1/_3$ cup)

ADJUST AN OVEN RACK TO THE MIDDLE POSITION and heat the oven to 425°F. Butter a 2-quart casserole dish that is at least 3 inches deep.

Separate the eggs, dividing them into three yolks and two whites, saving the remaining egg white for another use. Set aside.

In a 2-quart saucepan, over medium heat, combine 1 cup of water, milk, butter, jalapeño, 1 teaspoon of salt, and pepper; bring to a simmer. Slowly add the cornmeal, stirring vigorously with a whisk, making sure no lumps form. Cook, stirring occasionally, until the mixture is very thick, about 2 minutes. Slowly stir in the buttermilk until blended; remove from the heat. Let the mixture cool for 10 minutes. Mix in the egg yolks, one at a time, until incorporated. Fold in the artichokes and garlic; set aside.

Using an electric mixer, whip the egg whites at medium-high speed until soft peaks form. Gently fold the egg whites into the cornmeal mixture. Pour the mixture into the prepared casserole dish. Place the casserole dish in a larger pan lined with a kitchen towel; add enough hot water to the larger pan to reach halfway up the side of the casserole dish, taking care not to splash water into the cornmeal mixture. Bake until the spoonbread is puffed, the center jiggles slightly when shaken, and the surface is golden brown, 20 minutes.

WINE-BRAISED ARTICHOKES

BRAISING THESE LOVELY FLOWERS IN WINE ADDS AN EVEN SWEETER AND floral flavor. They are terrific alone, as a side dish, or use them in the Artichoke and Elephant Garlic Soufflé Spoonbread (page 152).

4 large artichokes

4 lemons, halved, divided

1 bottle Chardonnay

1 yellow onion, peeled and cut into 4 wedges

2 garlic bulbs, cut horizontally in half

8 sprigs thyme

12 sprigs flat-leaf parsley

2 bay leaves

$1/2$ cup olive oil

$1/2$ cup white balsamic vinegar

1 teaspoon kosher salt

$1/2$ teaspoon freshly ground black pepper

IN A LARGE STOCKPOT, place 2 lemons, wine, onion, garlic, thyme, parsley, bay leaves, oil, vinegar, salt, and pepper.

Peel off the small, tough, dark-green leaves from the artichokes. Cut the stem level with the base. Slice the top of the leaves to about 1 inch above the base. Rub each artichoke with the remaining lemons to prevent discoloring and place in the stockpot. Place a heatproof bowl on top of the artichokes to keep them submerged while cooking.

Place stockpot over high heat. Bring the liquid to a boil; reduce heat, and simmer until the artichokes are slightly tender and a knife can be inserted into the center with little resistance, about 20 minutes.

Transfer artichokes to a bowl of ice water; let cool for 10 seconds before removing. Slice artichokes in half and remove the thistle with a spoon.

Pass the cooking liquid through a fine-mesh sieve. Return liquid back into the stockpot over medium heat; simmer the liquid until reduced by half. Cool slightly and pour over the artichokes.

CANDIED YAMS

GROWING UP, THERE NEVER SEEMED TO BE ENOUGH OF THESE AT OUR HOLIDAY table. My mother would make more and more each year but there still were never any leftovers. I love the combination of apple and molasses in this recipe, since it adds great depth of flavor. These are a holiday must at the table and I can't guarantee any leftovers the first time you make them.

MAKES 8 SERVINGS

3 pounds sweet potatoes, peeled and cut into 1-inch thick diagonal slices

1/3 cup apple juice

3 tablespoons firmly packed brown sugar

3 tablespoons maple syrup

2 tablespoons molasses

1/8 teaspoon ground cinnamon

1/8 teaspoon ground allspice

Kosher salt

Freshly ground black pepper

ADJUST AN OVEN RACK TO THE MIDDLE POSITION and heat the oven to 375°F.

In a large rimmed baking sheet, toss the potatoes with the apple juice, sugar, syrup, molasses, cinnamon, and allspice. Arrange the potatoes in a single layer; cover tightly with foil and bake for 20 minutes. Flip the potatoes over; continue to bake, covered, until the potatoes are tender (a fork can easily pierce the flesh with no resistance), about 25 minutes. Uncover the potatoes; bake an additional 15 minutes. Flip potatoes again; bake until only a think layer of syrup remains on the bottom of the pan, about 5 minutes longer.

Arrange the potatoes on a serving dish; spoon the glaze over the potatoes; sprinkle with salt and pepper to taste.

DOUBLE-STUFFED BAKED POTATOES

*T*HESE POTATOES HAVE A SLIGHTLY CRISP, CHEWY SKINS AND A RICH, creamy filling. The perfect side dish to any beef entrée.

MAKES 6 TO 8 SERVINGS

4 medium russet potatoes (about 8 ounces each), scrubbed, dried, and rubbed lightly with vegetable oil

2 tablespoons unsalted butter

1 large shallot, finely chopped (about $\frac{1}{2}$ cup)

3 garlic cloves, finely chopped

$\frac{1}{4}$ cup heavy cream

8 ounces Camembert cheese, cut into pieces

$\frac{1}{4}$ cup crème fraîche

2 large eggs, separated

$\frac{1}{4}$ cup chopped fresh chives

Kosher salt

Freshly ground black pepper

$\frac{1}{4}$ cup Parmesan cheese

ADJUST AN OVEN RACK TO THE UPPER-MIDDLE POSITION and heat the oven to 400°F.

Bake the potatoes on a foil-lined baking sheet until the skin is crisp and deep brown and a skewer easily pierces the flesh, about 1 hour. Transfer the potatoes to a cooling rack and cool slightly, about 10 minutes. Leave the oven on.

Using an oven mitt or folded kitchen towel to handle the hot potatoes, cut each potato in half so that the long side sits on the work surface. Using a small spoon, scoop the flesh from each half into a medium bowl, leaving a $\frac{1}{4}$-inch thickness of the flesh in each shell. Arrange the shells on the foil-lined baking sheet and return the oven to dry and slightly crisp, about 10 minutes. Remove and set aside. Increase the oven setting to broil.

Meanwhile, pass the potato flesh through a ricer or food mill, or mash with a fork until smooth; set aside. Melt the butter in small skillet over medium-low heat; add the shallots and garlic, cook for 2 minutes; add the heavy cream and heat until cream just begins to simmer. Add the Camembert cheese and cook, stirring often, until the cheese has melted. Remove from the heat; set aside.

In a large bowl, combine the crème fraîche, egg yolks, and chives. Mix in the potato flesh and the cream mixture; season with salt and pepper to taste. (Recipe can be made to this point up to two days ahead. Cover and refrigerate until needed.) Place the egg whites in a medium bowl. Using an electric mixer on high speed, whip the egg whites until soft peaks form. Fold the whites into the potato mixture.

Holding the hot potato shells steady on the pan with an oven mitt, spoon the potato mixture into the crisped shells, mounding it slightly at the center. Sprinkle the Parmesan over the top. Broil until the cheese has melted and the tops are spotty brown and crisp, 10 to 15 minutes. Cool for 10 minutes and serve.

ROASTED BROCCOLI RABE *with* FENNEL *and* ORANGE

BROCCOLI RABE, ALSO KNOWN AS RAPINI, IS CLOSELY RELATED TO BROCCOLI. It is prized by chefs for its interesting flavor and slight bitterness, which pairs well with sweet fennel and orange.

MAKES 4 SERVINGS

1 pound broccoli rabe, rinsed, stems trimmed, and tough leaves removed

¼ cup extra-virgin olive oil plus 2 tablespoons, divided

Kosher salt

Freshly ground black pepper

½ cup pine nuts, toasted

2 teaspoons Champagne vinegar

4 young fennel bulbs, trimmed and cut into long strips

3 oranges, zest grated, then peeled and sliced ½-inch circles

2 tablespoons chopped flat-leaf parsley

2 tablespoons chopped fresh dill

ADJUST AN OVEN RACK TO THE MIDDLE POSITION and heat the oven to 400°F.

Toss the broccoli rabe in a rimmed baking sheet with ¼ cup of olive oil until evenly coated; spread in an even layer; sprinkle with salt and pepper to taste. Roast the broccoli rabe, stirring occasionally, until tender and tops of rabe are slightly crisp and golden brown, about 20 minutes.

While the broccoli rabe is cooking, place the pine nuts and 1 tablespoon of the oil in small nonstick skillet over medium-low heat, stirring occasionally, until the nuts are light golden brown and fragrant, about 3 minutes. Transfer nuts and oil to a large bowl; let cool.

Add the vinegar, the remaining 1 tablespoon of oil, the cooked broccoli rabe, the fennel, orange slices and zest, parsley, and dill to the toasted pine nuts. Toss to combine; season with salt and pepper to taste. Serve.

ROASTED CAULIFLOWER FLORETS

*U*SE A MIXTURE OF WHITE, GREEN, ORANGE, AND PURPLE HEADS OF CAULI-flower for a stunning and festive presentation. Serve with Black Mustard Beef Tenderloin with Red Wine Sauce (page 140).

MAKES 4 SERVINGS

4 cups cauliflower florets

2 tablespoons olive oil

2 tablespoons unsalted butter, melted

1 teaspoon kosher salt

1/2 teaspoon freshly ground black pepper

1 cup vegetable stock (page 193)

ADJUST AN OVEN RACK TO THE MIDDLE POSITION and heat the oven to 400°F.

In a large ovenproof skillet toss the cauliflower, oil, butter, salt, pepper, and stock. Roast, stirring occasionally, until the cauliflower is tender and slightly golden, about 20 minutes. Serve.

ROASTED SPAGHETTI SQUASH NOODLES

*T*HIS SQUASH IS NAMED PERFECTLY, AS ITS SWEET CRISP PULP RESEMBLES strands of pasta noodles. Serve with Crispy Flounder with Cara Cara Orange Sauce and Lump Crab (page 149).

(page 149)

MAKES 4 SERVINGS

3 cardamom pods

½ teaspoon whole allspice berries

3 star anise

1 large Granny Smith apple, cored and halved

1 lemon, juiced

1 (2-pound) spaghetti squash, cut in half lengthwise, seeds and pulp removed

3 tablespoons unsalted butter, melted

2 tablespoons honey

2 tablespoons packed golden brown sugar

1 teaspoon kosher salt

1 teaspoon freshly ground black pepper

½ cup apple cider (optional)

ADJUST AN OVEN RACK TO THE MIDDLE POSITION and heat the oven to 300°F.

Place the cardamom, allspice, and star anise in a small skillet over medium-low heat; toast the spices, shaking the pan often, until fragrant, about 4 minutes; remove from the heat and grind in a spice grinder; set aside.

In a small bowl, toss the apple with the lemon juice; set aside.

Place the squash on a rimmed baking sheet or a casserole dish skin-side down; brush the flesh of the squash with the butter and honey; evenly sprinkle the ground spices, sugar, salt, and pepper over the top. Place one apple half with juices into the cavity of each squash; add the apple cider to the inside of the cavity, if desired.

Bake, basting occasionally, until the squash is tender and offers no resistance when pierced with a paring knife, 1½ to 2 hours. Remove from the oven; discard the apple; and let cool for 10 minutes. Using a fork, scrape the cooked squash into a medium bowl and toss to separate the strands. Serve warm.

WHIPPED SWEET POTATOES

*B*AKING, RATHER THAN BOILING, THE POTATOES FOR THIS DISH CONCENtrates and intensifies their sweetness and maximizes the flavor.

2 pounds sweet potatoes
(about 5 small)

³/₄ cup apple juice or
apple cider

1 tablespoon grated
fresh ginger

2 tablespoons unsalted butter

¹/₄ cup heavy cream

Kosher salt

Freshly ground black pepper

ADJUST AN OVEN RACK TO THE MIDDLE POSITION and heat the oven to 400°F.

Bake the potatoes on a foil-lined baking sheet until the potatoes are tender and a knife can be inserted with little resistance, about 45 minutes.

Meanwhile, while the potatoes are baking, combine the apple juice and ginger in a small saucepan over medium-low heat. Keep the liquid at a simmer for 10 minutes. Pour the liquid through a fine-mesh sieve to remove the ginger; place back into the pot. Set aside and keep warm until needed.

Remove the potatoes from the oven; let cool enough until you are able to handle. Remove the peels and mash potatoes with a potato masher or pass through a ricer. Place the potatoes into the bowl of a stand mixer fitted with the whip attachment; set the speed to medium high; add the butter and cream. While mixer is still running slowly add the reserved apple juice until the desired consistency is reached (less juice for stiff potatoes, or more juice for smoother potatoes). Season the potatoes with salt and pepper to taste.

BOSTON BROWN BREAD

*D*RIED FIGS OR CURRANTS CAN ALSO BE USED IN THIS BREAD. SERVE WITH Green Apple and Pumpkin Butter (page 188).

MAKES 1 LOAF, SERVING 4 TO 6

2 tablespoons butter, softened

$^1/_2$ cup cornmeal

$^1/_2$ cup all-purpose flour

$^1/_2$ cup whole wheat flour

$^1/_2$ teaspoon salt

$^1/_2$ teaspoon baking soda

1 cup buttermilk

$^1/_4$ cup molasses

2 tablespoons packed dark brown sugar

$^2/_3$ cup raisins

ADJUST AN OVEN RACK TO THE MIDDLE POSITION and heat the oven to 350°F. Grease an 8 x 4 x $2^1/_2$-inch loaf pan with the butter.

In a large bowl, sift together the cornmeal, all-purpose flour, whole wheat flour, salt, and baking soda. In a separate bowl, whisk together the buttermilk, molasses, and sugar; add into the flour mixture; stir until mixture is just combined. Fold in the raisins. Fill the loaf pan three-quarters full with the batter. Cover the top with parchment paper and then with foil.

Place the loaf pan in large Dutch oven and fill the Dutch oven with enough water to come up halfway up the side of the loaf pan. Place the Dutch oven over high heat and bring the water to a boil. Cover; reduce the heat to medium and let the bread steam until the center is set and does not jiggle when pan is moved, 30 minutes. Carefully, remove the loaf pan from the Dutch oven, discard the foil and parchment paper, and place on a baking sheet.

Bake until bread pulls away from the sides of loaf pan, about 15 minutes. Cool loaf pan on a cooling rack for 15 minutes; then invert loaf onto the cooling rack, turn right side up, and continue to cool until warm, about 20 minutes. Cut into slices and serve.

NOTE: You can skip the steaming step and just bake the bread in the oven. Place the loaf pan in a larger pan lined with a kitchen towel. Carefully place the pan on the oven rack and fill the larger pan with enough hot water until it reaches two-thirds of the way up the side of the loaf pan, taking care not to splash water into the batter. Bake uncovered until the bread pulls away from the sides of the loaf pan, about 50 minutes.

CINNAMON BREAD *with* BROWN-SUGAR SWIRL

THESE LOAVES FREEZE WONDERFULLY AND MAKE GREAT HOSTESS GIFTS.

MAKES 4 LOAVES

BREAD

2 packages active dry yeast (4$\frac{1}{2}$ teaspoons)

1 teaspoon salt plus $\frac{1}{8}$ teaspoon

$\frac{1}{2}$ cup granulated sugar plus $\frac{1}{8}$ teaspoon

4 teaspoons cinnamon

$\frac{3}{4}$ teaspoon ground allspice

$\frac{3}{4}$ teaspoon freshly grated nutmeg

1$\frac{1}{4}$ cups cake flour

3$\frac{1}{2}$ cups all-purpose flour, plus more for dusting

6 tablespoons unsalted butter, softened, plus extra for greasing

3 large eggs plus 1 large egg yolk

1 cup raisins or chopped dried figs

Vegetable oil, for lightly coating the bread

Cooking spray

BROWN SUGAR SWIRL

1 cup packed brown sugar

6 tablespoons unsalted butter, softened

1 teaspoon vanilla

FOR THE BREAD: In a large bowl, whisk together 1 cup warm water, yeast, $\frac{1}{8}$ teaspoon of the salt, and $\frac{1}{8}$ teaspoon of the sugar. Let stand for 5 minutes.

In a small bowl, stir together the cinnamon, allspice, and nutmeg. Set the spice mixture aside.

Sift the flour and cake flour together into a medium bowl, whisk to thoroughly combine. Remove 1 cup of the flour mixture and add it to the yeast mixture, stir until combined. Let yeast mixture stand for 20 minutes.

Place the 6 tablespoons of butter and the $\frac{1}{2}$ cup of sugar in a large bowl. Beat with an electric mixer at medium speed until light and fluffy. Add the whole eggs, one at a time, beating well after each addition. Using a whisk, stir in 2 teaspoons of the spice mixture; set aside and reserve remaining spice mixture for the cinnamon swirl. Add the yeast mixture and salt; whisk until combined. Switch to a rubber spatula; add the remaining flour mixture, 1 cup at a time, stirring until a soft dough forms. Add the raisins and stir until incorporated.

Grease a large bowl with butter.

Transfer the dough onto a lightly floured work surface. Knead until smooth and elastic, about 8 minutes. Add additional flour as necessary, about 1 teaspoon at time, to prevent the dough from sticking to your hands. Transfer the dough to the prepared bowl; cover with plastic wrap. Let the dough rise in a warm place until it has doubled in size and an indention remains after you have poked the dough with your finger, about 1 hour.

WHILE THE DOUGH IS RISING PREPARE THE BROWN SUGAR SWIRL. In a small bowl, combine the brown sugar, 4 tablespoons of the butter, $3\frac{1}{2}$ teaspoons of the spice mixture, and vanilla; mix well; set aside.

Spray four loaf pans with cooking spray and line with parchment paper. Divide the dough into 4 equal pieces. Roll each piece of dough into a rectangle, about 1 inch thick; spread a quarter of the cinnamon swirl mixture over the dough, leaving a $\frac{1}{2}$-inch border. Beginning with the long edge nearest to you, roll the dough into a taught cylinder. Firmly pinch the seam and edges to seal and place the cylinder seam side down in the prepared loaf pan. Lightly brush the top with oil; cover with plastic wrap, and let rise until double in size, about 50 minutes.

Adjust an oven rack to the middle position and heat the oven to 350°F.

In a small bowl, thoroughly mix together a tablespoon of water and the egg yolk. Brush $\frac{1}{2}$ of the mixture equally over the loaves. Let sit for 10 minutes, then brush again with the remaining mixture. Bake until the loaves are golden brown and sound hollow when tapped, 20 to 25 minutes. Cool pans on a cooling rack for 10 minutes; then invert loaves onto the cooling rack and flip right-side up. Cool completely or serve warm.

NOTE: To freeze, wrap each loaf in plastic wrap then cover tightly with foil. Place in the freezer for up to two months. To thaw, just place on the counter overnight.

GREAT GIFTS FROM YOUR KITCHEN

I VIVIDLY RECALL NEIGHBORS, FRIENDS, AND EXTENDED FAMILY COMING TO visit during the holidays with some sort of homemade treat, compote, or dessert which I thought was terrific; I always enjoy gifts I can eat. Spread the same seasonal cheer I remember with personal and gracious gifts from your kitchen. Make the following recipes for hostess gifts, office presents, gift exchanges, or just thoughtful presents. Wrap the items in decorative paper or place in a nice jar with a stylish bow. Be sure to include a recipe card and serving suggestions.

Citrus-Cranberry Glaze (page 90)

Jellied Cranberry Sauce (page 93)

Persimmon Bread (page 77)

Spicy Glazed Walnuts (page 95)

Espresso Double-Chocolate Soufflé
   Brownies (page176)

Hot Fudge Sauce (page 185)

Green Apple and Pumpkin Butter (page 188)

Quince Compote (page 192)

Caramel Sauce (page 254)

Banana Blueberry Bread (page 243)

Crunchy Honey Lavender Almonds (page 35)

Spiced Plum BBQ Sauce (page 265)

CHIVE-ONION POPOVERS *with* TOASTED CARDAMOM

THESE FLAKY, AROMATIC POPOVERS PUFF MORE WHEN THE MILK AND EGGS are used at room temperature. For added flavor, ask your butcher for prime rib trimmings and render the fat at home. Don't be tempted to open the oven door to check on the popovers. Use an oven light and view them through the glass to see if they are golden brown.

MAKES 12 POPOVERS

1$\frac{1}{2}$ cups all-purpose flour

1 teaspoon salt

$\frac{1}{2}$ teaspoon freshly ground black pepper

$\frac{1}{8}$ teaspoon freshly ground toasted cardamom

4 large eggs

$\frac{1}{2}$ cup light beer

2 tablespoons horseradish

2 tablespoons finely chopped chives

2 tablespoons grated yellow onion

1 cup plus 2 tablespoons prime rib fat or grapeseed oil for greasing

IN A MEDIUM BOWL SIFT TOGETHER FLOUR, salt, pepper, and cardamom. In a separate medium bowl, whisk the eggs, $\frac{1}{2}$ cup of water, beer, and horseradish; once combined, stir in the chives and the onion. Make a well in the flour mixture and gradually whisk in the egg mixture until blended. Cover the bowl with plastic wrap and let the mixture sit at room temperature for at least 2 hours.

Adjust the oven rack to the lowest position and set the oven to 450°F.

Place the popover tray on a heavy sheet pan and fill each cup with 1$\frac{1}{2}$ tablespoons of the fat or oil. Place the tray in the oven to heat until the oil is smoking hot, 15 to 20 minutes. Carefully remove popover tray from the oven and pour the batter into the cups until $\frac{3}{4}$ full. Return the popover tray onto the sheet pan in the oven and bake for 20 minutes; reduce the temperature to 325°F and bake until popovers are golden brown and begin to pull away from sides of the tray, about 20 minutes more. Serve immediately.

NOTE: A muffin tin can be substituted for a popover tray; however, the popovers will be smaller so take five to ten minutes off the baking time.

SOFT ROLLS

*E*VERYONE LOVES THE AROMA AND FLAVOR OF FRESHLY BAKED BREAD. THESE soft rolls are perfect for any meal. If there are any leftover rolls make elegant mini sandwiches for brunch the next morning.

MAKES 24 ROLLS

2 packages (4½ teaspoons) active dry yeast

3½ tablespoons unsalted butter

⅓ cup granulated sugar

1 tablespoon salt

½ cup whole milk plus 1 tablespoon of whole milk, for brushing the rolls

¾ cup heavy cream

3 large eggs, 1 lightly beaten for brushing the rolls

4½ cups all-purpose flour, plus more for dusting

LINE A RIMMED BAKING SHEET WITH PARCHMENT PAPER; set aside.

Combine the yeast and ¼ cup of water in a medium bowl; stir until the yeast is dissolved; let stand for 10 minutes.

In a stand mixer fitted with the paddle attachment, beat the butter, sugar, and salt on medium speed until creamy, about 2 minutes. Decrease the speed to low; gradually add the yeast mixture, milk, cream, and 2 eggs; mix until thoroughly combined. Change mixer attachment to a hook, turn the mixer to low speed; slowly add the flour. Continue to mix on low speed until the dough is smooth and silky, 10 to 12 minutes. (If the dough creeps up on the attachment, stop the mixer and scrape it down.)

Transfer the dough onto a floured work surface and sprinkle the top with flour. Cut the dough in half; gently stretch each half into a 12-inch log. Cut 12 1-inch pieces from each log (you should have 24 pieces total); dust each piece with more flour. With floured hands, gently pick up each piece and roll in your palms to shape into a ball. Place in the prepared baking pan; repeat with the remaining dough. Loosely cover the pan with plastic wrap. Allow the rolls to rise until double in size, 1 to 2 hours. (Dough is ready when it springs back slowly when pressed lightly with a knuckle.)

Thirty minutes before baking, adjust an oven rack to the middle position and heat the oven to 400°F.

In a small bowl, mix the beaten egg and milk until combined. Remove the plastic wrap from the baking pan and lightly brush the rolls with the egg mixture and place in the oven. Bake until the tops of the rolls are browned, 15 minutes. Serve warm.

RED ONION *and* PARMESAN CRACKERS

DON'T BE INTIMIDATED BY MAKING YOUR OWN CRACKERS; IT IS REALLY VERY simple and the flavor and texture cannot be beat. Try these crackers with Broiled Oysters (page 130). To vary the flavor, add chopped fresh herbs like basil or thyme.

MAKES 36 (4 X 4-INCH) CRACKERS

$1\frac{1}{2}$ cups bread flour

1 tablespoon granulated sugar

$\frac{1}{2}$ teaspoon salt

$2\frac{1}{2}$ teaspoons shortening, chilled and cut into $\frac{1}{2}$-inch pieces

$2\frac{1}{2}$ teaspoons unsalted butter, chilled and cut into $\frac{1}{4}$-inch pieces

$\frac{1}{2}$ cup plus 3 tablespoons whole milk, if needed

1 large egg white, beaten

$\frac{1}{2}$ cup grated Parmesan cheese

1 small red onion, finely chopped ($\frac{1}{4}$ cup)

ADJUST AN OVEN RACK TO THE MIDDLE POSITION and heat the oven to 400°F. Line two baking sheets with parchment paper.

Process the flour, sugar, and salt together in a food processor until combined. Scatter the shortening and butter pieces over the flour and pulse until the mixture resembles coarse oatmeal, about 10 seconds. Slowly pour in the $\frac{1}{2}$ cup of milk and pulse until combined and a rough ball of dough is formed; add more milk, a tablespoon at a time, if necessary. Divide the dough into two equal pieces.

Remove the pre-fitted parchment paper from the baking trays and place half of the dough out onto each of the parchment papers; roll the dough into a very thin sheet. Place the parchment paper with the dough back onto the baking sheets. Cut the dough with a knife into even squares or any other desired shape. Using a fork, pierce each cracker approximately 6 times (this releases steam so crackers won't rise). Brush the dough with the egg white and evenly sprinkle the cheese and onions over the top. Bake until light golden brown; 10 minutes. Cool on a cooling rack to room temperature, about 20 minutes. Gently break the crackers apart along the precut lines.

CHOCOLATE BRIOCHE PUDDING

BREAD PUDDING WAS A FAVORITE WHEN I WAS GROWING UP. MY MOTHER would use leftover biscuits and whatever sandwich bread she had around the kitchen. I love this sophisticated and updated version of a nostalgic favorite. Add your favorite nut for additional crunch or serve with Champagne Sabayon (page 189).

MAKES 6 SERVINGS

COFFEE GANACHE

1 cup heavy cream

1 cup bittersweet chocolate, chopped

1 tablespoon coffee extract

BREAD PUDDING

2 tablespoons unsalted butter, softened, for greasing baking dish

3 cups diced brioche, egg, or raisin bread, crust trimmed, cut into 1-inch pieces

1 1/2 cups heavy cream, divided

2/3 cup dark brown sugar

4 large eggs

1/3 cup bourbon

1 teaspoon ground cinnamon

1 tablespoon vanilla extract

1 1/2 cups Champagne Sabayon (page 189), for garnish (optional)

Cocoa powder, for garnish

FOR THE GANACHE: Bring the cream to a simmer in a small saucepan over medium-high heat. Place the chocolate and extract in medium bowl; pour in the hot cream. Stir until chocolate has melted. Reserve 1/2 cup of the chocolate ganache; set the rest aside.

FOR THE BREAD PUDDING: Evenly spread the butter onto the bottom and sides of a medium baking dish; set aside.

In a large bowl, whisk together 1 cup of the heavy cream, sugar, and eggs until combined; set aside. Gently whisk the remaining 1/2 cup heavy cream into the chocolate ganache until well blended. Whisking slowly, add the unreserved chocolate ganache into the egg mixture until well blended and smooth. Stir in the bourbon, cinnamon, and vanilla. Pour 1 cup of the custard into the prepared pan and place half of the bread over the custard in an even layer. Distribute the reserved 1/2 cup of chocolate ganache, teaspoon by teaspoon, over the bread; add the remaining bread in an even layer. Pour the remaining custard over the bread. Cover with foil and place in the refrigerator for at least 4 hours, or up to overnight.

Adjust an oven rack to the middle position and heat the oven to 325°F.

Place the covered pudding in a larger pan lined with a kitchen towel. Carefully place the pan on the oven rack and fill larger pan with hot water to reach two-thirds of the way up the sides of the pudding dish.

Bake for 20 minutes; remove the cover, and bake until puffed, golden brown, and a knife inserted in the center of the custard comes out clean, an additional 25 minutes. Transfer the baking dish to a cooling rack and cool the custard until warm, about 10 minutes.

Place a serving of warm pudding onto an individual plate, dollop with an oval shaped portion of sabayon, and dust with powdered cocoa.

CHOCOLATE CREAM PUFFS

*T*HESE ELEGANT PUFFS ARE AN IDEAL ENDING FOR A FORMAL HOLIDAY FEAST: light, creamy, and with the perfect amount of chocolate to satisfy any sweet tooth.

$\frac{1}{2}$ cup cake flour

$\frac{1}{2}$ cup bread flour

3 tablespoons cocoa powder

4 tablespoons unsalted butter

$\frac{1}{4}$ teaspoon salt

2 tablespoons granulated sugar

4 large eggs

1 recipe Chocolate Whipped Cream (page 174)

Confectioners' sugar, for dusting

ADJUST ONE OVEN RACK TO THE MIDDLE POSITION and a second oven rack just below the first rack. Heat the oven to 425°F. Line two baking sheets with parchment paper.

Sift the cake four, bread flour, and cocoa powder together onto a sheet of parchment paper; set aside.

In a medium saucepan over high heat, combine 1 cup of water, the butter, salt, and sugar. Bring to a full rolling boil so the butter is not floating on the surface, but is dispersed throughout the liquid. Using a wooden spoon, stir the half of the flour mixture into the liquid, adding more as the liquid absorbs it. (The mixture will resemble a thick paste.) Reduce the heat to medium; cook the mixture, stirring constantly, until almost no steam rises from it and the mixture comes away from the sides of the pan, 3 to 5 minutes. Remove the pot from heat and let the mixture cool slightly, for about 5 minutes.

Transfer the mixture to a stand mixer fitted with the paddle attachment. Add one egg, beating at medium speed, until the egg is fully incorporated into the dough and the dough is very smooth. Repeat with each additional egg.

Transfer the dough into a large pastry bag with a $\frac{1}{4}$-inch plain round tip, or a gallon-size resealable plastic bag with one of the bottom corners clipped. Squeeze the dough onto the prepared baking sheets in the size of golf balls, or any desired shape, 1 inch apart.

Bake until fully puffed and just starting to lightly brown, about 10 minutes. Reduce the heat to 375°F; rotate and swap the baking sheets so the top one is now on the bottom rack and vice versa; bake until golden brown and firm, 10 to 12 minutes more (or longer depending

(continued)

on the size). Cool the puffs in the pan set on a cooling rack for 10 minutes. Remove the puffs from the baking pan and place onto the cooling rack; cool to room temperature. (At this stage the puffs can be frozen for up to one month if wrapped in plastic wrap. When ready to use the puffs, just place them on the counter and thaw to room temperature.)

Take a serrated knife and cut the top third from each puff and gently scoop out any moist interior. (At this point the puffs can be refrigerated for up to three days.)

Fill the cream puffs with the whipped cream, recap with the top. Dust with confectioners' sugar. Serve immediately.

NOTE: Fill the puffs with Kahlua Sabayon (page 190) for a nice alternative.

Wine pairing: port, Cabernet Sauvignon

CHOCOLATE WHIPPED CREAM

CHRISTMAS IS A DECADENT HOLIDAY. WHEN ORDINARY WHIPPED CREAM won't do, this rich chocolaty cream will satisfy any succulent craving and take your dessert to a new level for chocolate lovers. The addition of the Kahlua Sabayon to this whipped cream makes this filling unbelievably decadent and special.

MAKES 2 CUPS

$^3/_4$ cup heavy cream

$^1/_2$ teaspoon vanilla extract

2 teaspoons granulated sugar

2 ounces semisweet chocolate, finely chopped

1 recipe Kahlua Sabayon (page 190)

IN A LARGE CHILLED BOWL, whip $^1/_2$ cup of the heavy cream with an electric mixer on high speed until the cream forms soft peaks, 1 to 2 minutes. Add the vanilla and sugar and mix until combined; cover and refrigerate.

Place a medium glass bowl over a saucepan filled with 1 inch of simmering water. Add the chocolate and the remaining $^1/_4$ cup heavy cream and melt until smooth, stirring once or twice, about 5 minutes. Remove the bowl from the saucepan and retrieve the reserved whipped cream.

With an electric mixer on medium-high speed, beat the reserved whipped cream while slowly pouring in the melted chocolate in a thin stream; beat until thoroughly combined. Gently fold in the sabayon. Refrigerate until needed.

DEVIL'S FOOD CHOCOLATE CUPCAKES

*T*HESE FUN CUPCAKES HIT ALL YOUR CHOCOLATE SENSES WITH AN ALLURING combination of contrasting textures and chocolate flavors. Intensely rich, moist, and decadent cakes overflow with thick, rich, dark fudge sauce and cool ice cream. The beets may be a surprising addition, but are imperative to the exceptional moistness and sweetness of the cupcakes.

MAKES 12 CUPCAKES

Vegetable oil spray

1 cup all-purpose flour

$^1/_2$ cup cocoa powder

$^3/_4$ teaspoon baking soda

$^1/_4$ teaspoon baking powder

$^1/_4$ teaspoon salt

$^3/_4$ cup buttermilk

$^2/_3$ cup granulated sugar

2 large eggs

6 tablespoons unsalted butter, melted

$^1/_4$ cup sour cream

1 large red beet, uncooked, peeled and grated (about $^1/_2$ cup)

1 recipe Hot Fudge Sauce (page 185), warmed

Vanilla bean ice cream

Whipped cream

ADJUST AN OVEN RACK TO THE LOWER-MIDDLE POSITION and heat the oven to 350°F. Spray a standard-sized muffin pan with vegetable oil spray.

Sift the flour, cocoa, baking soda, baking powder, and salt together in a small bowl; set aside.

In a medium bowl with an electric mixer on medium speed, mix the buttermilk, sugar, and eggs until thick and homogeneous, about 45 seconds. Add the butter; mix until incorporated. Add half of the flour mixture to the egg mixture and beat until combined; add in the sour cream and beat until combined; then add the remaining flour mixture to the batter and beat until homogenous and thick. Gently fold the beets into the batter.

Divide the batter evenly among 12 muffin cups; batter should only come half way up muffin tin. Bake until a toothpick inserted into the center of the cupcakes comes out clean, 20 to 25 minutes, rotating the pan halfway through the baking time. Cool the cupcakes in the tin on a cooling rack until cool enough to handle, about 15 minutes. Carefully lift each cupcake from the muffin pan and set on a cooling rack until ready to use. (Cupcakes can be frozen at this point for later use.)

Split the cupcake in half horizontally. Place the bottom layer of the cake in a serving dish; place a scoop of vanilla bean ice cream on top; cap with the cupcake top. Ladle $^1/_4$ cup of the hot fudge sauce over the top and serve with a dollop of whipped cream. Serve immediately.

Wine pairing: port, Merlot, Cabernet Sauvignon

ESPRESSO DOUBLE-CHOCOLATE
SOUFFLÉ BROWNIES

CHEWY AND CHOCOLATY BROWNIES ARE AN UTTERLY SATISFYING AFFAIR. Reminiscent of the brownies your mom used to make with the addition of espresso to enhance the chocolate flavor and cater to adult tastes. Try them with the Chocolate Whipped Cream (page 174).

MAKES 1 DOZEN (3-INCH) SQUARES

2 tablespoons unsalted butter, for greasing baking dish, softened

6 ounces bittersweet chocolate, chopped

4 ounces dark chocolate, chopped

5 large eggs, 2 whole and 3 separated

10 ounces ($2^{1}/_{2}$ sticks) unsalted butter, softened

$1^{1}/_{2}$ cups granulated sugar

$^{1}/_{2}$ cup brewed espresso coffee

2 teaspoons vanilla extract

1 cup all-purpose flour

$^{1}/_{2}$ teaspoon salt

ADJUST AN OVEN RACK TO THE MIDDLE POSITION and heat the oven to 350°F. Grease a 13 x 9-inch baking pan with the 2 tablespoons of butter.

Melt the bittersweet and dark chocolate in a medium glass bowl set over a pot of simmering water. Once completely melted and smooth, remove from the heat, and cover with plastic wrap; set aside.

In a stand mixer fitted with the whisk attachment, beat the egg whites on high speed until soft peaks form; transfer whites to a small bowl and set aside. Take off the whisk attachment and put on the paddle attachment. In the same bowl, cream the $2^{1}/_{2}$ sticks of butter and sugar together on medium speed until light and fluffy; about 2 minutes. Add the 2 whole eggs and 3 egg yolks one at a time, incorporating completely after each addition. Reduce the mixer speed to low; add the melted chocolate, espresso, and vanilla; mix until well combined. Stir in the flour and salt; mixing to just combine; do not overmix. Gently fold in the egg whites. Pour the batter into the prepared baking dish.

Bake until slightly puffed and a toothpick inserted into the center of the brownies comes out with a few moist crumbs attached, 25 to 30 minutes. Let the brownies cool slightly and serve warm.

NOTE: The brownies can be wrapped in plastic wrap and refrigerated up to five days or placed in a freezer bag and frozen for up to one month.

CHRISTMAS ORANGE SHORTBREAD

*W*HAT'S GREAT ABOUT THIS SIMPLE AND VERSATILE SHORTBREAD IS YOU can easily change the flavor. I have made them with lemon zest, almond extract, vanilla bean, and even lavender. You can also substitute half a cup of ground blanched almonds for half a cup of the flour for added texture and flavor.

MAKES 8 SERVINGS

Cooking spray

4 ounces (1 stick) unsalted butter, softened

4 tablespoons granulated sugar, plus more for garnish

2 oranges, zest grated

1½ cups all-purpose flour

Confectioners' sugar, for rolling out dough

ADJUST AN OVEN RACK TO THE MIDDLE POSITION and heat oven to 375°F. Line a baking sheet with parchment paper and spray with cooking spray.

In a standing mixer fitted with the paddle attachment, cream the butter and sugar on medium speed until light and fluffy, about 5 minutes. Add the zest; then gradually add the flour until combined. Turn out dough on a large work surface lightly dusted with confectioners' sugar. Roll out the dough to ½-inch thickness. Cut or punch out dough into desired shapes, such as bars, strips, or rounds. Prick the dough with a fork a few times; sprinkle with sugar. Place dough on the prepared cookie sheet and bake until very light golden brown, about 20 minutes. Cool on the baking sheet for 2 minutes before transferring shortbread to a cooling rack to cook completely.

GINGER SNAP COOKIES *with* LEMON THYME

*A*DDING A FRESH HERB TO A COOKIE MAY BE NEW TO MANY OF YOU, BUT I insist you try this flavor combination. You won't be disappointed.

MAKES 4 DOZEN COOKIES

3 cups all-purpose flour

2$\frac{1}{2}$ teaspoons ground cinnamon

2$\frac{1}{2}$ teaspoons baking soda

2 teaspoons ground ginger

$\frac{1}{2}$ teaspoon ground cloves

$\frac{1}{2}$ teaspoon salt

$\frac{1}{2}$ teaspoons freshly ground pepper

$\frac{1}{2}$ teaspoon finely chopped lemon thyme

$\frac{1}{4}$ teaspoon ground nutmeg

8 ounces (2 sticks) unsalted butter, softened

1$\frac{1}{4}$ cup granulated sugar plus more for garnish

2 large eggs

$\frac{1}{4}$ cup molasses

1 teaspoon vanilla extract

ADJUST AN OVEN RACK TO THE MIDDLE POSITION and heat oven to 350°F. Line two baking sheets with parchment paper.

In a large bowl mix together the flour, cinnamon, baking soda, ginger, cloves, salt, pepper, thyme, and nutmeg until thoroughly combined; set aside.

In a standing mixer fitted with the paddle attachment, cream the butter and sugar on medium speed until light and fluffy, about 5 minutes. Add the eggs one at a time until incorporated; add the molasses and vanilla until incorporated, scraping down the sides and stirring the bottom of the bowl. Turn the mixer to low and gradually add the flour mixture until just incorporated; do not overmix. Form cookie balls with 2 teaspoons of dough each; flatten slightly with your palm. Dip one side of the dough in sugar and place sugar-side up on the prepared baking sheet.

Bake until cookies are fragrant, dark golden brown, and have slightly crisped edges, approximately 10 to 12 minutes, rotating the baking sheet halfway through the baking time. Allow the cookies to cool on the baking sheet for 2 minutes before transferring them to a cooling rack to cool completely.

PARSNIP COOKIES *with* MAPLE GLAZE

*T*HIS IS A VERY DEAR FRIEND'S DELICIOUS COOKIE RECIPE. I LOOK FORWARD to her dropping them by every holiday and managed to finally wear her down for the recipe. Parsnips are certainly an unusual ingredient in a dessert but they add a really wonderful earthy sweetness to this great cake-like winter cookie.

MAKES 2 DOZEN COOKIES

PARSNIP COOKIES

1 cup all-purpose flour

$3/4$ cup whole wheat flour

1 cup rolled oats

2 teaspoons baking powder

$1/2$ teaspoon salt

$1/2$ teaspoon ground cinnamon

$1/4$ teaspoon ground allspice

$1/4$ teaspoon nutmeg

4 ounces (1 stick) unsalted butter

$1/2$ cup packed brown sugar

$1/4$ cup granulated sugar

2 large eggs

1 teaspoon vanilla

1 cup cooked quinoa

$1/2$ cup buttermilk

1 cup packed finely grated parsnips

MAPLE GLAZE

$1^{1}/2$ cups confectioners' sugar

$1/4$ cup maple syrup

$1/8$ teaspoon salt

FOR THE COOKIES: Adjust an oven rack to the middle position and heat the oven to 375°F. Line 2 baking sheets with parchment paper.

In a large bowl mix together the flour, wheat flour, oats, baking powder, salt, cinnamon, allspice, and nutmeg until thoroughly combined; set aside.

In a standing mixer fitted with the paddle attachment, cream the butter and sugars on medium speed until light and fluffy, about 5 minutes. Add the eggs one at a time until incorporated; add the vanilla and quinoa until incorporated, scraping down the sides and stirring the bottom of the bowl. Turn the mixer to low and gradually add a third of the flour mixture followed by half of the buttermilk. Add half of the remaining flour followed by the remaining buttermilk and finish with the remaining flour; mix until just combined. Stir in the parsnips.

Drop 2 tablespoons of the dough for each cookie and place 1 inch apart. Bake until the edges are just golden, 10 to 13 minutes. Cool the cookies on the baking sheet for 2 minutes before transferring them to a cooling rack to cool completely.

FOR THE GLAZE: In a small bowl combine the sugar, syrup, and salt. Stir until smooth. Using the tines of a fork, drizzle the glaze over the cookies in a crisscross pattern.

HOLIDAY TANGERINE BARS

*T*HIS IS SUCH AN EASY AND FESTIVE COOKIE RECIPE. I CAN WHIP THESE UP IN no time for surprise holiday guests or last-minute dinners. Try sprinkling flaked coconut over the top for added flavor and texture.

MAKES 3 DOZEN COOKIES

TANGERINE CURD

4 large eggs, beaten

1$\frac{1}{2}$ cups granulated sugar

2 tablespoons cornstarch

$\frac{1}{2}$ teaspoon baking powder

1 tangerine, zest grated

$\frac{1}{4}$ cup freshly squeezed tangerine juice

$\frac{3}{4}$ cup whipping cream (optional)

SHORTBREAD

1 pound (4 sticks) unsalted butter, plus more for greasing

2 cups all-purpose flour

2 cups confectioners' sugar

ADJUST AN OVEN RACK TO THE MIDDLE POSITION and heat oven to 350°F. Grease a 13 x 9-inch baking dish with cooking spray or butter.

FOR THE SHORTBREAD: Place the butter, flour, and sugar in a food processor and pulse until the mixture resembles coarse oatmeal. Transfer the crumb mixture into the prepared baking dish and press into an even layer. Bake until crust has lightly browned, 15 to 20 minutes. While crust is baking make the curd.

FOR THE CURD: In a small non-reactive saucepan over medium-low heat, combine all of the ingredients. Keep mixture just under a simmer, stirring often, until thickened, glossy, and able to lightly coat the back of a spoon, 5 to 7 minutes. Place in a storage container and cool completely. Place a piece of plastic wrap directly on the surface of the curd then refrigerate until needed. Curd can be stored in the refrigerator for up to two weeks.

Pour the curd over the hot crust and bake until curd has set and does not jiggle when shook, about 25 minutes. Let cool completely then lightly sprinkle with confectioners' sugar.

NOTE: If you prefer a tarter curd, decrease the sugar by $\frac{1}{4}$ cup. Adding the whipped cream will make the curd more light and fluffy.

PUMPKIN COOKIES *with* LEMON CREAM CHEESE FROSTING

I ABSOLUTELY LOVE ANYTHING WITH PUMPKIN! IT IS DEFINITELY MY FAVORITE holiday food, so it wasn't difficult to come up with an amazing pumpkin cookie recipe.

MAKES 4 DOZEN COOKIES

PUMPKIN COOKIES

3 cups all-purpose flour

1 cup whole wheat flour

2 teaspoons baking soda

2 teaspoons baking powder

1½ teaspoons salt

2 teaspoons ground cinnamon

1 teaspoon ground allspice

1 teaspoon nutmeg

½ teaspoon ground cloves

8 ounces (2 sticks) unsalted butter, softened

2⅔ cups packed brown sugar

2½ cups canned unsweetened pumpkin purée

2 tablespoons honey

1 teaspoon vanilla extract

2 teaspoons grated fresh ginger

1 cup raisins

LEMON CREAM CHEESE FROSTING

8 ounces cream cheese, softened

½ cup superfine sugar

1 teaspoon freshly squeezed lemon juice

½ teaspoon vanilla extract

¾ cup finely chopped toasted walnuts or pecans (optional)

FOR THE COOKIES: Adjust an oven rack to the middle position and heat oven to 375°F. Line a baking sheet with parchment paper.

In a large bowl mix together the flour, wheat flour, baking soda, baking powder, salt, cinnamon, allspice, nutmeg, and cloves until thoroughly combined; set aside.

In a standing mixer fitted with the paddle attachment, cream the butter and sugar on medium speed until light and fluffy, about 5 minutes. Add the pumpkin, honey, vanilla, and ginger; mix until thoroughly combined, scraping down the sides and stirring the bottom of the bowl. Turn the mixer to low and gradually add the flour mixture until just incorporated; do not overmix. Using a rubber spatula, fold in the raisins.

Form balls with 2 tablespoons of batter each and place each cookie 1 inch apart. Bake until light golden brown around the edges, 13 to 15 minutes. Cool the cookies on the baking sheet for 2 minutes before transferring them to a cooling rack to cook completely before frosting.

FOR THE FROSTING: In a medium bowl mix together all the ingredients with an electric mixer on medium speed until smooth. Spread an even layer over the cookies. Sprinkle with nuts, if desired.

MILK CHOCOLATE *and* DRUNKEN PRUNE ICE CREAM

*I*CE CREAM IS A GREAT DESSERT THAT YOU CAN PREPARE AHEAD OF TIME. This rich flavor combination makes ordinary ice cream extraordinary. Try serving with Espresso Double-Chocolate Soufflé Brownies (page 176).

(page 176)

MAKES 4 CUPS

1 cup chopped prunes

1 cup dark rum

1 tablespoon brandy

1³/₄ cups heavy cream

1³/₄ cups whole milk

1 cup granulated sugar

¹/₈ teaspoon ground cinnamon

1 vanilla bean, split lengthwise in half

8 large egg yolks

1 teaspoon vanilla extract

4 ounces milk chocolate, chopped

2 tablespoons dark cocoa powder

IN A SMALL SAUCEPAN OVER MEDIUM-HIGH HEAT, bring the prunes, rum, and brandy to a boil. Turn off heat and let mixture sit until cooled to room temperature; set aside.

In a medium glass bowl set over a saucepan filled with 3 inches of simmering water, combine the cream, milk, sugar, and cinnamon. Using a paring knife, scrape the seeds from the vanilla bean into the mixture; discard the pod. Slowly heat the mixture, stirring occasionally, until it just begins to simmer.

Meanwhile, in a large bowl, whisk together the egg yolks, vanilla extract, chocolate, and cocoa powder. While whisking vigorously, slowly pour 2 cups of the hot cream mixture into the egg yolks; slowly pour the egg mixture back into the cream mixture, whisking constantly. Continue to cook mixture, stirring frequently, until the chocolate has melted and the custard thickens and coats the back of a spoon, about 8 minutes. Pour the custard through a fine-mesh sieve into a medium bowl; cover and refrigerate until completely cooled; about 1 hour.

Pour the mixture into an ice-cream maker and process according to the manufacturer's directions. When the ice cream is almost set, fold in the reserved prunes and liquid, continue to process.

HOT FUDGE SAUCE

*T*HIS PERFECT, RICH, AND SINFULLY DELICIOUS SAUCE CAN ACCOMPANY THE Devil's Food Chocolate Cupcakes (page 175) or be drizzled over cheesecake or ice cream. It also makes a thoughtful hostess gift.

MAKES 2 CUPS

12 ounces bittersweet chocolate, chopped

$^1/_3$ cup cocoa powder

$^1/_3$ cup granulated sugar

$^3/_4$ cup light corn syrup

$^1/_2$ cup heavy cream

$^1/_8$ teaspoon salt

1 teaspoon vanilla extract

6 tablespoons unsalted butter, cut into chunks

MELT THE CHOCOLATE IN A MEDIUM GLASS BOWL set over a saucepan filled with 2 inches of simmering water, stirring occasionally, until smooth. Whisk in the cocoa powder until completely incorporated. Set aside to cool slightly.

Heat the sugar, corn syrup, cream, and salt in a small saucepan over medium heat; simmer lightly until the sugar has dissolved, about 5 minutes. Remove the saucepan from the heat; let mixture cool slightly. Stir in the vanilla and butter until combined. Pour the sugar mixture into the chocolate and mix thoroughly to combine. Serve immediately, or cool to room temperature, cover, and refrigerate until needed.

NOTE: The sauce will keep in the refrigerator for up to two weeks.

HORSERADISH CRÈME FRAÎCHE

*T*HIS SPICY, TANGY, AND SLIGHTLY SOURED CREAM HAS A SHORT FERMENTATION period and will exceed your expectations with its simple preparation and light yet complex flavor. Serve this sophisticated crème with the Coffee-Spiced Prime Rib Roast (page 139) or Caviar Potato Puffs (page 131).

MAKES 2 CUPS

2 cups heavy cream

2 tablespoons buttermilk

1 tablespoon freshly squeezed lemon juice

$^{1}/_{2}$ teaspoon kosher salt

2 tablespoons freshly grated horseradish

IN A LARGE BOWL, COMBINE ALL THE INGREDIENTS except the horseradish and loosely cover but do not seal. Let mixture sit at room temperature (75 to 80 degrees) until cream has slightly thickened, 24 to 30 hours.

Stir in the horseradish; refrigerate for at least 8 hours before serving.

NOTE: The finished crème fraîche can be stored in refrigerator for at least seven days.

MIGNONETTE SAUCE

A DELIGHTFULLY SIMPLE SAUCE TO COMPLEMENT ANY SHELLFISH, RAW OR cooked. Serve with Broiled Oysters (page 130).

MAKES 1 CUP

$^{1}/_{2}$ cup Champagne vinegar

$^{1}/_{4}$ cup white wine

1 medium shallot, finely chopped (about 3 tablespoons)

2 tablespoons finely chopped flat-leaf parsley

1 teaspoon freshly ground black pepper

IN A SMALL BOWL, mix all of the ingredients together. Cover and refrigerate for at least 1 hour, or more. Serve with oysters or clams.

NOTE: The sauce can be made up to two days in advance.

PERSIMMON DRESSING

THIS GORGEOUS LITTLE FRUIT SHINES IN THIS FESTIVE DRESSING. SERVE OVER the simple Spinach Salad with Pomegranates and Blue Cheese (page 126).

MAKES 4 CUPS

4 star anise

5 medium Fuyu persimmons, peeled and chopped, 1 cup reserved for garnish

6 ripe Hachiya persimmons, seeded and pulp removed

2 cups freshly squeezed tangerine juice

1½ cups freshly squeezed Meyer lemon juice

1 cup fruity white wine

¼ cup olive oil

¼ teaspoon kosher salt

½ teaspoon freshly ground black pepper

IN A MEDIUM SKILLET OVER MEDIUM-LOW HEAT, toast the star anise until fragrant, about 3 minutes. Add the persimmon pulp, tangerine and lemon juices, wine, and pepper. Cook until the mixture has reduced by two thirds. Discard the star anise; pour the persimmon mixture through a fine-mesh strainer into a medium bowl and use the back of a spoon to press against the solids, extracting all of the liquid; discard solids. Cover liquid and cool completely in the refrigerator.

Stir the reserved cup of persimmons and oil into the chilled purée; season with salt and pepper to taste. Keep refrigerated until needed.

GREEN APPLE PUMPKIN BUTTER

SWEET AND TART. THE PERFECT COMBINATION FOR TOPPING ANY BREAD. THIS also makes a perfect hostess gift. Try it with the Boston Brown Bread (page 163). If using canned pumpkin, place the contents in a medium saucepan over medium-low heat with $\frac{1}{2}$ cup water, one quartered apple (chopped into small pieces), melted butter, $\frac{1}{2}$ of the ground spices, honey, $\frac{1}{2}$ cup of the cider, and $\frac{1}{2}$ of the lemon juice. Simmer gently until thick and the apples are very tender, about 30 minutes. Remove from heat; set aside until needed.

MAKES 4 CUPS

1 stick cinnamon

$\frac{1}{2}$ teaspoon whole allspice berries

4 star anise

5 whole cloves

2 tablespoons unsalted butter, melted

3 tablespoons honey, warmed

1$\frac{1}{2}$ cups apple cider

2 lemons, juiced

1 small (2- to 3-pound) sugar pumpkin, halved vertically and seeded, or 1 (28-ounce) can pumpkin purée

2$\frac{3}{4}$ pounds Granny Smith apples (about 6 large), cored and quartered, divided

$\frac{1}{4}$ cup packed dark brown sugar

1 orange, juiced

ADJUST AN OVEN RACK TO THE MIDDLE POSITION and heat the oven to 285°F.

Place the cinnamon, allspice, star anise, and cloves in a large skillet over medium-low heat; toast the spices, shaking pan occasionally, until fragrant, 3 to 4 minutes. Remove from the heat and grind in a spice grinder; set aside.

Place one quartered apple into a large bowl with the melted butter, $\frac{1}{2}$ of the ground spices, honey, $\frac{1}{2}$ cup of the cider, and $\frac{1}{2}$ of the lemon juice. Stir the mixture until blended and divide evenly inside the pumpkin cavities. Place the pumpkin halves, cut side up, on a baking dish and cook in the oven until the pumpkin is very tender and offers no resistance when pierced with a paring knife, about 2 hours. Remove the pumpkin from the oven and set on a clean dry surface until cool enough to handle. Scoop out the pumpkin pulp and stuffing into a medium bowl; set aside.

Place the remaining apples in a large saucepan over medium-high heat. Add the remaining spices, cider, and lemon juice. Add the brown sugar and orange juice; stir to combine; bring mixture to a boil. Reduce the heat to low; cover and cook, stirring occasionally, for 15 minutes. Remove the cover and add the reserved pumpkin mixture; stir to combine. Continue cooking, uncovered, stirring often, until the mixture has thickened and juice has evaporated, about 45 minutes. Remove from the heat and allow to cool in the pan for 10 minutes.

Pass mixture through a food mill or place in a food processor or and purée until very smooth. Cover and refrigerate until needed or place in sterilized jars.

CHAMPAGNE SABAYON

A LUXURIOUS SAUCE THAT IS DELICATELY FLAVORED, THICK, AND CREAMY. Don't let the sauce get too hot—it will turn grainy.

2 large egg yolks

3 tablespoons Champagne

2 tablespoons granulated sugar

$\frac{1}{8}$ teaspoon salt

$\frac{1}{2}$ cup Coffee Ganache (page 171), room temperature

$\frac{1}{2}$ cup heavy cream

WHISK TOGETHER THE EGGS, Champagne, sugar, and salt in a medium glass bowl until the sugar is dissolved, about 1 minute. Set the bowl over a saucepan filled with 1 inch of simmering water. Cook, whisking constantly, until the mixture is slightly thickened, creamy, and glossy, 5 to 10 minutes. At this stage, the mixture will form loose mounds when dripped from the whisk. Add the ganache and mix to incorporate. Remove from the heat and place in the refrigerator to cool completely.

In a small bowl, using an electric mixer, whip the heavy cream on medium-low speed until frothy, about 30 seconds. Increase the speed to high and continue to whip until the cream forms soft peaks, 1 to 2 minutes. Fold cream into the reserved mixture and use immediately or refrigerate until needed.

NOTE: Sabayon can be made 2 to 4 hours ahead and rewhipped with an electric mixer before using.

KAHLUA SABAYON

KAHLUA, WITH ITS RICH COFFEE FLAVOR, IS A WONDERFUL CO-STAR TO anything chocolate. Add it to the Chocolate Whipped Cream (page 174) and Hot Chocolate (page 115) or serve it with the Chocolate Brioche Pudding (page 171). You won't be disappointed any which way you serve it.

MAKES 1½ CUPS

⅓ cup Kahlua

¼ cup heavy cream

3 large egg yolks

3 tablespoons granulated sugar

1 tablespoon rum

2 ounces semisweet chocolate, finely chopped

WHISK TOGETHER THE INGREDIENTS in a medium glass bowl until the sugar is dissolved, about 1 minute. Set the bowl over a saucepan filled with 1 inch of simmering water. Cook, whisking constantly, until the mixture is frothy. Continue to cook, whisking constantly, until the mixture is slightly thickened, creamy, and glossy, 5 to 10 minutes. At this stage, the mixture will form loose mounds when dripped from the whisk. Remove the bowl from the saucepan and whisk constantly for 30 seconds to cool slightly. Place the bowl in the refrigerator and chill until the mixture is completely cool, about 10 minutes.

NOTE: The sabayon can be made up to five days ahead.

BEER BATTER

A N EXCELLENT COATING FOR SOFT-SHELL CRAB, FISH, OR ONIONS.

MAKES 1 CUP

¼ cup all-purpose flour

¼ cup cornstarch

1½ teaspoons baking powder

1 large egg, beaten

½ cup light beer

¼ cup chopped fresh chives

½ teaspoon kosher salt

¼ teaspoon freshly ground
    black pepper

IN A LARGE MIXING BOWL, sift together the flour, cornstarch, and baking powder. In a separate medium-sized bowl combine the egg, beer, chives, salt, and pepper. Add the wet ingredients into the dry ingredients and stir until the batter is smooth.

SEASONED FLOUR

U SE THIS FLOUR FOR DREDGING ALL TYPES OF MEATS AND VEGETABLES for frying.

MAKES ½ CUP

¼ cup all-purpose flour

¼ cup yellow corn flour

1 teaspoon kosher salt

½ teaspoon freshly ground
    black pepper

⅛ teaspoon cayenne pepper

IN A SMALL BOWL, combine all of the ingredients together and mix until well combined.

QUINCE COMPOTE

*I*F YOU WANT TO GIVE YOUR HOUSE A WONDERFULLY FRUITY HOLIDAY SCENT, set several quinces out in a bowl. This versatile compote can be served with Buttermilk Tangerine Soufflé Pancakes (page 250) or Twice-Baked Blue Cheese Soufflés (page 33). Try it as an accompaniment with chicken too.

2 large quinces, peeled and cut into $\frac{1}{2}$-inch pieces (about 2 cups)

2 cups freshly squeezed tangerine juice

1 cup freshly squeezed orange juice

$\frac{1}{2}$ cup freshly squeezed lemon juice

$\frac{1}{4}$ cup dried figs

1 stick cinnamon

1 vanilla bean, split lengthwise in half

$\frac{1}{8}$ teaspoon kosher salt

$\frac{1}{8}$ teaspoon freshly ground pepper

IN A LARGE SAUCEPAN OVER HIGH HEAT, combine all the ingredients with 1 cup of water; bring to a boil. Reduce the heat to maintain a simmer; cook until quinces are tender, rosy, and translucent, about 20 minutes. Remove the quinces with a slotted spoon to a bowl and reserve; continue to simmer the liquid until it becomes very thick and coats the back of a spoon. Remove from the heat, pour over the quinces and let cool. Serve.

NOTE: Compote will keep for two weeks in the refrigerator.

VEGETABLE STOCK

A WONDERFUL BASE FOR A SOUP; ADD RICE, NOODLES, VEGETABLES, AND mushrooms for a complete meal. The stock can be frozen in one cup portions for use in other recipes.

4 ears corn, husks and silk removed, cut into 2-inch pieces

3 medium carrots, halved

2 celery stalks, halved

1 medium red onion, quartered

1 medium fennel bulb, coarsely chopped (about 1 1/2 cups)

1 medium leek coarsely chopped (about 1 cup)

8 sprigs parsley

2 sprigs thyme

1 sprig marjoram

1/2 teaspoon red pepper flakes

1/2 bay leaf

COMBINE ALL THE INGREDIENTS plus 8 cups of water in a large Dutch oven over high heat and bring to a boil. Reduce the heat to low; simmer for 45 minutes. Pour the stock through a fine-mesh strainer into a large bowl; discard the solids. Cool to room temperature. Transfer the stock to an airtight container and refrigerate until needed.

NOTE: Stock can be made up to four days ahead or frozen for up to 3 months.

CHRISTMAS DINNER MENUS

A TRADITIONAL CHRISTMAS PARTY DINNER MENU

Drink:
Eggnog *(page 114)*

Appetizer:
Broiled Oysters with Mignonette Sauce *(page 130)*

Soup:
Beet and Apple Borscht *(page 118)*
with Caviar Potato Puffs *(page 131)*

Salad:
Spinach Salad with Pomegranates
and Blue Cheese with Persimmon Dressing
(page 126) and Spicy Glazed Walnuts *(page 126)*

Entrée:
Coffee-Spiced Prime Rib Roast *(page 139)*
with Horseradish Crème Fraîche *(page 186)*

Sides:
Chive-Onion Popovers with
Toasted Cardamom *(page 166)*;
Double-Stuffed Baked Potatoes *(page 157)*;
Roasted Cauliflower Florets *(page 160)*

Bread:
Soft Rolls *(page 168)* with Green Apple
and Pumpkin Butter *(page 188)*

Dessert:
Chocolate Cream Puffs *(page 172)*
with Chocolate Whipped Cream *(page 114)*
and Kahlua Sabayon *(page 190)*

"SOMETHING DIFFERENT" CHRISTMAS DINNER MENU

Drink:
Winter Citrus Punch with
Spiced Pomegranate Ice *(page 117)*

Appetizer:
Chicken Liver Pâté with
Pear and Currants *(page 134)*

Salad:
Winter Vegetable Salad *(page 129)*

Entrée:
Roasted Spiced Duck with Kumquat
and Pomegranate Glaze *(page 146)*

Sides:
Candied Yams *(page 154)*; Buttered Brussels
Sprouts with Chestnuts *(page 58)*

Bread:
Boston Brown Bread *(page 163)* with Green
Apple and Pumpkin Butter *(page 188)*

Dessert:
Espresso Double-Chocolate Soufflé
Brownies *(page 176)* with Milk Chocolate
and Drunken Prune Ice Cream *(page 184)*

INTIMATE CHRISTMAS DINNER
FOR TWO MENU

Salad:
Crispy Shrimp Salad with Cranberries
and Goat Cheese *(page 123)*

Entrée:
Grilled Cornish Game Hens with
Spiced Cherry Rub *(page 144)*

Sides:
Toasted Blood Orange
Couscous *(page 226)*; Roasted Broccoli Rabe
with Fennel and Orange *(page 158)*

Dessert:
Chocolate Brioche Pudding *(page 171)*

AN ELEGANT CHRISTMAS
DINNER PARTY

Drink:
Sparkling Pear Punch *(page 21)*

Appetizer:
Foie Gras Poppers *(page 135)*

Salad:
Shaved Fennel and Mushroom Salad *(page 125)*

Entrée:
Honey- and Cider-Vinegar-
Basted Rack of Pork *(page 143)*

Sides:
Artichoke and Elephant Garlic
Soufflé Spoonbread *(page 152)*; Roasted
Spaghetti Squash Noodles *(page 161)*

Dessert:
Chocolate Cream Puffs *(page 172)* with
Chocolate Whipped Cream *(page 174)*

CHRISTMAS MENU PREPARATION SCHEDULE

*F*OLLOWING A WELL-THOUGHT-OUT PLAN IS THE BEST WAY TO KEEP YOU ON track for your holiday dinner. Doing as much work ahead of time will allow you to spend time with family and friends. Follow this simple template to ensure a stress-free feast.

UP TO TWO WEEKS AHEAD:

Prepare the Green Apple and Sugar Pumpkin Butter.

UP TO ONE WEEK AHEAD:

Make the Spicy Glazed Walnuts.

Prepare the Horseradish Crème Fraîche.

UP TO FOUR DAYS AHEAD:

Prepare the Persimmon Dressing.

Prepare the Kahlua Sabayon.

Prepare the Coffee Ganache.

UP TO THREE DAYS AHEAD:

Prepare the Beet and Apple Borscht.

Prepare the Chocolate Cream Puffs to make-ahead point.

UP TO TWO DAYS AHEAD:

Prepare the base of the Eggnog recipe.

Prepare the Mignonette Sauce.

Prepare the Caviar Potato Puffs to make-ahead point.

Prepare the Chocolate Whipped Cream.

UP TO ONE DAY AHEAD:

Prepare the Coffee-Rubbed Rib Roast to make-ahead point.

Prepare the batter for the Chive-Onion Popovers with Toasted Cardamom.

Finish the Eggnog.

CHRISTMAS MORNING:

Prepare the Soft Rolls.

Assemble the Spinach Salad. Place the Persimmon Dressing on the bottom of a
salad bowl and top with spinach, followed by the blue cheese, pomegranate
seeds, and the Spicy Glazed Walnuts. Cover tightly and refrigerate.

A FEW HOURS BEFORE DINNER:

Place the roast in the oven.

Finish the Caviar Potato Puffs.

Finish the Chive-Onion Popovers with Toasted Cardamom.

Finish the Double-Stuffed Baked Potatoes.

Roast the Cauliflower Florets.

AT THE LAST MINUTE:

Broil the oysters.

Toss the Spinach Salad.

New Year's Day
Celebration

CELEBRATE THE NEW YEAR WITH A TRADITIONAL YET FLAVORFUL feast. Food is integral to most holiday celebrations but it is most symbolic during this holiday. What you eat is believed to weigh heavily on your fate in the coming year. Wishes for a healthy, happy New Year are happily consumed. In our culture, certain foods are considered especially auspicious: pork symbolizing prosperity, greens promising wealth, and beans symbolizing wealth.

I love beans and just don't eat them for their luck; I believe if there were a dish that could welcome you in from the cold, it would definitely be a bean stew. So embrace neighbors, family, and New Year well-wishers in from the cold with my delicious and hearty Bean Stew with Smoked Ham Hock and Kale (page 212). It will warm their souls and help them recover from the busy holiday season. This chapter contains simple yet elegant brunch items consisting of stews and other slow-cooked dishes that allow everyone to wake up on their own schedule and wander into the family gathering and festivities. After the hectic holidays it's time to relax.

I take particular advantage of wonderful and lucky legume treasures during this time of year for the hearty earthiness they impart to soups, stews, and chilies, and so will you. Whether thick or brothy, a stew simmering on the stove and warming the kitchen is just what the holidays ordered. It's so simple to place ingredients into a pot and let them simmer, almost unattended, while you spend time with your family and friends.

BLOOD ORANGE MIMOSAS, 204

STRAWBERRY SPARKLING WINE COCKTAIL, 204

EYE-OPENING BLOODY MARYS, 207

BLENDED COFFEE WITH KAHLUA SABAYON, 208

MANGO PINEAPPLE MARGARITAS, 208

MEYER LEMON SLUSH LEMONADE, 209

BEAN STEW WITH SMOKED HAM HOCK AND KALE, 212

GRANDMA'S CABBAGE AND SWEET-SAUSAGE SOUP, 213

WEDGE SALAD WITH BUTTERMILK DRESSING, 214

FRESH CHICKPEA DIP, 215

BLUE CORN CAKES WITH CAVIAR AND CRÈME FRAÎCHE, 216

FENNEL-CURED GRAVLAX, 219

BLACK-EYED PEAS WITH SMOKED BACON AND SPINACH, 220

BRAISED CHICKEN WITH CITRUS AND RAISINS, 222

BRAISED HAM HOCKS, 223

STEAK CHILI WITH BLACK BEANS, 224

TOASTED BLOOD ORANGE COUSCOUS, 226

SPICY CREAMY YELLOW GRITS WITH SHRIMP, 227

YANKEE POT ROAST, 229

LEEK AND SWEET POTATO "RISOTTO," 231

SOLE FILLETS WITH CITRUS BROWN BUTTER, 232

RAVIOLI WITH SWISS CHARD, 235

PASTA DOUGH, 236

ROASTED MUSHROOM RAGOÛT, 237

CRISPY POTATO AND CHIVE CAKES, 238

MIXED ROOT VEGETABLES, 239

BLUE CORN AND DILL MINI-MUFFINS, 240

FLATBREAD, 242

BANANA BLUEBERRY BREAD, 243

BANANA SOUR CREAM COFFEE CAKE, 245

COCONUT ANGEL CAKE WITH BANANA PUDDING, 246

BANANA PUDDING, 248

COCONUT FROSTING, 249

BUTTERMILK TANGERINE SOUFFLÉ PANCAKES, 250

CARAMEL SWIRL ANGEL FOOD CAKE, 253

CARAMEL SAUCE, 254

TOMATO HAM HOCK STOCK, 255

BLOOD ORANGE MIMOSAS

CELEBRATE THE NEW YEAR IN STYLE WITH THIS VIBRANTLY COLORED, fresh cocktail.

MAKES 4 SERVINGS

2 cups freshly squeezed blood orange juice

1 (750-milliliter) bottle sparkling wine, chilled

PLACE 4 CHAMPAGNE GLASSES IN FREEZER TO CHILL for 15 minutes.

Fill Champagne glasses two-thirds full with sparkling wine and top off with the juice.

STRAWBERRY SPARKLING WINE COCKTAIL

WHO DOESN'T LIKE STRAWBERRIES AND CHAMPAGNE? THEY MERGE perfectly in this ambrosial cocktail appropriate for all occasions.

MAKES 4 SERVINGS

2 cups strawberries, hulled

1 teaspoon vanilla extract

1 teaspoon freshly squeezed lemon juice

3 to 5 teaspoons granulated sugar, depending on the sweetness of the strawberries

1 (750-milliliter) bottle sparkling wine, chilled

PLACE THE STRAWBERRIES, VANILLA, LEMON JUICE, and sugar in a blender and purée until smooth. Pass the mixture through a fine-mesh strainer into a medium bowl. Fill the champagne glasses half full with the purée and top with the sparking wine.

A SPECIAL NOTE ON HANGOVER REMEDIES

A HANGOVER IS ONE OF THE MOST DREADED AILMENTS OF THE NEW YEAR. It easily replaces any positive memory of your beautiful evening with a stomach-turning recollection of how horrible you felt the day after. The best way to beat a hangover is to prevent one. Knowing your limit and drinking at least one glass of water between drinks can stave off the dreaded condition. However, when your head is spinning and you've definitely overindulged, you need to take serious measures before going to sleep to stop the hangover before it starts. My personal favorite is to eat a banana, take a bubbly antacid without aspirin, and drink as much water or sports drink as my stomach can handle before I crawl into bed. I usually wake up still feeling somewhat human and with no regrets.

However, if you've had a really good time and were unable to take preventative measures, here is what you can do to get through the day:

1. Drink plenty of fluids. Liquids such as sports drinks and orange juice, that replenish electrolytes and supply vitamin C, are good choices.
2. Get lots of rest.
3. Make a Bloody Mary or Hair of the Dog (gin, lemon juice, and hot sauce). These drinks work by forcing your body to process new alcohol. This gives your body a slight reprieve from all the toxic by-products from the previous alcohol you consumed. The fix is temporary but sometimes very necessary.
4. Taking a shower where you alternate between hot and cold water.
5. Despite popular beliefs, avoid the following: coffee, which can dehydrate you further; aspirin, which can magnify the very symptoms your trying to cure; and over-the-counter pain relievers, as they can harm your stomach and liver.

EYE-OPENING BLOODY MARYS

*T*RY THIS FRESH VERSION OF AN OLD FAVORITE. SOME FOLKS BELIEVE THIS drink can cure hangovers; it has always worked for me. Use fresh horseradish if you can find it.

MAKES 8 (8-OUNCE) SERVINGS

1 tablespoon celery seed

1 teaspoon red pepper flakes

10 garlic cloves

10 medium ripe tomatoes, cored and cut into quarters

2 medium cucumbers, peeled and roughly chopped

2 Granny Smith apples, cored and quartered

2 jalapeño chiles, stemmed and seeded

6 tablespoons prepared horseradish

1/2 cup freshly squeezed lime juice

1/2 cup freshly squeezed lemon juice

1/2 teaspoon Tabasco sauce

1 tablespoon Worcestershire sauce

Table salt

Freshly ground black pepper

Frozen vodka or gin, to taste

8 sprigs cilantro, for garnish

Pickled asparagus, beans, celery, and/or cucumber, for garnish

IN A SMALL SKILLET OVER LOW HEAT, toast celery seed and red pepper flakes, shaking the pan occasionally until fragrant and light golden, about 2 minutes; set aside.

In a food processor, purée the garlic, tomato, cucumber, apple, jalapeños, and horseradish until very smooth. Pass the mixture through a fine-mesh sieve into a large bowl, pressing the pulp with the back of a spoon to extract all the liquid; discard the solids. Stir in the reserved spices, lime juice, and lemon juice. Add the Tabasco, Worcestershire, and salt and pepper to taste. Pour mixture into a decorative pitcher and add the vodka or gin to taste. Serve over ice and garnish with cilantro and pickled vegetables.

BLENDED COFFEE *with* KAHLUA SABAYON

WHO NEEDS A COFFEE CHAIN WHEN YOU CAN MAKE YOUR OWN DELICIOUS concoction at home?

MAKES 4 SERVINGS

4 cups cold brewed coffee

1 cup Kahlua Sabayon (page 190)

12 to 18 ice cubes

PLACE ALL OF THE INGREDIENTS IN A BLENDER; purée until no large chunks of ice remain.

MANGO PINEAPPLE MARGARITAS

YOU HAVE TO PREPARE THE FRUIT THE DAY BEFORE SERVING THESE DRINKS, but the result is worth the wait.

MAKES 4 SERVINGS

5 ripe mangoes, cut into 2-inch pieces (about 4 cups)

1 ripe pineapple, cut into 2-inch pieces (about 3 cups)

$1/2$ cup granulated sugar

$1/2$ cup freshly squeezed lime juice

$1/2$ cup freshly squeezed lemon juice

$1/4$ cup (2 ounces) triple sec

$1/3$ cup (about 3 ounces) Cointreau

$3/4$ cup (6 ounces) gold tequila

2 cups crushed ice cubes

1 lime, cut into wedges, for garnish

PLACE THE MANGO AND PINEAPPLE IN A GLASS DISH; cover with plastic wrap and freeze for at least 8 hours or up to overnight.

Chill margarita glasses in the freezer.

In a small saucepan over medium-high heat, combine the sugar and 1 cup of water. Bring to a boil, stirring until the sugar is completely dissolved. Remove the simple syrup from the heat; cool or refrigerate until needed.

Place the frozen mango and pineapple, simple syrup, lime and lemon juices, triple sec, Cointreau, tequila, and ice in a blender. Purée until smooth. Serve immediately in chilled glasses garnished with a wedge of lime.

MEYER LEMON SLUSH LEMONADE

*M*EYER LEMONS ARE THOUGHT TO BE A CROSS BETWEEN A LEMON AND an orange. They have a sweeter and less acidic taste than conventional lemons and serve as a light refreshing flavor in this recipe.

MAKES 8 (8-OUNCE) SERVINGS

$\frac{1}{2}$ cup granulated sugar

4 Meyer lemons, peels reserved for lemon twists for garnish

2 oranges

1 cup freshly squeezed lemon juice

1 cup citrus-flavored soda

4 cups ice cubes

FOR THE SIMPLE SYRUP: In a medium saucepan over medium-high heat, combine sugar and $\frac{1}{2}$ cup of water. Bring to boil, stirring occasionally, until sugar has dissolved. Allow to cool to room temperature, about 30 minutes.

FOR THE BASE: Using a sharp knife, cut the ends of the lemons and oranges and place the fruit cut side down on a flat surface. Trim off all of the peel and the white pith by making a series of cuts along the curve of the fruit. Over a medium bowl, hold fruit in one hand and cut each segment from the fruit by inserting the blade between the membrane and pulp of each segment, allowing the segments and juice to fall into bowl.

In a blender, place the lemon and orange segments, lemon juice, and $\frac{1}{2}$ cup simple syrup and purée until smooth. Strain the purée through a fine-mesh strainer into a medium bowl. Place in the refrigerator until needed. (This may be done up to three days ahead.)

Chill glasses in the freezer.

To serve, place the juice mixture and citrus soda in a blender; fill with ice. Blend until smooth and frothy, 1 to 2 minutes; adjust sweetness with additional simple syrup to taste. Serve immediately in a chilled glass. Garnish with a lemon twist.

NOTE: Tequila or rum can be added for cocktails. Alternately, drizzle the slush over berries or mango slices, or use in a fruit smoothie.

A SPECIAL NOTE ON WINTER FRUIT

WINTERTIME DOESN'T NECESSARILY INVOKE THE THOUGHT OF A BOUNTIful fruit section at local markets. However, instead of barren produce sections for the cold winter months, many exotic winter fruits appear and, with them, many wonderful flavors and textures. Here is some basic information about how to pick and store some of winter's most delicious offerings:

Blood Oranges: Prized for their bright citrus flavor as well as their dramatic crimson-colored flesh with the subtle taste of raspberry. They are typically smaller, sweeter, and less acidic than most oranges. Moro and Ruby Red are popular varieties available from December through May. Select oranges that are heavy for their size, as they will be the juiciest. The skin may be tinged with red, and either smooth or pitted. Store in a loosely wrapped plastic bag in the refrigerator for two to four weeks.

Clementines: A cross between an orange and a Mandarin and usually seedless. They are very small, super sweet, and peel effortlessly; they are available from November through February. Choose clementines that are heavy for their size. They should be soft yet slightly firm to the touch. The color can vary from light to deep orange and skins should be glossy. Keep in the refrigerator for up to two weeks.

Kumquats: These miniature golden fruits can be eaten whole, skin and seeds included. They have a sweet, pungent rind and a bitter, dry flesh that lends to an intense sour-orange flavor. Kumquats are in season as early as October and as late as June, but are most plentiful from December through April. Pick only firm, dry, fully orange fruit with stems. The rounded variety is generally sweeter and milder than the oval variety. Store them at room temperature if you plan to use them within a few days or keep them for up to two weeks in the refrigerator loosely wrapped in a plastic bag.

Persimmons: The Hachiya persimmon is shaped like a long acorn with smooth, deep-orange skin. Select fruits that are softer than a baby's cheek and nearly liquid. If buying unripe persimmons, place them in a paper bag with a banana. Be prepared to wait since they may take several weeks to ripen. The Fuyu is another variety of persimmon. It is shaped like a tomato with a distinctive four-leaved, capped stem. Unlike the Hachiya variety, which would curl your tongue if eaten unripe, the Fuyu has no bitter tannins and can be eaten when crisp and hard. Ripe Fuyus should yield to gentle pressure and have yellow to orange unblemished skin. Look for persimmons from October through February.

Pomegranates: The pomegranate is actually a berry with delicious seeds encased in a uniquely flavored, ruby-red, sweet-tart pulp. They are in season August through December. Look for heavy, large, richly colored fruit. The skin should be uniform, free of blemishes, thin, and tough. Refrigerate whole pomegranates for up to three months or freeze the seeds for up to three months. Be careful with the juice, as it stains permanently.

Quinces: Available September through December, these fruits have a potent, tropical, and musky aroma. Shaped like a fat pear, its yellow skin can be smooth or fuzzy. Quinces are rarely eaten raw, but when cooked the flavor becomes similar to a combination of rich apple and pear. Select large, fragrant, smooth quinces with pale yellow skin. Store them at room temperature if they will be used right away. For longer storage, wrap each quince in plastic and refrigerate for up to three months.

BEAN STEW *with* SMOKED HAM HOCK *and* KALE

*I*T'S HARD TO BEAT A WARM AND COMFORTING BEAN STEW ON A COLD DAY. Serve with a simple green salad and crusty bread.

SPICE BAG

¹/₂ teaspoon red pepper flakes

1 teaspoon black peppercorns

¹/₂ bay leaf

2 sprigs thyme

STEW

¹/₂ cup dried flageolet beans or great Northern beans

2 slices smoked bacon, cut into 1-inch pieces

2 stalks celery, thinly sliced

2 small carrots, cut into 1-inch bias-cut pieces

¹/₂ medium yellow onion, chopped

8 garlic cloves, finely chopped

2 tablespoons seeded and finely chopped poblano chile

¹/₂ cup chopped roasted red bell pepper

2 cups Tomato Ham Hock Stock (page 255)

1 tablespoon red wine vinegar

2 tablespoons balsamic vinegar

1 teaspoon grated lemon zest

1 tablespoon olive oil

1 bunch kale (about 6 ounces), stems removed and leaves chopped into 1-inch pieces

1¹/₂ cups peeled, chopped tomato

1 cup smoked ham-hock meat, shredded

Kosher salt

Freshly ground black pepper

FOR THE SPICE BAG: Place items for the spice bag in cheesecloth and tie with butchers' twine; set aside.

FOR THE STEW: Soak the beans overnight in cold water. Drain the beans and place in a large pot. Cover with 1 inch of salted cold water and bring to a boil, cook for 3 minutes, drain the beans and cool completely; set aside.

In a large Dutch oven over medium heat, fry the bacon until just beginning to crisp and most of the fat has rendered, 4 to 5 minutes. Using a slotted spoon, transfer the bacon to paper towel–lined plate; set aside. Leave the bacon fat in the Dutch oven; add the reserved beans, celery, carrots, onion, garlic, poblano pepper, and roasted red pepper. Cook, stirring occasionally, until the vegetables have softened and have browned slightly, 7 to 8 minutes. Add 1 cup of water, the stock, and the spice bag; bring to a simmer. Reduce the heat to low, cover, and simmer until beans are tender, about 40 minutes. (If beans become too dry, add another cup of water.)

Discard the spice bag. Stir in the red wine vinegar, balsamic vinegar, and lemon zest; turn off the heat and set aside.

Place the reserved bacon and olive oil in a large skillet over high heat, and heat until sizzling, about 1 minute. Add the kale and cook, stirring occasionally, until lightly wilted, 2 to 3 minutes. Add the kale, tomatoes, and ham-hock meat to the beans and stir to combine. Season with salt and pepper to taste. Serve.

GRANDMA'S CABBAGE *and* SWEET-SAUSAGE SOUP

ITH A NAME LIKE "GRANDMA'S," YOU KNOW THIS STEW WILL BE WARM AND satisfying, just like one of her hugs.

MAKES 8 SERVINGS

3 tablespoons extra-virgin olive oil

1 medium yellow onion, diced (about 1 cup)

3 medium leeks (white and some green parts), thinly sliced (about 1 cup)

2 medium shallots, finely chopped (about $\frac{1}{2}$ cup)

5 red potatoes, cut into 2-inch pieces

8 garlic cloves, finely chopped

1 tablespoon fennel seed

2 teaspoons kosher salt

1 teaspoon freshly ground black pepper

8 cups chicken stock (page 101)

1 medium head napa cabbage, thinly sliced (about 5 cups)

5 ounces spinach, chopped (about 3 cups)

3 sweet Italian sausages, grilled, cut into $\frac{1}{2}$-inch pieces (about 2 cups)

2 tablespoons unsalted butter

HEAT THE OLIVE OIL IN A LARGE DUTCH OVEN over medium-high heat until the oil is shimmering. Add the onions, leeks, and shallots; cook, stirring occasionally, until the onions are slightly tender, about 3 minutes. Add the potatoes, garlic, fennel seed, salt, and pepper; cook, stirring occasionally, until the potatoes have softened and onions begin to brown lightly, 5 to 7 minutes. Add the stock and bring to a boil. Reduce the heat to low, cover, and simmer for 25 minutes.

Add the cabbage, spinach, sausage, and butter to the pot; cover and simmer until the potatoes are cooked through and tender, about 10 minutes. Serve.

Wine pairing: Chardonnay, Pinot Noir, Zinfandel

WEDGE SALAD *with* BUTTERMILK DRESSING

*T*HE SIMPLICITY OF THIS SALAD REQUIRES THE USE OF THE BEST INGREDIENTS in order to shine. Use a creamy high-quality blue cheese to impart a sweet and savory bite in this tangy dressing.

MAKES 1½ CUPS

BUTTERMILK DRESSING

2 large garlic cloves, minced (about 2 teaspoons)

1 large egg yolk

¼ teaspoon dry mustard

¼ cup grapeseed oil or light olive oil

½ cup crumbled blue cheese, softened

¾ cup buttermilk

¼ teaspoon kosher salt

¼ teaspoon freshly ground black pepper

⅛ teaspoon cayenne pepper

1 tablespoon freshly squeezed lemon juice

WEDGE SALAD

1 head iceberg lettuce, cut into quarters

2 plum tomatoes, cored and chopped

2 green onions, finely chopped

6 strips bacon, cooked and crumbled (about 1 cup)

FOR THE DRESSING: In a blender on low speed, combine the garlic, egg yolk, and dry mustard. Add the oil slowly in a steady stream to make an emulsion. Blend until a smooth mayonnaise has formed; set aside.

In a medium bowl, gently stir the blue cheese and the buttermilk together. Add the salt, pepper, cayenne, and lemon juice; stir gently to combine; fold in the prepared mayonnaise. Dressing will keep for two weeks in the refrigerator.

FOR THE SALAD: On each salad plate, place one wedge of lettuce on its side. Pour the dressing over each wedge and sprinkle the top with the tomatoes, green onions, and bacon. Serve immediately.

FRESH CHICKPEA DIP

*I*NDIAN, ASIAN, OR MIDDLE EASTERN GROCERS MAY CARRY INDIAN LONG peppers, or Pippali long peppers, as they are also called. With their hot and sweet earthy undertones, Indian long peppers really have no substitute for their unique flavor—however, in a pinch, any peppercorn will do.

1 Indian long pepper or 1 teaspoon black peppercorns

1 teaspoon cumin seeds

1 teaspoon fennel seeds

1 teaspoon coriander seeds

1 teaspoon red pepper flakes

$1/4$ cup extra-virgin olive oil

1 tablespoon unsalted butter

$1/2$ pound fresh chickpeas, sprouted (see note), or 2 (14-ounce) cans chickpeas, rinsed

1 small yellow onion, sliced

1 small bulb fennel, stalks removed and bottom trimmed, sliced

4 garlic cloves, crushed

$1/2$ bay leaf

3 sprigs thyme

1 cup vegetable stock (page 193)

Kosher salt

Freshly ground black pepper

$1/4$ teaspoon paprika

$1/8$ teaspoon cayenne

$1/4$ cup freshly squeezed lemon juice

1 teaspoon lemon zest

3 tablespoons finely chopped red onion, for garnish

$1/4$ finely chopped cilantro, for garnish

IN A SMALL SKILLET OVER LOW HEAT, toast the Indian long pepper, cumin, fennel, coriander, and red pepper flakes, shaking the pan occasionally, until light golden and fragrant, about 3 minutes. Grind in a spice grinder; set aside.

Melt the butter and 2 tablespoons of the oil in a large saucepan over low heat. Add the chickpeas, onions, fennel, garlic, bay leaf, and thyme sprigs; cover and cook, stirring often, until the vegetables are very soft and lightly browned, 20 minutes. Add half of the ground spices and all of the stock; uncover and cook, stirring often, about 10 minutes longer. Remove and discard the bay leaf and thyme; stir in the paprika and cayenne. Taste; adjust seasoning with salt, pepper, and reserved ground spices, if needed.

Transfer the mixture to a food processor or blender and purée until smooth. Transfer to a medium bowl or pass the purée through a fine-mesh strainer for a smoother consistency. Stir in the lemon juice and zest. Garnish with the remaining oil, red onion, and cilantro. Serve with sliced grilled flat bread.

NOTE: To sprout chickpeas, soak dried chickpeas for 24 hours in room-temperature water; drain. Then spread chickpeas out into a single layer at room temperature, uncovered, until small $1/4$-inch tails sprout, about 24 to 48 hours.

BLUE CORN CAKES *with* CAVIAR *and* CRÈME FRAÎCHE

*T*HE BLUE CORNMEAL ADDS A DISTINCTLY NUTTY FLAVOR AND BRILLIANT HUE. If you cannot find blue cornmeal, just substitute yellow or white cornmeal.

MAKES 24 CAKES, SERVING 6

1 cup whole milk

¼ cup buttermilk

1 large egg, separated

3 tablespoons butter, melted

1 teaspoon kosher salt

½ teaspoon granulated sugar

½ cup blue cornmeal

¼ cup all-purpose flour

½ teaspoon baking powder

½ teaspoon freshly ground black pepper

⅛ teaspoon cayenne pepper

Vegetable oil spray

1½ cups crème fraîche or sour cream

1 cup caviar or chopped smoked salmon

IN A MEDIUM BOWL, combine the milk, buttermilk, egg yolk, butter, salt, and sugar; mix until thoroughly combined; set aside.

Whisk the egg white in a small bowl until it forms soft peaks; set aside.

In large bowl, sift together the cornmeal, flour, baking powder, pepper, and cayenne. Make a well in the center; pour in the milk mixture and gently stir until just combined. Gently fold in the beaten egg white.

Coat the bottom of a large nonstick saucepan or griddle with vegetable spray. Place over medium heat. Using a tablespoon, drop the batter into the pan to make small cakes, being careful not to crowd the pan. Cook until the edges of the cakes are set and the bottom is golden brown, about 1 minute. Flip and cook until golden on the second side, about 30 seconds. Transfer cakes to a sheet pan and repeat with remaining batter. Top the cakes with a dollop of crème fraîche and a generous spoonful of caviar. Serve.

NOTE: If you don't like fish or want a vegetarian option, substitute the caviar with chopped hard-boiled eggs, sprinkling chopped capers over the top.

FENNEL-CURED GRAVLAX

THIS DISH IS EFFORTLESS TO MAKE BUT IT DOES TAKES SOME TIME TO CURE. The reward of sweetly spiced salmon is well worth the wait. Serve gravlax at your party and devour morning-after leftovers with cream cheese and bagels or added to scrambled eggs.

MAKES 5 SERVINGS

2 cups kosher salt

2 cups granulated sugar

$^3/_4$ cup freshly ground black pepper

5 bunches fennel tops, chopped (about 6 cups), plus sprigs for garnish

2 (1-pound) skin-on fresh salmon fillets, pin bones removed

Caviar, for garnish (optional)

IN A MEDIUM BOWL, combine the salt, sugar, and pepper until well mixed. Rub the mixture evenly on both sides of the fillets. Use all of the spice mixture.

In a glass baking dish that is wide enough to hold one salmon fillet, place one-fourth of the fennel in an even layer. Place one fillet, skin-side down, on top of the fennel; cover the top of the fillet with one-half of the fennel; the herb should be thick and well distributed. Lay the second fillet on top, skin-side up, and press the remaining fourth of the fennel over the top of it. Cover the dish tightly with plastic wrap and refrigerate for 24 hours.

Unwrap the dish, drain the liquid, flip the fillets over, cover, and return the dish to the refrigerator for another 24 hours. Repeat for two more days.

After the full 72 hours, unwrap the dish, separate the fillets, and scrape away the herbs and seasonings.

Using a thin, sharp knife—with a scalloped, not serrated, edge—held at a 10-degree angle, begin slicing the gravlax starting from the tail end into slices no thicker than $^1/_{16}$ of an inch. The slices should be so thin that you can see the knife's movement through the flesh. After you have sliced the gravlax, remove the brownish-grey bloodline by folding each slice in half, so that the bloodline forms a triangle and using a small, sharp, straight-edged knife to remove the triangle with one slice. Garnish the gravlax with fennel sprigs and caviar; serve.

Wine pairing: Sauvignon Blanc, Sancerre, Chenin Blanc, or sparkling wine

BLACK-EYED PEAS
with SMOKED BACON *and* SPINACH

THIS EARNEST STEW DEFINES THE NEW YEAR'S DAY HOLIDAY TRADITION. Promising black-eyed peas, prosperous pork, and auspicious spinach all symbolize good fortune in the New Year. Serve this lucky and hearty stew with a side of grilled sausage and crusty bread.

MAKES 4 SERVINGS

SPICE BAG

¼ teaspoon red pepper flakes

1 teaspoon black peppercorns

½ bay leaf

2 sprigs thyme

STEW

½ cup black-eyed peas

2 thick slices (2 ounces) smoked bacon, cut into 1-inch pieces

2 stalks celery, thinly sliced

2 small carrots, peeled and cut into 1-inch bias-cut pieces

½ medium yellow onion, chopped

8 garlic cloves, finely chopped

¼ cup seeded and finely diced poblano chile

½ cup chopped roasted red bell pepper

2 cups chicken stock (page 101)

2 tablespoons sherry vinegar

1 tablespoon red wine vinegar

1 cup balsamic vinegar

1 tablespoon olive oil

6 cups chopped fresh spinach

1 cup chopped tomato

Kosher salt

Freshly ground black pepper

FOR THE SPICE BAG: Place the items for the spice bag in cheesecloth. Tie closed with butchers' twine.

FOR THE STEW: Soak the peas overnight in cold water. Drain the peas and place in a large saucepan. Cover the peas with 1 inch of salted cold water and bring to a boil and cook for 3 minutes; drain the beans and cool completely.

Place the bacon in a large Dutch oven over medium-high heat; cook until the bacon is slightly crispy. Remove the bacon with a slotted spoon to a paper towel–lined plate to drain; set aside. Add the celery, carrots, onion, garlic, peas, poblano chile, and roasted peppers to the pot; cook for 5 minutes. Add the stock, sherry vinegar, red wine vinegar, balsamic vinegar, 1 cup of water, and the spice bag. Bring to a simmer; reduce the heat to low. Cover and cook until the peas are tender, about 40 minutes, stirring halfway through and adding water if beans need more liquid. Remove the spice bag and discard.

In a large sauté pan over high heat, add the reserved bacon and olive oil and cook for 1 minute. Add the spinach and wilt lightly, 30 seconds. Off the heat, stir in the tomatoes. Add the spinach mixture to the stew; season with salt and pepper to taste and serve.

BRAISED CHICKEN *with* CITRUS *and* RAISINS

*E*NJOY THIS SIMPLE DISH IN WINTER OR EARLY SPRING WHEN CITRUS IS STILL at its peak. Buy a free-range organic chicken; it's worth the extra expense for the pure, clean flavor.

MAKES 4 SERVINGS

2 pounds bone-in chicken pieces (breasts split and cut in half, drumsticks, and/or thighs)

2 tablespoons extra-virgin olive oil

2 medium yellow onions, chopped (about 2 cups)

1 small red bell pepper, chopped (about $^1/_2$ cup)

4 garlic cloves, finely chopped

1 tablespoon grated fresh ginger

$^1/_2$ teaspoon cinnamon

$^1/_2$ teaspoon turmeric

$^1/_2$ cup dry white wine

$^1/_2$ cup freshly squeezed tangerine juice

$^1/_2$ cup freshly squeezed orange juice

1 cup vegetable stock (page 193)

$^1/_2$ teaspoon kosher salt, plus more for seasoning

$^1/_4$ teaspoon freshly ground black pepper, plus more for seasoning

$^1/_4$ cup raisins

$^1/_2$ cup chopped orange sections

$^1/_2$ cup chopped tangerine sections

3 tablespoons chopped lemon sections

3 tablespoons chopped flat-leaf parsley

3 tablespoons chopped cilantro

$2^1/_2$ cups Toasted Blood Orange Couscous (page 226)

PAT THE CHICKEN PIECES DRY AND SEASON with salt and pepper. Heat the olive oil in a large Dutch oven over medium heat until just smoking. Add the chicken, skin-side down; cook until golden brown, about 5 minutes. Turn the chicken over and cook until golden brown on the second side, about 3 minutes. Stir in the onions, red bell pepper, garlic, ginger, cinnamon, and turmeric; reduce the heat to low, and cook, stirring occasionally, for 15 minutes.

Add the wine, tangerine and orange juices, stock, salt, and pepper; bring to a boil. Reduce the heat to medium low, cover, and simmer until the chicken is fully cooked and tender, about 1 hour. Off the heat, add the raisins, orange, tangerine, and lemon segments, parsley, and cilantro; stir to combine. Serve over couscous.

Wine pairing: Pinot Blanc, Sauvignon Blanc

INSTRUCTIONS ON SEGMENTING CITRUS

*S*TART BY SLICING A $^1/_2$-INCH PIECE FROM THE TOP and bottom of the citrus.

With a cut side of the fruit flat against a work surface, use a very sharp paring knife to slice off the rind, including the white pith, following the natural curve in the fruit. Continue working your way around the fruit until it is completely peeled.

While holding the citrus fruit over a bowl, carefully slip the knife blade between each of the membrane walls of the fruit and slice to the center to completely release the segment into the bowl.

BRAISED HAM HOCKS

*H*AM HOCKS WERE ABSOLUTELY MEANT TO BE BRAISED. IT'S SUCH A FOOL-proof method. This easy and simple dish really cooks itself and makes a perfect supper on a busy weekend. Serve over Mashed Red Potatoes with Garlic (page 67) or over your favorite pasta or gnocchi.

MAKES 8 SERVINGS

1 large yellow onion, sliced (about 2 cups)

2 Anaheim chiles, stemmed and chopped

8 garlic cloves, crushed

4 cups chicken stock (page 101)

3 large ham hocks

¼ cup balsamic vinegar

¼ cup chopped flat-leaf parsley

¼ cup chopped basil

2 tablespoons olive oil

ADJUST AN OVEN RACK TO THE MIDDLE POSITION and heat the oven to 350°F.

Heat the oil in a large Dutch oven over medium heat until shimmering. Add the onions, chile, and garlic; cook, stirring occasionally, until the onions are lightly brown and translucent, about 5 minutes. Add the remaining ingredients to the pot, cover, and bring to a simmer. Transfer the pot to the oven; cook until a fork easily slips in and out of the meat, about 1½ hours. Use tongs to turn the meat twice during cooking.

Transfer the hocks to a platter to cool, enough to handle. Pour the braising liquid through a fine-mesh strainer into a medium serving bowl; discard the solids. Remove the meat from the hocks and add to the braising liquid. Serve.

STEAK CHILI *with* BLACK BEANS

A HEARTY SPICY CHILI TO BRING IN THE NEW YEAR. DON'T BE INTIMIDATED by the long ingredient list, you can make the beans and chili separately and several days in advance.

MAKES 4 TO 5 SERVINGS

BLACK BEANS

1 cup dried black beans, rinsed and picked over

1 medium yellow onion, cut in half

1 whole head garlic, cloves peeled and crushed with the flat side of a knife

1 bay leaf

$\frac{1}{2}$ teaspoon red pepper flakes

1 bottle (12-ounce) light beer

STEAK CHILI

2 teaspoons cumin seeds

2 teaspoons coriander seeds

3 tablespoons olive oil

3 medium yellow onions, cut into $\frac{1}{2}$-inch dice

2 green bell peppers, stemmed, seeded, and chopped

2 red bell peppers, stemmed, seeded, and chopped

2 Anaheim or pasilla chiles, stemmed, seeded, and finely chopped

2 jalapeño chiles, stemmed, seeded, and finely chopped

12 garlic cloves, finely chopped

3 (28-ounce) cans whole organic tomatoes, drained

1 (12-ounce) bottle light or dark beer

FOR THE BEANS: Soak beans overnight in 4 cups of cold water.

Drain beans; place in a large saucepan and cover with 1 inch of water. Place over medium-high heat, cover, and bring to a boil; turn off the heat and let the beans soak for 1 hour. Drain the beans and place them back into the saucepan; add the onion, garlic, bay leaf, pepper flakes, beer, and 6 cups of cold water. Cover the pot, place over medium heat; simmer until the beans are tender, $1\frac{1}{2}$ to 2 hours. Drain and reserve beans; discard onion, garlic, and bay leaf. Beans can be made up to four days ahead.

FOR THE CHILI: In a small skillet over medium-low heat, lightly toast the cumin and coriander seeds until light brown and fragrant, 2 to 3 minutes. Place them in a spice grinder and grind until fine; set aside.

Heat the olive oil in a large Dutch oven over medium-high heat until shimmering; add the onions, green and red peppers, and Anaheim and jalapeño chiles; cook, stirring occasionally, for 2 minutes. Reduce the heat to low, add the garlic, and cover; continue to cook, stirring often, until vegetables are tender, about 10 minutes longer. Add the tomatoes, beer, cilantro stems, vinegar, chili powder, reserved black beans, salt, pepper, and ground cumin and coriander. Gently simmer, uncovered, stirring occasionally, until sauce has thickened slightly, about 25 minutes.

Heat the vegetable oil in a large cast-iron skillet over medium-high heat until thin wisps of smoke appear. Add steak, sprinkling with salt and pepper, and cook for 2 minutes, stirring occasionally; set aside.

- 1 bunch cilantro, leaves and stems separated, stems tied together for chili, leaves chopped for garnish
- 1/2 cup red wine vinegar
- 3 tablespoons chili powder
- 1 teaspoon kosher salt, plus more for seasoning
- 1/2 teaspoon freshly ground black pepper, plus more for seasoning
- 2 teaspoons vegetable oil
- 12 ounces rib-eye steak, cut into 1-inch cubes
- 2 cups grated aged white cheddar
- 1 avocado, chopped, for garnish
- 1 lemon, cut into 6 wedges, for garnish
- 1 small red onion, finely chopped, for garnish
- 1/2 cup sour cream, for garnish

Season the chili with additional salt and pepper to taste. Equally divide steak into serving bowls, top with the chili. Garnish with the cheese, avocado, onion, lemon wedges, and sour cream.

Wine pairing: Cabernet Sauvignon

TOASTED BLOOD ORANGE COUSCOUS

*T*HE TOASTY NUTTINESS OF THE COUSCOUS AND CRANBERRY-LIKE ZING FROM the blood orange will round out the complex flavors of any dish, and is especially complementary to the Braised Chicken with Citrus and Raisins (page 222).

MAKES 4 SERVINGS

1$\frac{1}{2}$ cups couscous

$\frac{3}{4}$ cup freshly squeezed blood orange juice

$\frac{1}{2}$ cup chicken stock (page 101)

$\frac{1}{4}$ teaspoon kosher salt

$\frac{1}{8}$ teaspoon freshly ground black pepper

2 tablespoons chopped flat-leaf parsley (optional)

IN LARGE SKILLET OVER MEDIUM-LOW HEAT, toast the couscous, shaking the pan often, until the couscous turns light golden brown, about 4 minutes; set aside.

Bring the juice and chicken stock to a boil in a medium saucepan over high heat. Add the salt and pepper; stir in the couscous. Remove the pot from the heat; cover and let stand until the liquid is absorbed, about 5 minutes. Stir in the parsley, if using. Serve.

SPICY CREAMY YELLOW GRITS *with* SHRIMP

A CREAMY MOUND OF HOT SPICY GRITS IS A COMFORTING DISH ON A COLD day. Cooking the grits in milk and chicken stock impart extra creaminess and depth of flavor. Serve with the Grilled Spicy Sole Fillets (page 55).

MAKES 6 SERVINGS

4 tablespoons unsalted butter, divided

8 ounces andouille or chorizo sausage, chopped (about 1 cup)

1 poblano chile, seeded and finely diced

6 large garlic cloves, finely chopped (about 2 tablespoons)

4 cups chicken stock (page 101) or vegetable stock (page 193)

4 cups whole milk

1 cup stone-ground yellow grits

$\frac{1}{4}$ teaspoon freshly grated nutmeg

Kosher salt

Freshly ground black pepper

1 pound (25 to 30 per pound) shrimp, peeled, deveined, and tails removed

1 cup grated Pepper Jack cheese

$\frac{1}{4}$ cup finely chopped chives

$\frac{1}{4}$ cup chopped flat-leaf parsley

ADJUST AN OVEN RACK TO THE MIDDLE POSITION and heat the oven to 350°F.

Melt 2 tablespoons of the butter in a large ovenproof skillet over medium-high heat; add the sausage and poblano. Cook until the sausage is lightly browned and crisp, about 4 minutes; add the garlic and cook until fragrant, about 1 minute. Add the stock and milk; bring to a simmer. Reduce the heat to medium low and gradually pour the grits in a very slow stream, all the while whisking in a circular motion to prevent lumps. Simmer gently, stirring occasionally, until the grits become soft and smooth, 15 to 20 minutes. Stir in the remaining 2 tablespoons of butter, nutmeg, salt, and pepper to taste. Cover the skillet with foil and transfer to the oven.

Bake for 15 minutes; remove from the oven. Place the shrimp over the top; cover and bake until the shrimp are pink and cooked through and the center of the grits has set, about 10 minutes. Remove from the oven, uncover, and sprinkle with the cheese, chives, and parsley. Serve immediately.

YANKEE POT ROAST

THERE ARE TWO METHODS NECESSARY FOR MAKING THIS FLAVORFUL AND tender pot roast. One is browning the meat over high heat, which both caramelizes the sugars on the meat and leaves you with flavorful crust left on the bottom of the pot, helping to flavor the sauce. Second is proper braising—cooking the roast at a low temperature for a long time—which guarantees the roast is very tender. Serve with Mashed Red Potatoes with Garlic (page 67) and Mixed Root Vegetables (page 239).

MAKES 6 TO 8 SERVINGS

8 stems flat-leaf parsley, plus chopped leaves for garnish

1 bay leaf

1 teaspoon black peppercorns

$\frac{1}{4}$ teaspoon red pepper flakes

4 sprigs thyme

1 (2$\frac{1}{2}$-pound) boneless chuck-eye roast (see note)

Kosher salt, plus more for seasoning

Freshly ground black pepper, plus more for seasoning

3 tablespoons olive oil

3 medium carrots, cut in $\frac{1}{2}$-inch slices (about 1$\frac{1}{2}$ cups)

2 medium yellow onions, diced

2 stalks celery, chopped

2 medium leeks (white and light green part only), diced (about 1 cup)

12 garlic cloves, peeled

1 (28-ounce) can organic whole tomatoes, chopped, with juice

1$\frac{1}{2}$ cups dry red wine

1 cup Tomato Ham Hock Stock (page 255)

$\frac{1}{2}$ cup balsamic vinegar, plus more for seasoning

2 medium tomatoes, cored and quartered

PLACE THE PARSLEY STEMS, BAY LEAF, PEPPERCORNS, chili, and thyme in the center of a piece of cheesecloth, bundle it into a bag, and tie the top with butchers' string; set aside. Adjust an oven rack to lower-middle position and heat the oven to 275°F.

Thoroughly pat the roast dry with paper towels; sprinkle generously salt and pepper. Heat the oil in a large Dutch oven over medium-high heat until shimmering. Add the roast and brown on all sides, reducing the heat if the fat begins to smoke, 6 to 8 minutes in total. Transfer the roast to a large plate; set aside. Reduce the heat to medium; add the carrots, onion, celery, and leeks. Cook, stirring occasionally, until the vegetables are tender and lightly browned, 6 to 8 minutes. Add the garlic and cook for another 2 to 3 minutes. Add the canned tomatoes, wine, stock, vinegar, fresh tomatoes, poblano chile, and spice bag; stir and scrape the bottom of the pan with a wooden spoon to loosen the browned bits. Return the roast and any accumulated juices to the pot. Add enough water to come halfway up the sides of the roast. Bring the liquid to a simmer, place a large piece of foil over the pot and cover tightly with the lid, then transfer the pot to the oven. Cook, turning the roast every 30 minutes, until fully tender and a fork or sharp knife easily slips in and out of the meat, 3$\frac{1}{2}$ to 4 hours.

Transfer the roast to a carving board; tent with foil to keep warm. Allow the liquid in the pot to settle, about 5 minutes. Discard the spice bag. Use a wide spoon to skim the fat off the surface. Strain the sauce

(continued)

1 poblano chile pepper, roasted, seeded, and diced

Mashed Red Potatoes with Garlic (page 67)

Mixed Root Vegetables (page 239)

into a medium saucepan and transfer the solids to a food processor and purée until smooth. Pour purée through a fine-mesh strainer into the saucepan with the sauce; the purée will thicken the sauce (depending on the consistency you desire, you may not need all of the purée). Season with additional vinegar, salt, and pepper to taste.

Using a chef's knife or carving knife, cut the meat into $\frac{1}{2}$-inch-thick slices or pull apart into large pieces. Place a portion of the Horseradish Whipped Yukon Gold Potatoes in the middle of a plate; top with a serving of roast and pour $\frac{1}{2}$ cup of sauce over the top; arrange the Mixed Root Vegetables around the plate; sprinkle with the parsley.

NOTE: A chuck-eye roast is preferred in this recipe because it is the most tender of the chuck roasts. It is also sold under the names chuck filet, bones chuck roll, chuck tender, and scotch tender. Many markets sell this roast with twine tied around the perimeter; if they do not, ask the butcher to tie the meat for you, or do it yourself. Also, ask the butcher to trim the extra fat from the roast. Seven-bone and top-blade roasts are also good choices for this recipe. Remember to add only enough water to come halfway up the sides of these thinner roasts and begin checking for doneness after 2 hours.

Wine pairing: Zinfandel, Cabernet Sauvignon, Pinot Noir

LEEK *and* SWEET POTATO "RISOTTO"

*A*N INTERESTING, HEALTHY, AND EXCITING PLAY ON THE FAMOUS RICE DISH. There is no rice here—the sweet potato takes its place. Like a risotto, a seasoned stock is constantly added to the pot until everything is tender and cooked through, imparting lots of flavor.

MAKES 4 SERVINGS

---

2 pounds sweet potatoes, peeled and cut into $^1/_2$-inch dice

5 cups vegetable stock (page 193)

1 medium Granny Smith apple, cored and quartered

1 medium zucchini, ends trimmed and cut crosswise into 1-inch chunks

2 tablespoons olive oil

2 tablespoons unsalted butter

$1^1/_2$ to 2 pounds medium leeks (white and light green parts only), halved lengthwise, sliced crosswise $^1/_2$-inch thick (about 4 cups)

$^1/_2$ cup grated Parmesan cheese

Freshly squeezed lemon juice, to taste

Kosher salt

Freshly ground black pepper

SOAK SWEET POTATOES IN ENOUGH WATER TO COVER for 10 minutes; drain.

In a medium saucepan over medium heat, bring the stock, apple, and zucchini to a simmer for 10 minutes. Remove from the heat; set aside and keep warm.

In a large Dutch oven, melt the butter and oil together; add the leeks and sweet potatoes; cover and cook, stirring occasionally, until leeks are tender and translucent, about 15 minutes. Remove the cover, stir in 1 cup of the reserved stock, stirring constantly until absorbed, about 3 minutes; repeat with additional stock until the vegetables are tender. Off the heat, stir in the cheese and lemon juice. Season with salt and pepper to taste.

SOLE FILLETS *with* CITRUS BROWN BUTTER

*F*LOUNDER CAN BE SUBSTITUTED FOR SOLE. SERVE WITH LEEK AND SWEET Potato "Risotto" (page 231).

MAKES 4 SERVINGS

1 cup pea shoots

3 lemons; 2 lemons, zest grated and juice freshly squeezed; 1 lemon, segmented

3 tangerines, zest grated and segmented

1 tablespoon extra-virgin olive oil

Kosher salt

Freshly ground black pepper

1½ pounds skin-on sole fillets

½ cup grapeseed or vegetable oil

4 tablespoons unsalted butter

3 (2-inch) sprigs thyme

1 recipe Leek and Sweet Potato "Risotto" (page 231)

12 medium shrimp, peeled, deveined, and tails left on (optional)

Black truffle, shaved (optional)

TOSS THE PEA SHOOTS, LEMON AND TANGERINE SEGMENTS, olive oil, and 1 teaspoon of the lemon juice in a medium bowl. Season with salt and pepper to taste; set aside.

In a large skillet over medium-high heat, add enough oil to come ⅛-inch up the side of the pan; heat the oil until shimmering but not smoking. Sprinkle the fillets with salt and pepper. Add the fillets skin-side down in the hot oil and cook without moving the fillets until the edges of the fillet are opaque and the bottoms are golden brown and crispy, 2 to 3 minutes. Using a fish spatula, gently flip the fillets and cook on the second side until the thickest part of the fillet easily separates into flakes when a toothpick is inserted, about 2 minutes longer. Carefully remove fillets from the pan and transfer to paper towel–lined plate to drain. Add the shrimp, if using, to the hot pan. Season with salt and pepper and cook until just pink, about 2 minutes on each side. Remove and transfer to paper towel–lined plate.

Discard the oil from the pan; reduce the heat to low. Add the butter and thyme sprigs; cook, simmering gently, until the butter it turns deep golden and frothy, about 5 minutes. Remove the browned butter from heat and take out the thyme sprigs; stir in the lemon and tangerine zest and remaining lemon juice.

Spoon the Leek and Sweet Potato "Risotto" into soup plates; arrange two fillets on top, garnish with three shrimp, optional, and spoon the hot butter mixture over the fish. Garnish with dressed pea shoots and citrus and shaved black truffle, if using. Serve immediately.

Wine pairing: Chardonnay

RAVIOLI *with* SWISS CHARD

THE CHARD AND BASIL GIVE THE RAVIOLI A WONDERFULLY EARTHY, HERBY flavor, perfectly complemented by the savory mushrooms and smoky, tender ham hocks. Wonton or gyoza wrappers, found in the refrigerated section of most markets, make a decent substitute for the homemade pasta.

MAKES 6 SERVINGS

---

1 bunch red Swiss chard, coarsely chopped (about 2 cups)

1 tablespoon plus $\frac{1}{2}$ teaspoon kosher salt, divided

$\frac{1}{2}$ cup ricotta cheese

$\frac{1}{4}$ cup crème fraîche

2 large garlic cloves, finely chopped (about 2 teaspoons)

1 tablespoon chopped basil

$\frac{1}{4}$ teaspoon freshly ground black pepper

1 recipe Pasta Dough (page 236)

Olive oil, for drizzling

1 cup grated Monterey Jack cheese

2 cups Braised Ham Hocks (page 223), both meat and broth, for garnish

1 recipe Roasted Mushroom Ragoût (page 237), for garnish

LINE TWO RIMMED BAKING SHEETS with parchment paper; set aside.

Bring 4 cups of water to a boil in a medium saucepan; add 1 tablespoon of salt and chard. Cook for 30 seconds; transfer the chard, with a slotted spoon, to a medium bowl filled with ice water. Let soak for 2 minutes then place the chard onto a dry kitchen towel. Twist the towel around the chard and squeeze tightly to remove any excess water; remove the chard from the towel and finely chop.

In a medium bowl, combine the chard, ricotta, crème fraîche, garlic, basil, the $\frac{1}{2}$ teaspoon of salt, and pepper; mix thoroughly.

On a pasta machine, roll the prepared pasta dough to the second thinnest setting. With a 3-inch biscuit cutter, cut out 24 circles; using a $3\frac{3}{4}$-inch biscuit cutter, cut out 24 additional circles. Place a heaping tablespoon of ricotta filling in the center of each of the smaller circles; moisten the edges of the circles with water. Place the larger circles on top of the filling; working from the center out, gently press the top pasta over the filling and seal the edges, removing any air pockets. Crimp edges with a fork to seal. Place the ravioli on the parchment paper–lined baking sheets; cover and refrigerate. (Ravioli can be made to this step up to two days in advance.)

Bring 4 quarts of water to a boil in a large pot. Add 1 tablespoon of salt and the ravioli to the boiling water and cook, stirring often, until the ravioli are tender and floating, 5 or 6 minutes. Remove ravioli with a slotted spoon to prepared sheet pans; drizzle lightly with olive oil. Place three ravioli on each plate, top with some of the ham hock meat and braising liquid, the mushroom ragoût, and sprinkle with the Jack cheese. Serve immediately.

235

NEW YEAR'S DAY CELEBRATION

PASTA DOUGH

*I*TALIANS MAKE THEIR DOUGH FOR A REASON: IT'S SUPER SIMPLE AND ONCE you have made your own dough you will never want to buy the dried commercial stuff again. Experiment by adding different flavors to the dough like lemon zest, black pepper, or basil.

MAKES 6 SERVINGS

1 cup all-purpose flour
1 large egg, beaten
1 teaspoon olive oil

POUR THE FLOUR IN A MOUND onto a smooth work surface; make a well in the middle of the flour; add the egg and oil. Using a fork, begin stirring to incorporate the flour starting with the inner rim of the well. Mix together until a stiff dough has formed. Not all the flour will be used.

Knead the dough until smooth and elastic, about 3 minutes. Wrap the dough tightly in plastic wrap and let the dough rest at room temperature for 1 hour before rolling.

Starting with the widest setting, roll the dough between the rollers of a pasta machine. Fold the rolled dough in thirds and pass through the machine two more times at that setting. Then set the machine's setting smaller each time you pass the dough through until you get the desired thickness.

For fettuccini or other noodles, let the dough dry for 2 minutes before cutting into strands. For ravioli, keep the pasta sheets covered with a damp towel and use as soon as possible. Fresh pasta cooks in half the time as dried pasta so start checking for doneness within the first 3 minutes of cooking.

ROASTED MUSHROOM RAGOÛT

ROASTING CARAMELIZES THE MUSHROOMS AND CREATES FLAVORFUL browned bits that eventually season the sauce. Hearty and earthy, this ragoût is perfect for saucing any pasta—just top with freshly grated Parmesan and *mangia*!

4 cups shiitake, chanterelle, cremini, or button mushrooms, stems discarded, wiped clean, and quartered

8 garlic cloves, thinly sliced

5 shallots, thinly sliced

3 sprigs rosemary

3 sprigs thyme

3 tablespoons olive oil

$\frac{1}{4}$ cup balsamic vinegar

Kosher salt

Freshly ground black pepper

1 cup Zinfandel

$1\frac{1}{2}$ cups chicken stock (page 101)

3 tablespoons unsalted butter

$\frac{1}{4}$ cup chopped flat-leaf parsley

ADJUST AN OVEN RACK TO THE MIDDLE POSITION and heat the oven to 425°F.

In a large bowl, toss together the mushrooms, garlic, shallots, rosemary, thyme, oil, vinegar, salt, and pepper. Transfer the mushrooms to a heavy bottomed roasting pan; spread in an even layer. Roast the mushrooms, stirring occasionally, until they are tender and lightly browned, about 15 minutes. Remove the mushrooms from the pan, set them aside, and keep them warm; reserve pan.

Place the roasting pan on the stovetop over medium heat; pour in the wine and simmer, stirring up the browned bits from the bottom of the pan, until wine has reduced by half. Add the chicken stock. Continue to simmer until the sauce has reduced by a third. Add the butter, parsley, and reserved mushrooms; simmer for 5 minutes.

CRISPY POTATO *and* CHIVE CAKES

MAKE THESE DELICATE AND CRISPY CAKES INSTEAD OF HASH BROWNS FOR breakfast or brunch. Serve with Fennel-Cured Gravlax (page 219).

MAKES 4 CAKES

2 medium russet potatoes
(1 pound), peeled

2 tablespoons lemon juice

1 small yellow onion, grated
(about $\frac{1}{3}$ cup)

$\frac{1}{4}$ cup chives, cut into $\frac{1}{4}$-inch pieces

$1\frac{1}{2}$ teaspoons kosher salt

$\frac{1}{4}$ teaspoon freshly ground
black pepper

$\frac{1}{8}$ teaspoon cayenne pepper

8 tablespoons (1 stick)
unsalted butter, melted

PLACE THE LEMON JUICE IN A LARGE MIXING BOWL. Use a box grater to coarsely grate the potatoes into the bowl and toss to combine the shreds with the juice. Add the onion, chives, salt, pepper, and cayenne, stir to combine. Let the mixture stand at room temperature for 20 minutes.

Heat 2 tablespoons of the butter in a small nonstick skillet over medium heat until shimmering. Squeeze one quarter of the potato mixture with your hands to remove any liquid. Sprinkle the potatoes evenly and thinly over the bottom of the pan—you should be able to see the bottom of the pan between the shreds of potato. Cook until the edges turn crisp and light golden, about 5 minutes. Flip the cake over and cook the second side until golden and crispy, 3 to 4 minutes more. Transfer cooked potato cake to a paper towel–lined plate. Repeat 3 more times with the remaining potato mixture. Serve immediately.

MIXED ROOT VEGETABLES

CHIOGGIA BEETS, PRONOUNCED KEE-OH-GEE-YA, ARE STUNNING RED-AND-white-striped Italian heirloom beets often found at farmers' markets. They are also known as "candy stripe" or "bull's-eye" beets, and are often sweeter than red or golden beets. Use more red or orange beets if you cannot find the Chioggia variety. Serve with Yankee Pot Roast (page 229).

MAKES 4 SERVINGS

1 small rutabaga, peeled and cut into 8 wedges

1 turnip, peeled and cut into 8 wedges

8 tablespoons (1 stick) unsalted butter, softened, divided

Kosher salt

Freshly ground black pepper

4 small Chioggia beets

4 small red beets

4 small golden beets

Olive oil

5 ounces green beans, trimmed (about 1 cup)

8 baby carrots

1/4 cup finely chopped flat-leaf parsley

ADJUST AN OVEN RACK TO THE MIDDLE POSITION and heat the oven to 400°F.

Toss the rutabaga and turnips with 3 tablespoons of the butter, 2 tablespoons of water, salt, and pepper; place in a small broiler pan. Roast the rutabaga and turnips in the oven until lightly browned and tender (a paring knife should insert into the vegetables with slight resistance), 15 minutes. Shake pans several times during roasting to brown the vegetables on each side. Remove from the oven, set aside.

On a baking sheet, toss the different beets with enough olive oil to coat; sprinkle with salt and pepper. Roast the beats until almost tender (a paring knife should insert into the beets with slight resistance), 15 to 20 minutes. Remove beets from oven and let stand until cool enough to handle. Gently rub the skins off the beets with a paper towel. Cut the beets in quarters, set aside.

While the beets are roasting, bring 3 cups of water to a boil in a medium saucepan over high heat and fill a large bowl with ice water. Add 1 teaspoon of salt and green beans, return to a boil and cook until the beans are bright green and crisp-tender, 2 to 3 minutes. Drain the beans and transfer them immediately to the ice water for 1 minute, drain again and dry with paper towels. Set aside until needed. Repeat blanching process for carrots.

Melt the remaining butter in large sauté pan over medium-high heat. Add all of the cooked vegetables; cook to warm through. Season with additional salt and pepper to taste and sprinkle with parsley. Serve immediately. (This dish can be made up to two days ahead, but keep the beets separate until ready to serve.)

BLUE CORN *and* DILL MINI-MUFFINS

BLUE CORNMEAL DIFFERS FROM YELLOW CORNMEAL WITH ITS SWEETER flavor and coarser grains, which gives these muffins a luscious and dense texture. Its grayish-blue color turns into a beautiful purple when cooked. If you cannot find blue cornmeal, substitute yellow cornmeal—the flavor and texture will be slightly different but will still be delicious.

2 ears corn, husks and silk removed

1 cup all-purpose flour

²/₃ cup blue cornmeal

¹/₂ teaspoon baking powder

1 teaspoon baking soda

³/₄ cup buttermilk

¹/₂ cup sour cream

2 large eggs

¹/₄ cup melted butter, plus more for greasing muffin pans

2 tablespoons granulated sugar

2 tablespoons honey, melted

¹/₂ teaspoon white vinegar

¹/₂ teaspoon kosher salt

¹/₄ cup chopped fresh dill

ADJUST AN OVEN RACK TO THE MIDDLE POSITION and heat the oven to 375°F. Lightly butter the mini-muffin pans or use paper liners. Stand the corn upright inside a large bowl and, using a paring knife, carefully cut the kernels from the corn; use the back of a butter knife to scrape off any pulp remaining on the cobs; you should have about 1 cup; set aside.

In a large bowl, sift together the flour, cornmeal, baking powder, and baking soda.

In a separate medium bowl, whisk together the buttermilk, sour cream, eggs, butter, sugar, honey, vinegar, and salt. Add the wet ingredients into the dry ingredients and gently mix with a rubber spatula until the batter is just combined and evenly moistened. Do not overmix. Gently fold in the corn and dill.

Fill the muffin cups two-thirds full. Place the muffin tin on a sheet pan and bake until they are light golden brown and a toothpick inserted into the center of them comes out clean, about 15 minutes. Rotate the pan halfway through the baking time. Cool the muffins in the pan for 5 minutes, then transfer them to a cooling rack and cool for 5 minutes before serving.

NOTE: If standard-size muffins are desired, increase the baking time by approximately 8 minutes.

FLATBREAD

*T*HERE IS NOTHING LIKE THE TASTE AND SMELL OF FRESHLY BAKED BREAD. Onion and chive perfume this bread and give it a delightful texture. These flatbreads can also be made on the stovetop in a cast-iron skillet. Serve with Fresh Chickpea Dip (page 215) or as a base for pizza.

MAKES 6 FLATBREADS

1 small red onion, finely chopped (about $^1/_3$ cup)

4 teaspoons olive oil

2 tablespoons finely chopped chives

1 tablespoon active dry yeast

3 cups bread flour, plus more as needed

2 teaspoons kosher salt

COMBINE THE ONION, $^3/_4$ CUP OF COLD WATER, oil, chives, and yeast in the bowl of a standing mixer fitted with the hook attachment. Add the flour and salt; mix on low speed until a roughly combined and shaggy dough forms, about 1 minute. Scrape down the sides of the bowl as necessary. Increase the speed to medium low and continue mixing, adding more flour as necessary, until the dough becomes a uniform mass that collects on the paddle and pulls away from the sides of the bowl, 4 to 6 minutes. Turn the dough out of mixing bowl onto a very lightly floured work surface and knead until smooth and elastic, 12 to 15 minutes. (If the dough is too sticky, sprinkle with flour.) Place the dough in a medium bowl, cover with plastic wrap, and place in warm spot until dough doubles in size, 30 to 45 minutes. (At this point, dough can be punched down, wrapped tightly in plastic wrap, and refrigerated for up to two days.)

About 30 minutes prior to cooking, adjust an oven rack to the lowest position, line the rack with unglazed baking tiles, a pizza stone, or a baking sheet, and heat oven to 500°F.

Using a chef's knife, divide the dough into 6 equal portions. Roll each portion of dough on the work surface to form a round ball, roll each ball out into a 4-inch circle, and let rest for 10 minutes. Then roll the 4-inch circles into 6-inch circles; lift and stretch each dough round slightly to achieve a 7-inch round circle.

Bake dough rounds directly on preheated tiles or pizza stone until bread is puffed and golden brown on bottom, 5 to 6 minutes. Transfer flatbreads to a cooling rack to cool for 5 minutes; wrap in clean kitchen towels and serve warm or at room temperature.

BANANA BLUEBERRY BREAD

SUBSTITUTE FRESH STRAWBERRIES FOR THE BLUEBERRIES FOR A NICE variation. Frozen blueberries or strawberries can be used in place of the fresh; however, add them frozen to the batter or dust them with flour to prevent them from "bleeding" into the batter.

2 cups all-purpose flour, plus more for dusting

2 tablespoons whole wheat flour

1 teaspoon baking soda

1 teaspoon ground cinnamon

$\frac{1}{4}$ teaspoon ground allspice

$\frac{1}{4}$ teaspoon ground cloves

$\frac{1}{4}$ teaspoon ground nutmeg

$\frac{1}{4}$ teaspoon salt

1 cup granulated sugar, plus 1 tablespoon for sweetening berries, if needed

8 tablespoons (1 stick) unsalted butter, softened, plus more for greasing

2 large eggs

2 teaspoons vanilla

4 very ripe bananas, mashed well (about 2$\frac{1}{2}$ cups)

1 cup blueberries or strawberries (sweetened with 1 tablespoon sugar, if needed)

ADJUST AN OVEN RACK TO THE MIDDLE POSITION; do not turn on the oven. Grease and flour a 9 x 5-inch loaf pan; set aside. Sift together the flour, wheat flour, baking soda, cinnamon, allspice, cloves, nutmeg, and salt; set aside.

In a standing mixer fitted with the paddle attachment, beat the 1 cup of sugar and butter together at medium-high speed until light and fluffy, about 2 minutes. Decrease the speed to low; add the eggs one at a time until well incorporated. Add the vanilla. Add one-third of the dry ingredients and mix on low speed until just until incorporated, about 5 seconds. Add one-third of the bananas. Scrape the bowl with a rubber spatula, and repeat using half of the remaining flour mixture and half of the banana mixture; mix until just combined. Add the remaining flour mixture and beat until just incorporated; add the remaining banana mixture until just combined; do not overmix. Using a rubber spatula, very gently fold in the blueberries.

Pour the batter into the prepared pan, smoothing out the top with a rubber spatula. Place the loaf pan in the cold oven. Set the oven to 300°F.

Bake until the loaf is golden brown and a toothpick inserted into the center comes out clean, 60 to 90 minutes. Cool the bread in the pan on a cooling rack for 5 minutes; invert the bread directly onto the cooling rack and turn right side up. Serve warm or at room temperature.

BANANA SOUR CREAM COFFEE CAKE

*T*HE SOUR CREAM AND BANANA MAKE THIS CAKE SINFULLY MOIST AND DELI-cious; it will keep on your counter for days without drying out.

TOPPING

1 cup packed light brown sugar

1/4 cup unbleached all-purpose flour

2 tablespoons old-fashioned oats

4 tablespoons unsalted butter, chilled and cut into 1/4-inch pieces

COFFEE CAKE

4 very ripe bananas, mashed well (about 2 cups)

1 tablespoon freshly squeezed lemon juice

1 cup granulated sugar plus 1 tablespoon, divided

2 cups cake flour

1 teaspoon baking powder

1 teaspoon baking soda

1 teaspoon ground cinnamon

1/2 teaspoon ground ginger

1/4 teaspoon ground allspice

1/4 teaspoon ground nutmeg

1/4 teaspoon salt

8 tablespoons (1 stick) unsalted butter, softened, plus more for greasing

3 large eggs

2 teaspoons vanilla extract

1 cup sour cream

ADJUST AN OVEN RACK TO THE MIDDLE POSITION and heat the oven to 350°F. Butter a 13 x 9-inch baking dish.

FOR THE TOPPING: In a small bowl, combine the brown sugar, flour, oats, and butter. Using the back of a fork, mash the butter into the flour, sugar, and oats until the mixture resembles course crumbs; set aside.

FOR THE CAKE: In a small bowl, mix the bananas with the lemon juice and 1 tablespoon of sugar; set aside. In a medium bowl, sift together the flour, baking powder, baking soda, cinnamon, ginger, allspice, nutmeg, and salt; set aside.

In a large bowl, using an electric mixer, beat the remaining butter and sugar on medium-high speed until fluffy, about 2 minutes. Add the eggs, one at a time, beating until just incorporated. Add the vanilla. Reduce the speed to medium and beat in one-third of the flour mixture until incorporated; beat in 1/2 cup of the sour cream until blended. Beat in half of the remaining flour mixture, then the remaining 1/2 cup of sour cream, and finally the remaining flour mixture until just blended. Using a rubber spatula, gently fold in the banana mixture. Spread the batter into the prepared pan. Evenly sprinkle the crumb topping over the top of the batter.

Bake until a toothpick inserted in the center of the cake comes out clean, 30 minutes. Cool in the pan for 20 minutes. Serve warm or at room temperature.

NOTE: The cake can be stored in an airtight container at room temperature for up to three days or frozen for up to one month.

COCONUT ANGEL CAKE *with* BANANA PUDDING

*T*HE BANANA PUDDING ADDS A LUXURIOUS CREAMINESS AS WELL AS A WON-derful contrast to the coconut flavor.

MAKES ONE (9-INCH) CAKE, SERVING 10 TO 12

$^1/_3$ cup unsalted butter plus 1 tablespoon, softened, divided

2$^1/_4$ cups cake flour, plus more for dusting cake pans

2$^1/_4$ teaspoons baking powder

$^1/_2$ teaspoon salt

1$^2/_3$ cups granulated sugar

2 large eggs

1 (14-ounce) can coconut milk

1 tablespoon plus 2 teaspoons vanilla extract

1 recipe Banana Pudding (page 248), chilled

1 cup sweetened coconut flakes

1 recipe Coconut Frosting (page 249)

ADJUST AN OVEN RACK TO THE MIDDLE POSITION and heat the oven to 350°F. Coat two 9 x 2-inch-high round cake pans with 1 tablespoon of the butter and dust with the flour, tap out the excess flour; line the bottom of the pans with parchment paper.

Whisk the flour, baking powder, and salt in a medium bowl to combine; set aside.

In a large bowl, combine the sugar and the remaining $^1/_3$ cup of butter; beat with an electric mixer at medium speed until light and fluffy, about 5 minutes; scrape down the bowl with a rubber spatula. Beat in one egg at a time, fully incorporating each egg before adding the next one. Reduce the mixer speed to low and beat in one-third of the flour mixture, followed by half of the coconut milk. Repeat with half of the remaining flour mixture and the remaining coconut milk. Beat in the remaining flour mixture until just combined; add the vanilla and scrape down the bowl.

Give the batter a final stir with a rubber spatula to make sure it is thoroughly combined. Evenly pour the batter into the prepared pans, smooth the top, and lightly tap the pans against the countertop two or three times to settle the batter. Bake the cake until a toothpick inserted in the center comes out with a few moist crumbs attached, 30 to 35 minutes, rotating the pans halfway through the baking time.

Cool the cakes in the pans on a cooling rack for 15 minutes. Run a small knife around the edge of the cakes, flip them out, peel off the parchment paper, then flip the cakes right side up onto the racks. Cool completely before frosting, about 2 hours.

Line the edges of a cake platter with strips of parchment to keep the
(continued)

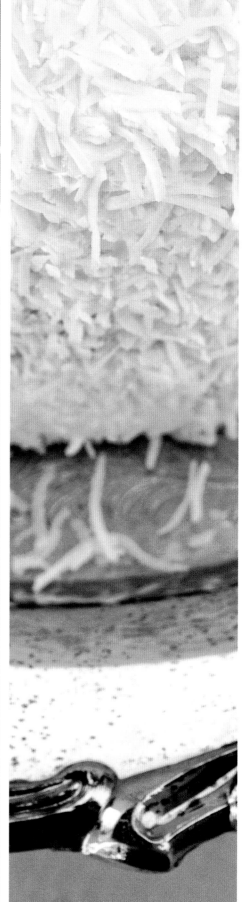

platter clean while you assemble the cake. Place one of the cakes on the cake platter. With a spatula, spread the banana pudding filling evenly across the top of the cake; sprinkle with $\frac{1}{4}$ cup of the coconut. Place the second cake layer on top, and spread the coconut frosting evenly over the top and sides of the cake. Sprinkle the remaining flaked coconut on top and sides of cake. Remove the parchment strips from the platter before serving.

BANANA PUDDING

THIS PUDDING HAS A MARVELOUS SATINY TEXTURE AND INTENSE BANANA flavor. Use it as the filling in the Coconut Angel Cake with Banana Pudding or by itself; topping the pudding with fresh whipped cream and chopped nuts makes a delightfully delicious dessert.

MAKES 4 SERVINGS

2 large ripe bananas, coarsely mashed (about 2 cups)

1 tablespoon freshly squeezed lemon juice

$\frac{1}{8}$ teaspoon salt

5 large egg yolks

$\frac{3}{4}$ cup heavy cream

$\frac{3}{4}$ cup whole milk

$\frac{1}{3}$ cup granulated sugar

2 tablespoons honey

2 teaspoons vanilla extract

$\frac{1}{2}$ vanilla bean, cut in half and seeds scraped

ADJUST AN OVEN RACK TO THE MIDDLE POSITION and heat the oven to 275°F.

In a food processor, purée the bananas, lemon juice, and salt until very smooth; set aside.

In a medium glass bowl set over a pot with 1 inch of simmering water, whisk the egg yolks, cream, milk, sugar, honey, vanilla extract, and vanilla seeds until combined. Pour in the banana purée; cook, stirring frequently, until the mixture has thickened and coats the back of a spoon, about 15 minutes.

Pour the mixture through a fine-mesh strainer into a large measuring cup or clean medium bowl. Transfer the mixture into a one-quart baking dish and place dish in a larger pan lined with a kitchen towel. Carefully place the pan on the oven rack and fill the pan with enough hot water until it reaches two-thirds of the way up the side of the baking dish, taking care not to splash water into the pudding. Bake until the center of the pudding is set and no longer jiggles when shaken, about 30 minutes. Let stand 5 minutes before serving, or cover and place in refrigerator until needed.

COCONUT FROSTING

*T*HE FROSTING BASE HERE IS AN ITALIAN MERINGUE—ONE OF THE SILKIEST AND smoothest icings for cakes or cupcakes.

1 cup granulated sugar
4 large egg whites
½ teaspoon cream of tartar
⅛ teaspoon salt
1 teaspoon vanilla extract
½ teaspoon coconut extract

IN A SMALL SAUCEPAN OVER LOW HEAT, combine the sugar and ¼ cup of water; swirl the pot over the burner to dissolve the sugar completely; do not stir. Increase the heat to high and boil until the liquid reaches 235°F on a candy thermometer; set aside.

In a large bowl, whip the egg whites with a hand mixer on low speed until foamy. Add the cream of tartar and salt; increase the speed to medium and beat until soft peaks form.

With the mixer running, slowly pour the hot sugar syrup in a thin steady stream over the beaten egg whites; add the vanilla and coconut extracts. Continue to beat until glossy, stiff peaks have formed. Refrigerate until needed.

NOTE: This versatile frosting's flavor can be easily changed. For Italian buttercream frosting, slowly beat in 6 sticks of unsalted softened butter after you have added all the hot syrup. For raspberry frosting, omit the coconut extract and add ¼ cup of raspberry purée for every 2 cups of frosting. For lemon frosting, omit the coconut extract and add ½ cup of lemon curd for every 2 cups of frosting.

BUTTERMILK TANGERINE SOUFFLÉ PANCAKES

N UPSCALE TWIST ON REGULAR PANCAKES, THESE PANCAKES ARE DELIGHT-fully light and flavorful. Serve with Quince Compote (page 192) to warm up a winter day.

MAKES 16 2-INCH PANCAKES

¹/₂ cup buttermilk

¹/₄ cup freshly squeezed tangerine juice

2 lemons, zest grated, 1 tablespoon freshly squeezed juice reserved

1 large egg yolk

3 tablespoons superfine sugar (see note)

¹/₄ teaspoon salt

1 teaspoon vanilla extract

2 tablespoons unsalted butter, melted

¹/₂ cup all-purpose flour

2 teaspoons baking powder

2 large egg whites

Cooking spray

Confectioners' sugar, for garnish

Quince Compote (page 192), for garnish

IN A SMALL BOWL, MIX THE BUTTERMILK, tangerine and lemon juices, lemon zest, egg yolk, superfine sugar, salt, and vanilla extract; stir in the butter; set aside.

In a large mixing bowl, sift together the flour and baking powder. Make a well in the center of the flour mixture; add the buttermilk mixture, stirring until the dry ingredients are just moistened. Be careful not to overmix; set aside.

Using an electric mixer, beat the egg whites in a small bowl until soft peaks form. Gently fold the egg whites into the batter until just a few traces of egg white are visible.

Heat a large nonstick pan over medium heat for 3 minutes. Spray the bottom of the pan with cooking spray and spoon 2 tablespoons of batter into the skillet per pancake. Cook the pancakes until large bubbles begin to appear, the edges are set, and the bottoms are golden, 1 to 2 minutes. Flip the pancakes over and cook until golden brown on the second side, 1 to 2 minutes longer. Place three on a plate; dust the pancakes with confectioners' sugar; top with compote, if using; serve immediately.

NOTE: To make 3 tablespoons of superfine sugar, just place 1/4 cup of sugar into a food processor and process until sugar granules are very fine, about 10 seconds.

A VERY SPECIAL NOTE ON
BUYING ORGANIC AND LOCAL FOOD

*M*OST CHEFS AGREE THAT THEIR FOOD IS ONLY AS GOOD AS THEIR ingredients. To ensure they have access to the best flavor, they buy organic meats and produce, preferably local. When given the opportunity, I have to speak about how important buying local organic food is to me. I love going down to my local farmers' market and purchasing seasonal produce at the peak of its freshness and flavor. Organic and local food not only tastes better, but it also benefits farmers, animals, the environment, and your health.

Organic has many definitions these days, depending on shipping practices, genetic modification, or processing techniques. But to me, *organic* means food with no chemicals, fertilizers, coloring, additives, or preservatives.

Fruits and vegetables grown on organic farms are proven to have more nutrients, vitamins, and minerals because they are allowed to grow in a more natural way, without synthetic fertilizers. Also, fewer and safer pesticides are used due to organic regulations. That already tastes better to me.

Organic meats should be free-range and raised without antibiotics or growth hormones and, preferably, animals should be raised humanely. Organic free-range chickens have better flavor and nutrients since they eat a vegetarian diet, are able to walk, and have access to sunlight. Organic, one-hundred-percent grass-fed and finished beef has all of the amazing, rich, beefy flavor you expect from meat but somehow forgot since the market is full of unnatural, fatty, grain-fed beef. Purchase pork that has been pasture raised and look for the "humanely raised" seal on the packaging or ask your grocer to purchase meats that carry the seal.

Using local and organic ingredients is the most delicious and satisfying way to cook. Please do some research on the benefits of buying organic and supporting your local farmers' market. It may be slightly more expensive but the cost is worth the flavor and the long-term benefits to farmers, animals, the environment, and your health.

CARAMEL SWIRL ANGEL FOOD CAKE

*E*VERYONE LIKES ANGEL FOOD CAKE; IT PROVIDES A LIGHT, SWEET ENDING TO any meal. This is great with the Chocolate Whipped Cream (page 174).

MAKES 8 SERVINGS

1 1/3 cups cake flour

2 cups superfine sugar, divided (see note)

12 large egg whites, room temperature

3/4 teaspoon kosher salt

1 1/2 teaspoons cream of tartar

1 1/2 teaspoons vanilla extract

1 lemon, zest grated

1 orange, zest grated

1/2 cup Caramel Sauce (page 254), divided, plus more for garnish

Whipped cream, for garnish

ADJUST AN OVEN RACK TO THE MIDDLE POSITION and heat the oven to 350°F. Line the bottom of a 10-inch tube pan with parchment paper but do not grease.

Whisk the flour and 1/2 cup of the sugar together in a medium bowl; set aside.

With an electric mixer on high speed, whip the egg whites, salt, and cream of tartar together until the whites form soft, billowy mounds, about 2 minutes. Reduce the speed to medium, slowly sprinkle the remaining 1 1/2 cups of sugar over the egg whites, beat until mixture is thick and stiff peaks have formed, about 4 minutes. Add the vanilla, lemon zest, and orange zest, and continue beating for 1 minute longer.

Sift 1/4 cup of the flour mixture over the top of the egg whites; using a rubber spatula, gently fold the flour into the whites until a few streaks of flour remain. Repeat with the remaining flour mixture, 1/4 cup at a time. Be gentle and do not overmix.

Gently pour half the batter into the prepared pan and then pour 1/4 cup of the caramel sauce around the center of the batter. Using a long wooden skewer, gently swirl the caramel into the cake batter. Pour the remaining batter over, followed by the remaining caramel, repeating the swirl procedure and then smoothing the top with a rubber spatula. Wipe any drops of batter off the sides of the pan and lightly tap the pan against the countertop two or three times to settle the batter. Bake the cake until golden brown and the top springs back when pressed firmly, 30 minutes.

Invert the tube pan over the neck of a sturdy bottle. Completely cool the cake upside down, 2 to 3 hours. Run a small knife around the edge of the cake to loosen; gently tap the pan upside down on the countertop

(continued)

to release the cake. Peel off the parchment paper and turn the cake right side up onto a serving platter. Serve with additional caramel sauce and a dollop of whipped cream. Do not refrigerate.

NOTE: To make 2 cups of superfine sugar, just place 2½ cups of sugar into a food processor and process until sugar granules are very small, about 30 seconds.

CARAMEL SAUCE

AN EFFORTLESS SAUCE TO MAKE. POUR IT OVER THE APPLE CRUMB PIE (page 80) or the Caramel Swirl Angel Food Cake (page 253), or serve it with ice cream.

MAKES 1½ CUPS

8 ounces (2 sticks) unsalted butter

1 cup granulated sugar

¾ cup heavy cream

⅛ teaspoon salt, or more to taste

2 teaspoons vanilla

MELT THE BUTTER IN A LARGE SAUCEPAN over medium heat. Add the sugar; cook, stirring often, until the sugar begins to foam and turn dark brown; remove from the heat. Add the heavy cream and stir until smooth and shiny. Stir in the salt and vanilla. Cool to room temperature; adjust seasoning with salt, if necessary. Serve warm or store in refrigerator until needed.

TOMATO HAM HOCK STOCK

A MULTIPURPOSE STOCK THAT CAN BE USE TO ENHANCE ANY DISH. USE IN Bean Stew with Smoked Ham Hock and Kale (page 212) or Ravioli with Swiss Chard (page 235).

MAKES 5 CUPS

4 cups chicken stock (page 101)

2 large smoked ham hocks

8 large ripe tomatoes or 1 (28-ounce) can Italian plum tomatoes, drained

8 garlic cloves, crushed

2 medium Anaheim chiles, stems removed, halved, and seeded

1 large yellow onion, sliced

$\frac{1}{2}$ cup balsamic vinegar

2 tablespoons olive oil

$\frac{1}{4}$ cup chopped flat-leaf parsley

$\frac{1}{4}$ cup chopped basil

1 tablespoon chopped thyme

1 bay leaf

ADJUST AN OVEN RACK TO THE MIDDLE POSITION and heat the oven to 350°F.

Combine all of the ingredients plus 4 cups of water in a large roasting pan. Bake, basting frequently, until the meat is tender and a knife easily slips in and out of the meat, about $1\frac{1}{2}$ hours.

Transfer the hocks to a plate; set aside and cool to room temperature. Pour stock through a fine-mesh strainer into a large bowl and let cool to room temperature; discard solids. Flake the meat from the bones of the hock, discarding the skin; add the meat to the finished stock. Transfer the stock to an airtight container and refrigerate until needed. (Stock can be made up to four days ahead.)

NOTE: If you are not going to use the stock right away, freeze the stock in 1-cup portions; divide the flaked ham hock meat evenly among the containers. Freeze for up to two months.

∾ SAMPLE MENUS FOR NEW YEAR'S DAY ∾

A NEW YEAR CASUAL BRUNCH MENU

Drink:
Blood Orange Mimosas *(page 204)*

Brunch:
Buttermilk Tangerine Soufflé Pancakes
with Quince Compote *(page 250)*; Fennel-Cured
Gravlax *(page 219)*; Crispy Potato and Chive
Cakes *(page 238)*; Black-Eyed Peas with
Smoked Bacon and Spinach *(page 220)*

Bread:
Soft Rolls *(page 168)*

Dessert:
Banana Sour Cream Coffee Cake *(page 245)*

AN INTIMATE LUNCH FOR TWO

Drink:
Strawberry Sparkling Wine Cocktail *(page 204)*

Salad:
Green Goddess Salad with Shrimp *(page 124)*

Entrée:
Braised Chicken with
Citrus and Raisins *(page 220)*

Side:
Toasted Blood Orange Couscous *(page 226)*

Dessert:
Banana Pudding *(page 248)*

A FOOTBALL DINNER PARTY

Drink:
Meyer Lemon Slush Lemonade *(page 209)*

Appetizer:
Fresh Chickpea Dip *(page 215)*
with Flatbread *(page 242)*

Entrée:
Steak Chili with Black Beans *(page 224)*

Breads:
Blue Corn and Dill Mini-Muffins *(page 240)*;
Flatbread *(page 242)*

Dessert:
Devil's Food Chocolate Cupcakes
with Hot Fudge and Ice Cream *(page 175)*

A HEARTY WINTER'S SUPPER

Salad:
Wedge Salad with Buttermilk Dressing *(page 214)*

Entrée:
Yankee Pot Roast *(page 229)*

Sides:
Mashed Red Potatoes with Garlic *(page 67)*;
Mixed Root Vegetables *(page 239)*

Dessert:
Coconut Angel Cake
with Banana Pudding *(page 246)*

A SPECIAL NOTE ABOUT

Warm Weather Holidays

LTHOUGH MANY OF THE MAJOR HOLIDAYS HAPPEN OVER THE FALL and winter, I couldn't resist the temptation to add some of my favorite warm-weather recipes. Since my move to the West Coast, I rarely experience weather I cannot grill in. However, I look forward to the bounty of perfectly ripe, locally grown produce that summer has to offer. So celebrate the sunshine wherever you are and step outside for fun summer holiday gatherings or outdoor grilling.

When planning a barbecue event, whether indoors or out, think about chilled drinks, dishes that can be served at room temperature, and fresh fruit cobblers. If you can't make it to an outdoor grill, the grilling recipes can all be cooked on an indoor grill pan or oven broiler. Many of the recipes can be made ahead, leaving you plenty of time to unwind and enjoy the beautiful evenings with friends and family.

SUMMER CELEBRATION MENU

SPARKLING PEACH AND APRICOT SANGRÍA, 261

GRILLED APRICOT AND GOAT CHEESE SALAD, 262

GRILLED MARINATED FLANK STEAK, 264

SPICED PLUM BARBECUE SAUCE, 265

HEIRLOOM POTATO SALAD WITH MUSHROOMS, 266

STUFFED SQUASH BLOSSOMS, 267

SPICY BBQ DRY RUB, 268

BERRY COBBLER, 269

SPARKLING PEACH *and* APRICOT SANGRÍA

I MAKE THIS LOVELY LIBATION FOR MANY OF MY OUTDOOR PARTIES. IT IS SO refreshing and the perfect drink to celebrate the wonderful summer fruits and sip with family and friends in the warm weather.

MAKES 6 SERVINGS

2 (750-milliliter) bottles sparkling wine or Champagne

5 peaches, peeled and cut into 6 wedges, one peach reserved for garnish

6 apricots, peeled and cut into 6 wedges

1 pint blackberries

2 lemons, sliced

2 apples, cored and cut into 6 wedges

1 orange, sliced

1 recipe Spiced Simple Syrup (page 21)

½ cup brandy

¼ cup Cointreau

12 mint leaves, plus sprigs for garnish

1 (2-inch) piece of fresh ginger, peeled and thinly sliced

IN A GLASS PITCHER, combine all the sangría ingredients except garnishes; refrigerate for at least 1 hour or up to 1 day. Before serving, stir briskly to distribute the settled fruit and pulp; serve immediately over ice. Garnish with wedges of peach and a mint sprig.

GRILLED APRICOT *and* GOAT CHEESE SALAD

THIS IS ONE OF MY FAVORITE SALADS AND I'M CERTAIN IT WILL SOON BE YOURS too. The combination of sweet grilled apricots with tangy goat cheese, crisp lettuce, and the delicate flavor and crunch of the nuts is simply delightful.

MAKES 4 SERVINGS

BROKEN APRICOT VINAIGRETTE

1 small red onion

1 medium garlic clove

1 lemon, zested and juiced

1 teaspoon Dijon mustard

$1/4$ cup extra-virgin olive oil

1 tablespoon Champagne vinegar

1 tablespoon sherry vinegar

2 tablespoons chopped chives

2 tablespoon finely chopped flat-leaf parsley

3 apricots

GRILLED APRICOT AND GOAT CHEESE SALAD

4 tablespoons goat cheese

2 tablespoons mascarpone cheese

$1/2$ teaspoon white balsamic vinegar

$1/2$ teaspoon freshly squeezed lemon juice

$1/4$ teaspoon kosher salt

4 apricots, halved and pitted

$1/4$ teaspoon freshly ground black pepper

2 tablespoons extra-virgin olive oil

4 small heads Bibb lettuce

24 Crunchy Honey Lavender Almonds (page 35)

PREPARE AN OUTDOOR GRILL or indoor grill pan.

FOR THE VINAIGRETTE: Finely chop the red onion (about $1/4$ cup) and the garlic clove (about 1 teaspoon). Using all the lemon zest and 1 tablespoon of lemon juice, whisk together all of the ingredients except the apricots. Cut the apricots into $1/4$-inch pieces (about 1 cup) and gently stir them in. Add kosher salt and freshly ground black pepper to taste. Let the dressing sit for at least 30 minutes before serving.

FOR THE SALAD: In a small bowl, mix together the goat cheese, mascarpone cheese, vinegar, lemon juice, and salt until well combined. Place 1 tablespoon of the cheese mixture on the cut side of the apricots and lay them cheese-side up on a plate; sprinkle with the pepper and drizzle with the olive oil.

Place apricots cheese-side up on the grill and cook until slightly tender and the cheese begins to melt, 1 to 2 minutes. Remove from the grill; set aside.

Place the leaves from one head of lettuce on a salad plate in a blooming flower formation; drizzle with $1/4$ cup of the dressing; top with 2 apricot halves; sprinkle with 6 almonds. Repeat with the remaining heads of lettuce. Serve.

TIPS FOR GREAT GRILLING

ADDING ANY FOOD TO THE SMOKY FIRE OF A GILL IS A DEPENDABLE WAY TO add great flavor. In the summer months, grilling is the perfect cooking method to get you out of the hot kitchen and into the outdoors. In some warmer regions of the United States, grilling can happen year-round. To ensure your safety and to guarantee your food has all the flavor cooking over an open flame can provide, follow these guidelines.

1. Avoid fires by making sure that your grill is on level, stable ground. Have a small fire extinguisher, garden hose, bucket of sand, or baking soda (if it's a grease fire) nearby. Never put water on a grease fire.

2. Have all the items you may need near you, such as tongs, a fish spatula, sauces, foil, and clean platters. Use the proper utensils for the food you are cooking. Fish and hamburgers can fall apart if you use tongs—a fish spatula will ensure that they stay in one piece.

3. Make sure to clean and oil the grate to prevent your food from sticking. Here is the easiest way: After your grill has thoroughly heated, use a grill brush to remove any charred residue—it should easily scrape off. Just before adding the food, dip a wad of paper towels into oil and, using tongs to hold the paper towel, wipe the grates evenly.

4. Build either a single or double-level fire. The coals should be in an even layer for a single fire, so as to heat the grate uniformly. This is a good method for quick cooking items such as vegetables or fish. Leave a small area with no coals to transfer the food in case of a flare-up.

   A double-level fire is where all the hot coals are moved to one side of the grill to create two distinct temperature zones: one with direct heat, the other with indirect heat. Use this method for meats. Get a nice char over the direct heat side, then move the meat over to the indirect heat side to finish cooking. This allows the interior of the meat to finish cooking before the exterior burns.

5. Cook meats to the proper internal temperature using an instant-read thermometer. It is the best and safest way to gauge when the meat is done. In a pinch, you can use your finger to poke the middle of steaks, burgers, or fish; the flesh should feel firm and barely give to your touch for medium well.

6. Glaze food in the last minutes of cooking to avoid a charred, burned mess.

7. Do not place cooked meats back onto their original plate; use a clean plate to prevent cross-contamination.

GRILLED MARINATED FLANK STEAK

SPICY MUSTARD, SWEET SPICED PLUM BARBECUE SAUCE (PAGE 265), AND TANGY vinegar make a flavorful paste to marinate the meat. Save the extra BBQ sauce for dipping.

MAKES 4 SERVINGS

2 tablespoons Dijon mustard

2 tablespoons Spiced Plum Barbecue Sauce (page 265), plus more for garnish

2 tablespoons red wine vinegar

2 tablespoons vegetable oil

2 teaspoons freshly ground black pepper, plus more to taste

2 teaspoons Spicy BBQ Dry Rub (page 268)

1 teaspoon finely chopped thyme

1 (1½- to 2-pound) flank steak, trimmed

1 teaspoon kosher salt

Freshly ground black pepper

1 recipe Heirloom Potato Salad with Mushrooms (page 266)

IN A SMALL BOWL, COMBINE THE MUSTARD, barbecue sauce, vinegar, oil, pepper, dry rub, and thyme; set the marinade aside. Pat the steak dry with paper towels and place it in a glass baking dish just large enough to hold it. Using a fork, prick the steak about 20 times on each side. Rub both sides evenly with the salt and cover with the marinade. Cover the dish with plastic wrap and refrigerate for at least 4 hours or up to 24 hours, flipping the steak once or twice while it marinates.

Remove the steak from the marinade and bring to room temperature, about 30 minutes.

Meanwhile, prepare a double-level fire in an outdoor grill or use an indoor grill pan set over medium-high heat.

Grill the steak directly over the coals until well browned and charred, 4 to 6 minutes. Flip the steak; grill on the second side until well browned, 3 to 6 minutes for medium. (If the exterior of the meat is browned but the meat has not yet cooked through, move the steak to the cooler side of the grill and continue to grill to the desired doneness.) Transfer the steak to a carving board, tent loosely with foil, and let rest for 15 minutes before slicing.

Spoon the potato salad onto four plates; slice the steak very thinly against the grain and lay over the salad. Drizzle additional BBQ sauce over the top; season with pepper to taste. Serve.

Wine pairing: Cabernet Sauvignon, Shiraz

SPICED PLUM BARBECUE SAUCE

A SPECIAL BBQ SAUCE ELEVATES A GOOD BARBECUE TO A GREAT ONE. This sauce also makes an excellent hostess gift or parting gift from your barbecue.

$^1/_2$ teaspoon coriander seed

$^1/_2$ teaspoon mustard seed

$^1/_2$ teaspoon cumin seed

1 tablespoon unsalted butter

1 small yellow onion, finely chopped (about $^1/_4$ cup)

6 plums, pitted and quartered (about 2 cups)

1 cup ketchup

$^1/_2$ cup firmly packed brown sugar

$^1/_4$ cup bourbon

3 tablespoons cider vinegar

3 tablespoons molasses

2 tablespoons Worcestershire sauce

1 tablespoon Dijon mustard

2 garlic cloves, crushed

$^1/_8$ teaspoon ground cloves

1 teaspoon vanilla extract

1 (1-inch) stick cinnamon

1 (3-inch) piece fresh ginger, peeled and sliced

$^1/_2$ teaspoon freshly ground black pepper

IN A SMALL SAUCEPAN OVER MEDIUM-LOW HEAT, toast the coriander, mustard, and cumin seeds, shaking the pan often, until lightly browned and fragrant, about 3 minutes. Transfer the spices to a spice grinder and grind until fine; set aside.

Melt the butter in a medium saucepan over medium-high heat. Add the onions and plums; cook, stirring occasionally, until the onions begin to soften, about 3 minutes. Add the ground spices and the remaining ingredients. Bring the sauce to a simmer. Reduce the heat to low; cook until sauce has thickened slightly and plums are very soft, about 20 minutes. Pour the sauce through a fine-mesh strainer into a medium bowl; press the solids to extract all their juices (don't forget to scrape the bottom of the strainer for additional sauce); discard solids. Refrigerate until needed.

NOTE: The sauce can be refrigerated for up to four weeks or frozen for several months.

HEIRLOOM POTATO SALAD *with* MUSHROOMS

*L*IKE MOST POTATO SALADS, THIS CAN BE MADE UP TO TWO DAYS AHEAD AND refrigerated. For the best flavor, bring it back to room temperature before serving. Because there is no dairy in this potato salad, it holds up remarkably well during outdoor gatherings.

MAKES 4 SERVINGS

8 ounces small heirloom potatoes

8 ounces brown mushrooms, sliced ¼-inch thick

8 marinated sun-dried tomato halves, thinly sliced

½ medium yellow or red onion, thinly sliced

4 cloves garlic, finely chopped

1 small head of radicchio, torn into bite-size pieces

½ cup chopped basil

½ cup extra-virgin olive oil

⅓ cup white balsamic vinegar

½ teaspoon cayenne pepper

1 tablespoon plus one teaspoon kosher salt, divided

2 teaspoons freshly ground black pepper

PLACE THE POTATOES IN A LARGE SAUCEPAN, cover with 1 inch of water, and bring to a boil over medium-high heat. Reduce the heat to medium; add 1 tablespoon of salt and simmer, stirring occasionally, until the potatoes are tender and a paring knife can be slipped in and out of the potatoes with little resistance, about 15 minutes.

Drain the potatoes; cut them into ½-inch circles and place in large bowl. Add the mushrooms, tomato, onion, garlic, radicchio, basil, oil, vinegar, cayenne, 1 teaspoon of salt and pepper; toss to combine. Serve or refrigerate until needed.

STUFFED SQUASH BLOSSOMS

THIS MAKES AN EXQUISITE GARNISH, APPETIZER, SALAD TOPPER, OR SIDE DISH. The best source for blossoms are at farmers' markets or specialty markets. They don't store well, so use the blossoms soon after you get them.

MAKES 4 SERVINGS

4 ounces goat cheese (about ½ cup), softened

1 teaspoon kosher salt, plus more to taste

½ teaspoon freshly ground black pepper, plus more to taste

1 cup fresh breadcrumbs

1 cup Seasoned Flour (page 191)

2 eggs

½ cup milk

1 cup vegetable oil, or more as needed

4 squash blossoms, rinsed and dried

IN A MEDIUM BOWL, COMBINE THE GOAT CHEESE, salt, and pepper; mix well to combine. Stuff about 2 tablespoons of the goat cheese mixture into each blossom.

Mix the breadcrumbs and flour together in a shallow dish. In a separate shallow dish, whisk the eggs and milk together. Working with one blossom at a time; dredge the blossom in the flour mixture, shaking off the excess; coat with the egg mixture, allowing the excess to drip off. Then coat again with the flour; shaking off the excess. Place the coated blossoms in a single layer on a cooling rack set over a rimmed baking sheet.

In a 12-inch nonstick skillet, add enough oil to come up ⅛-inch of the side of the pan. Heat the oil over high heat until it registers 375°F on an instant-read thermometer, or until shimmering. Add the blossoms, one at a time, and cook until golden brown on each side, 2 to 3 minutes. Transfer the blossoms to a paper towel–lined plate and roll the blossoms several times to blot the excess oil. Sprinkle with salt and pepper to taste. Serve immediately.

SPICY BBQ DRY RUB

A GOOD RUB ADDS GREAT FLAVOR AND TEXTURE TO MEATS. I LIKE THIS RUB because it has a good combination of sweet and heat and can be used on beef, chicken, pork, or lam. Feel free to adjust the heat by adding $\frac{1}{2}$ teaspoon more cayenne pepper for an even spicier rub.

MAKES $\frac{3}{4}$ CUP

1 teaspoon cumin seeds

$\frac{1}{2}$ teaspoon coriander seeds

8 tablespoons brown sugar

3 tablespoons kosher salt

1 tablespoon chili powder

$\frac{1}{2}$ teaspoon freshly ground black pepper

$\frac{1}{2}$ teaspoon cayenne pepper

$\frac{1}{2}$ teaspoon red pepper flakes

$\frac{1}{2}$ teaspoon celery seed

$\frac{1}{2}$ teaspoon dry mustard

$\frac{1}{4}$ teaspoon ground cloves

IN A DRY SKILLET OVER MEDIUM-LOW HEAT, toast the cumin seeds and coriander seeds until lightly browned and fragrant, 2 to 4 minutes. Remove from the heat; grind in spice grinder. Place in a medium bowl and add the remaining spices; mix well. Rub will last one month in a tightly sealed container.

BERRY COBBLER

*I*F YOU CAN, USE WILD VARIETIES AT YOUR FARMERS' MARKET. IN A PINCH, frozen berries can be substituted for fresh. For the best flavor, use a combination of berries. Serve with Buttermilk Ice Cream (page 81).

MAKES 1 2-QUART COBBLER, SERVING 6 TO 8

FILLING

4 pints assorted berries (blueberries, blackberries, cherries, raspberries, strawberries) (about 4 cups)

$^2/_3$ cup granulated sugar

2 oranges or lemons, 2 tablespoons zest grated, 1 tablespoon juice freshly squeezed

$^1/_4$ cup tapioca flour

2 tablespoons vanilla

DOUGH

1$^1/_2$ cups all-purpose flour

2 tablespoons whole oats

1 teaspoon baking powder

$^1/_4$ teaspoon baking soda

2 tablespoons granulated sugar

2 teaspoons ground cinnamon

$^1/_4$ teaspoon freshly grated nutmeg

$^1/_4$ teaspoon salt

4 tablespoons unsalted butter, cut into $^1/_4$-inch pieces and frozen for 10 to 15 minutes

$^3/_4$ cup buttermilk

1 large egg, separated, egg white lightly beaten

1 teaspoon whole milk or cream

Coarse (crystal) or granulated sugar, for sprinkling

ADJUST AN OVEN RACK TO THE MIDDLE POSITION and heat the oven to 375°F.

In a large bowl, toss the berries with the sugar, juice, zest, tapioca flour, and vanilla. Place the mixture in a 2-quart baking dish. Bake, stirring once, until the fruit is cooked and the juices are bubbling, about 35 minutes. Remove from the oven and set aside. Keep the oven on.

About 10 minutes before the berries have finished cooking, whisk together the flour, oats, baking powder, baking soda, sugar, cinnamon, nutmeg, and salt in a large bowl. Using the back of a fork, mash the butter into the flour mixture until the mixture resembles coarse oatmeal. Add the buttermilk and stir with a rubber spatula until just combined. Add the egg yolk and milk; gently stir until just incorporated. Drop the dough in dollops onto the cooked fruit in a single layer. Brush the top of the dough with the egg white; sprinkle with the coarse sugar. Bake until the filling is bubbling and the dough is golden brown, about 15 to 20 minutes longer. Cool for 15 minutes before serving.

A SPECIAL NOTE ABOUT WARM WEATHER HOLIDAYS

INDEX

A

Acorn squash, 73
  Pan-Roasted Turkey Breast with Sweet Squash Matchsticks, 13, 44, 45 (photo)
  Roasted Harvest Squash Soup, 24 (photo), 25
  Winter Panzanella, 70, 71 (photo)
Almonds
  Crunchy Honey Lavender Almonds, 35, 165
Appetizers
  Blue Corn Cakes with Caviar and Crème Fraîche, 216, 217 (photo)
  Caviar Potato Puffs, 119 (photo), 131
  Chicken Liver Pâté with Pear and Currants, 109, 134
  Corn and Shrimp Fritters, 31
  Crunchy Honey Lavender Almonds, 35, 165
  Fennel-Cured Gravlax, 218 (photo), 219
  Foie Gras Poppers, 135
  Fresh Chickpea Dip, 215
  Spicy Glazed Walnuts, 95, 165
  Stuffed Squash Blossoms, 267
  Twice-Baked Blue Cheese Soufflés with Citrus-Fennel Salad, 32 (photo), 33–34, 34 (photo)
Apple cider and juice
  Apple Juice with Cranberry and Ginger, 18, 19 (photo)
  Hot Mulled Cider, 20
Apples
  Apple Crumb Pie, 80
  Apple Juice with Cranberry and Ginger, 18, 19 (photo)
  Beet and Apple Borscht, 118, 119 (photo)
  Braised Napa Cabbage with Apple and Bacon, 56 (photo), 57
  Chilled Apple Soup with Lobster Salad, 22
  Green Apple Pumpkin Butter, 165, 188
  Yankee Salad with Apple, Walnuts, and Blue Cheese, 30
Apricots
  Broken Apricot Vinaigrette, 262
  Grilled Apricot and Goat Cheese Salad, 262
  Sparkling Peach and Apricot Sangría, 261
Artichokes
  Artichoke and Elephant Garlic Soufflé Spoonbread, 152
  Wine-Braised Artichokes, 153

B

Bacon
  Black-Eyed Peas with Smoked Bacon and Spinach, 220, 221 (photo)
  Braised Napa Cabbage with Apple and Bacon, 56 (photo), 57
Bain-marie, 36
Bananas
  Banana Blueberry Bread, 165, 243
  Banana Pudding, 248
  Banana Sour Cream Coffee Cake, 244 (photo), 245
  Coconut Angel Cake with Banana Pudding, 246–249, 247 (photo)
  hangover remedies, 206
Basil Gnocchi, 151
Batters and breadings
  Beer Batter, 191
  Seasoned Flour, 191
  Spicy BBQ Dry Rub, 268
Beans, 201
  Bean Stew with Smoked Ham Hock and Kale, 201, 212
  Braised Lamb Shoulder with Butter Beans, 136–137
  Steak Chili with Black Beans, 224–225, 225 (photo)
Beef
  Black Mustard Beef Tenderloin with Red Wine Sauce, 109, 140, 141 (photo)
  Braised Short Ribs with Onions and Sugar Pumpkin, 53
  Coffee-Spiced Prime Rib Roast, 138 (photo), 139
  Grilled Marinated Flank Steak, 264
  organic and local, 251
  Steak Chili with Black Beans, 224–225, 225 (photo)

Yankee Pot Roast, 228 (photo), 229–230, 230 (photo)

Beer

Beer Batter, 191

Steak Chili with Black Beans, 224–225, 225 (photo)

Beets

Beet and Apple Borscht, 118, 119 (photo)

Devil's Food Chocolate Cupcakes, 175

Mixed Root Vegetables, 230 (photo), 239

Winter Vegetable Salad, 128 (photo), 129

Berry Cobbler, 269

Beverages, 78

Apple Juice with Cranberry and Ginger, 18, 19 (photo)

Blended Coffee with Kahlua Sabayon, 208

Blood Orange Mimosas, 204, 205 (photo)

Eggnog, 114–115

Eye-Opening Bloody Marys, 205 (photo), 207

Hot Chocolate with Champagne Sabayon, 115

Hot Mulled Cider, 20

Mango Pineapple Margaritas, 208

Meyer Lemon Slush Lemonade, 209

Sparkling Peach and Apricot Sangría, 261

Sparkling Pear Punch, 21

Strawberry Sparkling Wine Cocktail, 204

Winter Citrus Punch with Spiced Pomegranate Ice, 116 (photo), 117

Biscuits

Dill Buttermilk Drop Biscuits, 76

Black-Eyed Peas with Smoked Bacon and Spinach, 220, 221 (photo)

Blue cheese

Spinach Salad with Pomegranates and Blue Cheese, 126, 127 (photo)

Twice-Baked Blue Cheese Soufflés with Citrus-Fennel Salad, 32 (photo), 33–34, 34 (photo)

Wedge Salad with Buttermilk Dressing, 214

Yankee Salad with Apple, Walnuts, and Blue Cheese, 30

Blueberries

Banana Blueberry Bread, 165, 243

Berry Cobbler, 269

Bourbon

Chocolate Brioche Pudding, 170 (photo), 171

Onion-Bourbon-Horseradish Mustard, 98

Spiced Plum Barbecue Sauce, 165, 265

Brandy

Eggnog, 114–115

Hot Mulled Cider, 20

Persimmon Bread, 77, 165

Sparkling Pear Punch, 21

Bread pudding

Chocolate Brioche Pudding, 170 (photo), 171

Breadings. See Batters and breadings

Breads and rolls, 7

Banana Blueberry Bread, 165, 243

Blue Corn and Dill Mini-Muffins, 240, 241 (photo)

Boston Brown Bread, 163

Chive-Onion Popovers with Toasted Cardamom, 166, 167 (photo)

Cinnamon Bread with Brown-Sugar Swirl, 164–165

Cornbread, 74

Cranberry Scones with Orange Glaze, 75

Dill Buttermilk Drop Biscuits, 76

Flatbread, 242

Persimmon Bread, 77, 165

Soft Rolls, 168

Breakfast dishes

Banana Sour Cream Coffee Cake, 244 (photo), 245

Buttermilk Tangerine Soufflé Pancakes, 250

Crispy Potato and Chive Cakes, 238

Leftover Turkey Hash, 52

Broccoli rabe

Roasted Broccoli Rabe with Fennel and Orange, 158, 159 (photo)

Brownies

Espresso Double-Chocolate Soufflé Brownies, 165, 176

Brussels sprouts

Buttered Brussels Sprouts and Chestnuts, 58, 59 (photo)

Butter, flavored

Lemon-Thyme-Mustard Butter, 96

Roasted Pepper Butter, 63

Butter, fruit

Green Apple Pumpkin Butter, 165, 188

Buttermilk

Artichoke and Elephant Garlic Soufflé Spoonbread, 152

Blue Corn and Dill Mini-Muffins, 240, 241 (photo)

Boston Brown Bread, 163

Buttermilk Ice Cream, 81

Buttermilk Tangerine Soufflé Pancakes, 250

Buttermilk, *continued*
Dill Buttermilk Drop Biscuits, 76
Wedge Salad with Buttermilk Dressing, 214
Butternut squash, 73
Butternut Squash Gratin, 60
Pan-Roasted Turkey Breast with Sweet Squash
Matchsticks, 13, 44, 45 (photo)
Roasted Harvest Squash Soup, 24 (photo), 25
Winter Panzanella, 70, 71 (photo)

C

Cabbage
Braised Napa Cabbage with Apple and Bacon, 56
(photo), 57
Grandma's Cabbage and Sweet-Sausage Soup, 213
Cakes and cupcakes
Banana Sour Cream Coffee Cake, 244 (photo), 245
Caramel Swirl Angel Food Cake, 252 (photo), 253-
254
Coconut Angel Cake with Banana Pudding, 246-249,
247 (photo)
Devil's Food Chocolate Cupcakes, 175
Persimmon Walnut Upside-Down Cake, 87-88
Strawberry Rhubarb Upside-Down Cake, 88
Candles, 16, 78
Caramel
Caramel Sauce, 165, 254
Caramel Swirl Angel Food Cake, 252 (photo), 253-254
Carrots
Mixed Root Vegetables, 230 (photo), 239
Winter Vegetable Salad, 128 (photo), 129
Yankee Pot Roast, 228 (photo), 229-230, 230
(photo)
Cauliflower
Roasted Cauliflower Florets, 109, 160
Caviar
Blue Corn Cakes with Caviar and Crème Fraîche,
216, 217 (photo)
Caviar Potato Puffs, 119 (photo), 131
Celery Root and Pear Purée, 13, 61
Centerpieces, 16, 78
Champagne, 132
Champagne Sabayon, 189
Hot Chocolate with Champagne Sabayon, 115
Sparkling Peach and Apricot Sangría, 261
Sparkling Pear Punch, 21
Cheese
Double-Stuffed Baked Potatoes, 156 (photo), 157

Red Onion and Parmesan Crackers, 169
See also Blue cheese; Goat cheese
Cherries and cherry juice, 7
Berry Cobbler, 269
Grilled Cornish Game Hens with Spiced Cherry
Rub, 144, 145 (photo)
Chestnuts
Buttered Brussels Sprouts and Chestnuts, 58, 59
(photo)
Chestnut and Oyster Gratin, 62
Chicken
Braised Chicken with Citrus and Raisins, 222
Grilled Chicken and Caramelized Pear Salad, 38
organic and local, 251
Turkey or Chicken Stock, 101
Chicken Liver Pâté with Pear and Currants, 109, 134
Chickpeas
Fresh Chickpea Dip, 215
Chili. See Soups, stews, chili, and chowders
Chimichurri, 91
Chocolate, 36
Chocolate Brioche Pudding, 170 (photo), 171
Chocolate Cream Puffs, 172-174, 173 (photo)
Chocolate Whipped Cream, 174
Devil's Food Chocolate Cupcakes, 175
Espresso Double-Chocolate Soufflé Brownies, 165,
176
Hot Chocolate with Champagne Sabayon, 115
Hot Fudge Sauce, 165, 185
Kahlua Sabayon, 190
Milk Chocolate and Drunken Prune Ice Cream, 184
Chowders. See Soups, stews, chili, and chowders
Christmas
memories of, 109
menus, 194-195
preparation schedule, 196-197
recipes for, 109-111
traditions, 112
Cinnamon Bread with Brown-Sugar Swirl, 164-165
Citrus fruit
Braised Chicken with Citrus and Raisins, 222
Citrus-Cranberry Glaze, 90, 165
Crab Cake and Citrus Salad, 122
segmenting instructions, 222
Sole Fillets with Citrus Brown Butter, 232, 233
(photo)
Twice-Baked Blue Cheese Soufflés with Citrus-
Fennel Salad, 32 (photo), 33-34, 34 (photo)

Winter Citrus Punch with Spiced Pomegranate Ice, 116 (photo), 117
Clams
Shellfish Chowder, 23
Clementines, 211
Coconut
Coconut Angel Cake with Banana Pudding, 246–249, 247 (photo)
Coconut Frosting, 247 (photo), 249
Coffee and espresso
Blended Coffee with Kahlua Sabayon, 208
Coffee Ganache, 171
Coffee-Spiced Prime Rib Roast, 138 (photo), 139
Espresso Double-Chocolate Soufflé Brownies, 165, 176
Coffee cake
Banana Sour Cream Coffee Cake, 244 (photo), 245
Cointreau
Mango Pineapple Margaritas, 208
Sparkling Pear Punch, 21
Winter Citrus Punch with Spiced Pomegranate Ice, 116 (photo), 117
Cookies and bars
Christmas Orange Shortbread, 177
Espresso Double-Chocolate Soufflé Brownies, 165, 176
Ginger Snap Cookies with Lemon Thyme, 178
Holiday Tangerine Bars, 180, 181 (photo)
Parsnip Cookies with Maple Glaze, 179
Pumpkin Cookies with Lemon Cream Cheese Frosting, 182 (photo), 183
Corn
Blue Corn and Dill Mini-Muffins, 240, 241 (photo)
Corn and Sage Stuffing, 64 (photo), 65
Corn and Shrimp Fritters, 31
Corn Stock, 99
Grilled Corn with Roasted Pepper Butter, 63
Cornmeal
Artichoke and Elephant Garlic Soufflé Spoonbread, 152
Blue Corn and Dill Mini-Muffins, 240, 241 (photo)
Blue Corn Cakes with Caviar and Crème Fraîche, 216, 217 (photo)
Cornbread, 74
Couscous
Toasted Blood Orange Couscous, 226
Crabmeat
Crab Cake and Citrus Salad, 122

Crispy Flounder with Cara Cara Orange Sauce and Lump Crab, 148 (photo), 149–150, 150 (photo)
Elephant Garlic Soup with Dungeness Crab Salad, 120 (photo), 121
Shellfish Chowder, 23
Crackers
Red Onion and Parmesan Crackers, 169
Cranberries
Apple Juice with Cranberry and Ginger, 18, 19 (photo)
Citrus-Cranberry Glaze, 90, 165
Cranberry Scones with Orange Glaze, 75
Cranberry-Orange Vinaigrette, 28, 29 (photo)
Crispy Shrimp Salad with Cranberries and Goat Cheese, 123
Hot Mulled Cider, 20
Jellied Cranberry Sauce, 93, 165
Cream
Chocolate Whipped Cream, 174
Coffee Ganache, 171
Horseradish Crème Fraîche, 186
Cream cheese
Pumpkin Cookies with Lemon Cream Cheese Frosting, 182 (photo), 183
Crème fraîche
Blue Corn Cakes with Caviar and Crème Fraîche, 216, 217 (photo)
Horseradish Crème Fraîche, 186
Culinary Institute of America (CIA), 8
Currants. See Raisins and currants

D

Desserts, 78
Berry Cobbler, 269
Chocolate Brioche Pudding, 170 (photo), 171
Chocolate Cream Puffs, 172–174, 173 (photo)
Espresso Double-Chocolate Soufflé Brownies, 165, 176
See also Cakes and cupcakes; Cookies and bars; Pies and piecrust
Dill Buttermilk Drop Biscuits, 76
Dinner party, preparing for, 78
Double boilers, 36
Dry rubs
Spicy BBQ Dry Rub, 268
Duck
Roasted Spiced Duck with Kumquat and Pomegranate Glaze, 109, 146–147

E

Eggs
  Champagne Sabayon, 189
  Chive-Onion Popovers with Toasted Cardamom, 166, 167 (photo)
  Chocolate Brioche Pudding, 170 (photo), 171
  Chocolate Cream Puffs, 172–174, 173 (photo)
  Eggnog, 114–115
  Kahlua Sabayon, 190
  Milk Chocolate and Drunken Prune Ice Cream, 184
  Twice-Baked Blue Cheese Soufflés with Citrus-Fennel Salad, 32 (photo), 33–34, 34 (photo)
Endive Salad with Tangerines and Kumquats, 26

F

Fennel
  Fennel-Cured Gravlax, 218 (photo), 219
  Roasted Broccoli Rabe with Fennel and Orange, 158, 159 (photo)
  Shaved Fennel and Mushroom Salad, 125
  Twice-Baked Blue Cheese Soufflés with Citrus-Fennel Salad, 32 (photo), 33–34, 34 (photo)
Fish
  Crispy Flounder with Cara Cara Orange Sauce and Lump Crab, 148 (photo), 149–150, 150 (photo)
  Fennel-Cured Gravlax, 218 (photo), 219
  Grilled Spicy Sole Fillets, 55
  Sole Fillets with Citrus Brown Butter, 232, 233 (photo)
Flatware, 16–17
Flour
  Seasoned Flour, 191
Flowers, 16, 78
Foie Gras Poppers, 135
Fritters
  Corn and Shrimp Fritters, 31
Frosting
  Coconut Frosting, 247 (photo), 249
  Lemon Cream Cheese Frosting, 182 (photo), 183
Fruits
  organic and local, 7, 8, 251
  winter fruit, 211
  See also specific kinds

G

Game hens, Cornish
  Grilled Cornish Game Hens with Spiced Cherry Rub, 144, 145 (photo)
Garlic
  Artichoke and Elephant Garlic Soufflé Spoonbread, 152
  Chimichurri, 91
  Elephant Garlic Soup with Dungeness Crab Salad, 120 (photo), 121
  Mashed Red Potatoes with Garlic, 67
Gifts from your kitchen, 165
Gin
  Eye-Opening Bloody Marys, 205 (photo), 207
  Hair of the Dog, 206
Ginger
  Apple Juice with Cranberry and Ginger, 18, 19 (photo)
  Ginger Snap Cookies with Lemon Thyme, 178
Glazes. See Sauces, glazes, and gravies
Goat cheese
  Crispy Shrimp Salad with Cranberries and Goat Cheese, 123
  Grilled Apricot and Goat Cheese Salad, 262
  Roasted Pear and Goat Cheese Salad, 28, 29 (photo)
  Stuffed Squash Blossoms, 267
Gravies. See Sauces, glazes, and gravies
Green beans
  Green Bean and Persimmon Salad, 27
  Mixed Root Vegetables, 230 (photo), 239
Greens, 201
Grilling recipes, 259
  Grilled Apricot and Goat Cheese Salad, 262
  Grilled Chicken and Caramelized Pear Salad, 38
  Grilled Corn with Roasted Pepper Butter, 63
  Grilled Cornish Game Hens with Spiced Cherry Rub, 144, 145 (photo)
  Grilled Marinated Flank Steak, 264
  Grilled Spicy Sole Fillets, 55
  Thanksgiving dinner menu, 103
  tips for grilling, 263
  Wood-Grilled Butterflied Leg of Lamb, 54
  Wood-Grilled Turkey Chop with Wild Mushroom Gravy, 46 (photo), 47–48, 48 (photo)
Grits
  Spicy Creamy Yellow Grits with Shrimp, 227

H

Ham and ham hocks
  Bean Stew with Smoked Ham Hock and
    Kale, 201, 212
  Braised Ham Hocks, 223
  Ravioli with Swiss Chard, 234 (photo), 235
  Spiced Honey-Baked Ham, 39
  Tomato Ham Hock Stock, 255
Hangover remedies, 206
Herbs, purchase and storage tips, 137
Holiday meals
  importance of, 8, 13
  preparing for a dinner party, 78
  recipes for, 9
  at the restaurants, 8–9
  setting the holiday table, 16–17
Honey
  Crunchy Honey Lavender Almonds, 35, 165
  Honey- and Cider-Vinegar-Basted Rack of Pork, 142
    (photo), 143
  Spiced Honey-Baked Ham, 39
  Spicy Glazed Walnuts, 95, 165
Horseradish
  Eye-Opening Bloody Marys, 205 (photo), 207
  Horseradish Crème Fraîche, 186
  Onion-Bourbon-Horseradish Mustard, 98
Hubbard squash, 73
  Winter Panzanella, 70, 71 (photo)

I

Ice cream, 7, 8
  Buttermilk Ice Cream, 81
  Milk Chocolate and Drunken Prune Ice Cream, 184

K

Kabocha squash, 73
  Winter Panzanella, 70, 71 (photo)
Kahlua
  Blended Coffee with Kahlua Sabayon, 208
  Kahlua Sabayon, 190
Kumquats, 211
  Endive Salad with Tangerines and Kumquats, 26
  Roasted Spiced Duck with Kumquat and
    Pomegranate Glaze, 109, 146–147

L

Lamb
  Braised Lamb Shoulder with Butter Beans, 136–137
  Wood-Grilled Butterflied Leg of Lamb, 54
Lark Creek, 8
Lavender
  Crunchy Honey Lavender Almonds, 35, 165
Leeks
  Leek and Sweet Potato "Risotto," 231
  Yankee Pot Roast, 228 (photo), 229–230, 230
    (photo)
Lemons and lemon juice
  Braised Chicken with Citrus and Raisins, 222
  Citrus-Cranberry Glaze, 90, 165
  Crab Cake and Citrus Salad, 122
  Hot Mulled Cider, 20
  Lemon-Basil Vinaigrette, 96
  Lemon-Thyme-Mustard Butter, 96
  Meyer Lemon Slush Lemonade, 209
  Pumpkin Cookies with Lemon Cream Cheese
    Frosting, 182 (photo), 183
  segmenting instructions, 222
  Winter Citrus Punch with Spiced Pomegranate Ice,
    116 (photo), 117
Limes and lime juice
  Mango Pineapple Margaritas, 208
  segmenting instructions, 222
Lobster
  Chilled Apple Soup with Lobster Salad, 22
  Lobster Salad, 26
  Lobster Stock, 100
  Shellfish Chowder, 23
Local and fresh ingredients, 7, 8, 251

M

Mango Pineapple Margaritas, 208
Maple syrup
  Parsnip Cookies with Maple Glaze, 179
Menus
  Christmas, 194–195
  New Year's Day, 256
  Thanksgiving, 102–103
Mignonette Sauce, 186
Muffins
  Blue Corn and Dill Mini-Muffins, 240, 241 (photo)

Mushrooms
  Heirloom Potato Salad with Mushrooms, 266
  Ravioli with Swiss Chard, 234 (photo), 235
  Roasted Mushroom Ragoût, 234 (photo), 237, 237
    (photo)
  Shaved Fennel and Mushroom Salad, 125
  Winter Vegetable Salad, 128 (photo), 129
  Wood-Grilled Turkey Chop with Wild Mushroom
    Gravy, 46 (photo), 47–48, 48 (photo)
Mustard
  Black Mustard Beef Tenderloin with Red Wine
    Sauce, 109, 140, 141 (photo)
  Lemon-Thyme-Mustard Butter, 96
  Onion-Bourbon-Horseradish Mustard, 98

N

Napkins, 17
New Year's Day
  hangover remedies, 206
  menus, 256
  recipes for, 201–203
  traditions, 112, 201

O

Onions
  Braised Short Ribs with Onions and Sugar
    Pumpkin, 53
  Chive-Onion Popovers with Toasted Cardamom,
    166, 167 (photo)
  Flatbread, 242
  Onion-Bourbon-Horseradish Mustard, 98
  Red Onion and Parmesan Crackers, 169
  Red Onion and Tomato Relish, 94
Orange flavored liquor. See Cointreau
Oranges and orange juice, 211
  Blood Orange Mimosas, 204, 205 (photo)
  Braised Chicken with Citrus and Raisins, 222
  Christmas Orange Shortbread, 177
  Citrus-Cranberry Glaze, 90, 165
  Cranberry Scones with Orange Glaze, 75
  Cranberry-Orange Vinaigrette, 28, 29 (photo)
  Crispy Flounder with Cara Cara Orange Sauce and
    Lump Crab, 148 (photo), 149–150, 150 (photo)
  Hot Mulled Cider, 20
  Red Curry Turkey Scaloppini, 13, 49
  Roasted Broccoli Rabe with Fennel and Orange,
    158, 159 (photo)
  segmenting instructions, 222

Toasted Blood Orange Couscous, 226
Twice-Baked Blue Cheese Soufflés with Citrus-
  Fennel Salad, 32 (photo), 33–34, 34 (photo)
Winter Citrus Punch with Spiced Pomegranate Ice,
  116 (photo), 117
Organic and sustainable produce and meats, 7, 8, 251
Oysters
  Broiled Oyster, 130
  Chestnut and Oyster Gratin, 62
  Kumamoto Oyster and Sausage Stuffing, 66

P

Pancakes
  Blue Corn Cakes with Caviar and Crème Fraîche,
    216, 217 (photo)
  Buttermilk Tangerine Soufflé Pancakes, 250
Parsnips
  Parsnip Cookies with Maple Glaze, 179
  Winter Vegetable Salad, 128 (photo), 129
Pasta
  Basil Gnocchi, 151
  Pasta Dough, 236
  Ravioli with Swiss Chard, 234 (photo), 235
Peaches
  Sparkling Peach and Apricot Sangría, 261
Pears
  Celery Root and Pear Purée, 13, 61
  Chicken Liver Pâté with Pear and Currants, 109, 134
  Grilled Chicken and Caramelized Pear Salad, 38
  Roasted Pear and Goat Cheese Salad, 28, 29
    (photo)
  Sparkling Pear Punch, 21
Peppers
  Grilled Corn with Roasted Pepper Butter, 63
  Leftover Turkey Hash, 52
  Winter Panzanella, 70, 71 (photo)
Peppers, Indian long
  Braised Lamb Shoulder with Butter Beans, 136–137
  Fresh Chickpea Dip, 215
  Grilled Cornish Game Hens with Spiced Cherry
    Rub, 144, 145 (photo)
Persimmons, 211
  Green Bean and Persimmon Salad, 27
  Persimmon Bread, 77, 165
  Persimmon Dressing, 187
  Persimmon Walnut Upside-Down Cake, 87–88
Pies and piecrust
  Apple Crumb Pie, 80

Classic Pumpkin Pie, 82 (photo), 83
Sour Cream Piecrust, 89
Three-Layer Pumpkin Pie, 13, 84–86, 85 (photo)
Pineapples and pineapple juice
Mango Pineapple Margaritas, 208
Winter Citrus Punch with Spiced Pomegranate Ice,
116 (photo), 117
Plums
Spiced Plum Barbecue Sauce, 165, 265
Pomegranates and pomegranate juice, 211
Roasted Spiced Duck with Kumquat and
Pomegranate Glaze, 109, 146–147
Spinach Salad with Pomegranates and Blue Cheese,
126, 127 (photo)
Winter Citrus Punch with Spiced Pomegranate Ice,
116 (photo), 117
Popovers
Chive-Onion Popovers with Toasted Cardamom,
166, 167 (photo)
Pork, 201
Honey- and Cider-Vinegar-Basted Rack of Pork, 142
(photo), 143
organic and local, 251
Potatoes
Basil Gnocchi, 151
Caviar Potato Puffs, 119 (photo), 131
Chestnut and Oyster Gratin, 62
Crispy Potato and Chive Cakes, 238
Double-Stuffed Baked Potatoes, 156 (photo), 157
Heirloom Potato Salad with Mushrooms, 266
Leftover Turkey Hash, 52
Mashed Red Potatoes with Garlic, 67
Prunes
Milk Chocolate and Drunken Prune Ice Cream, 184
Puddings and custards, 36
Banana Pudding, 248
Pumpkin, 73
Braised Short Ribs with Onions and Sugar
Pumpkin, 53
Classic Pumpkin Pie, 82 (photo), 83
Green Apple Pumpkin Butter, 165, 188
Pumpkin Cookies with Lemon Cream Cheese
Frosting, 182 (photo), 183
Three-Layer Pumpkin Pie, 13, 84–86, 85 (photo)

Quinces, 211
Quince Compote, 165, 192

Raisins and currants
Boston Brown Bread, 163
Braised Chicken with Citrus and Raisins, 222
Chicken Liver Pâté with Pear and Currants, 109, 134
Persimmon Bread, 77, 165
Red Curry Turkey Scaloppini, 13, 49
Relishes
Red Onion and Tomato Relish, 94
Rhubarb
Strawberry Rhubarb Upside-Down Cake, 88
Roasting racks, 43
Rum
Eggnog, 114–115
Hot Mulled Cider, 20
Meyer Lemon Slush Lemonade, 209
Milk Chocolate and Drunken Prune Ice Cream, 184
Winter Citrus Punch with Spiced Pomegranate Ice,
116 (photo), 117

Salad dressings and vinaigrettes
Broken Apricot Vinaigrette, 262
Buttermilk Dressing, 214
Cranberry-Orange Vinaigrette, 28, 29 (photo)
Green Goddess Dressing, 124
Lemon-Basil Vinaigrette, 96
Louis Dressing, 31
Persimmon Dressing, 187
Salads, 78
Citrus-Fennel Salad, 33–34, 34 (photo)
Crab Cake and Citrus Salad, 122
Crispy Shrimp Salad with Cranberries and Goat
Cheese, 123
Endive Salad with Tangerines and Kumquats, 26
Green Bean and Persimmon Salad, 27
Green Goddess Salad with Shrimp, 124
Grilled Apricot and Goat Cheese Salad, 262
Grilled Chicken and Caramelized Pear Salad, 38
Heirloom Potato Salad with Mushrooms, 266

Salads, *continued*
    Lobster Salad, 26
    Roasted Pear and Goat Cheese Salad, 28, 29
       (photo)
    Shaved Fennel and Mushroom Salad, 125
    Spinach Salad with Pomegranates and Blue Cheese,
       126, 127 (photo)
    Wedge Salad with Buttermilk Dressing, 214
    Winter Vegetable Salad, 128 (photo), 129
    Yankee Salad with Apple, Walnuts, and Blue
       Cheese, 30
Salmon
    Fennel-Cured Gravlax, 218 (photo), 219
Sauces, glazes, and gravies
    Cara Cara Orange Sauce, 148 (photo), 149–150,
       150 (photo)
    Caramel Sauce, 165, 254
    Champagne Sabayon, 189
    Chimichurri, 91
    Citrus-Cranberry Glaze, 90, 165
    Green Apple Pumpkin Butter, 165, 188
    Horseradish Crème Fraîche, 186
    Hot Fudge Sauce, 165, 185
    Jellied Cranberry Sauce, 93, 165
    Kahlua Sabayon, 190
    Kumquat and Pomegranate Glaze, 146–147
    Louis Dressing, 31
    Maple Glaze, 179
    Mignonette Sauce, 186
    Onion-Bourbon-Horseradish Mustard, 98
    Quince Compote, 165, 192
    Red Wine Sauce, 141 (photo)
    Spiced Plum Barbecue Sauce, 165, 265
    Turkey Gravy, 97
    Wild Mushroom Gravy, 47–48, 48 (photo)
Sausage
    Grandma's Cabbage and Sweet-Sausage Soup, 213
    Kumamoto Oyster and Sausage Stuffing, 66
    Spicy Creamy Yellow Grits with Shrimp, 227
Scones
    Cranberry Scones with Orange Glaze, 75
Seasonal ingredients, 7, 16
Shrimp
    Corn and Shrimp Fritters, 31
    Crispy Shrimp Salad with Cranberries and Goat
       Cheese, 123
    Green Goddess Salad with Shrimp, 124
    Spicy Creamy Yellow Grits with Shrimp, 227

Silverware, 16–17
Simple syrup
    Spiced Simple Syrup, 21
Soufflés
    Twice-Baked Blue Cheese Soufflés with Citrus-
       Fennel Salad, 32 (photo), 33–34, 34 (photo)
Soups, stews, chili, and chowders, 201
    Bean Stew with Smoked Ham Hock and Kale,
       201, 212
    Beet and Apple Borscht, 118, 119 (photo)
    Black-Eyed Peas with Smoked Bacon and Spinach,
       220, 221 (photo)
    Chilled Apple Soup with Lobster Salad, 22
    Elephant Garlic Soup with Dungeness Crab Salad,
       120 (photo), 121
    Roasted Harvest Squash Soup, 24 (photo), 25
    Shellfish Chowder, 23
    Steak Chili with Black Beans, 224–225, 225 (photo)
Sour cream
    Banana Sour Cream Coffee Cake, 244 (photo), 245
    Sour Cream Piecrust, 89
Spaghetti squash, 73
    Roasted Spaghetti Squash Noodles, 161
Spinach
    Black-Eyed Peas with Smoked Bacon and Spinach,
       220, 221 (photo)
    Spinach Salad with Pomegranates and Blue Cheese,
       126, 127 (photo)
Squash, winter, 73
    Pan-Roasted Turkey Breast with Sweet Squash
       Matchsticks, 13, 44, 45 (photo)
    Roasted Harvest Squash Soup, 24 (photo), 25
    Winter Panzanella, 70, 71 (photo)
    See also specific kinds
Squash blossoms
    Stuffed Squash Blossoms, 267
Stews. *See* Soups, stews, chili, and chowders
Stocks
    Corn Stock, 99
    Lobster Stock, 100
    Tomato Ham Hock Stock, 255
    Turkey or Chicken Stock, 101
    Vegetable Stock, 193
Strawberries
    Berry Cobbler, 269
    Strawberry Rhubarb Upside-Down Cake, 88
    Strawberry Sparkling Wine Cocktail, 204
Stuffing

Corn and Sage Stuffing, 64 (photo), 65
Kumamoto Oyster and Sausage Stuffing, 66
Summer celebrations, 259–260
Sweet potatoes
    Candied Yams, 154, 155 (photo)
    Leek and Sweet Potato "Risotto," 231
    Sweet Potato Gratin, 68, 69 (photo)
    Whipped Sweet Potatoes, 162
Swiss chard
    Ravioli with Swiss Chard, 234 (photo), 235

Table, setting the holiday, 16–17
Tangerines and tangerine juice
    Braised Chicken with Citrus and Raisins, 222
    Buttermilk Tangerine Soufflé Pancakes, 250
    Citrus-Cranberry Glaze, 90, 165
    Crab Cake and Citrus Salad, 122
    Endive Salad with Tangerines and Kumquats, 26
    Holiday Tangerine Bars, 180, 181 (photo)
    Sole Fillets with Citrus Brown Butter, 232, 233
        (photo)
    Winter Citrus Punch with Spiced Pomegranate Ice,
        116 (photo), 117
Tanz Haus, 8
Tequila
    Mango Pineapple Margaritas, 208
    Meyer Lemon Slush Lemonade, 209
Thanksgiving
    menus, 102–103
    preparation schedule, 104–105
    recipes for, 13–15
    traditions, 112
Thermometers, instant-read, 43
Tomatoes
    Eye-Opening Bloody Marys, 205 (photo), 207
    Red Onion and Tomato Relish, 94
    Tomato Ham Hock Stock, 255
Turkey
    carving technique, 50, 51 (photo)
    Leftover Turkey Hash, 52
    Pan-Roasted Turkey Breast with Sweet Squash
        Matchsticks, 13, 44, 45 (photo)
    Red Curry Turkey Scaloppini, 13, 49
    rules for preparing, 43

Sage-Butter-Roasted Turkey, 13, 40, 41 (photo)
size of, 43
Turkey Gravy, 97
Turkey or Chicken Stock, 101
varieties available, 43
Wood-Grilled Turkey Chop with Wild Mushroom
    Gravy, 46 (photo), 47–48, 48 (photo)

Vegetables
    Mixed Root Vegetables, 230 (photo), 239
    organic and local, 7, 8, 251
    Vegetable Stock, 193
    Winter Vegetable Salad, 128 (photo), 129
    Yankee Pot Roast, 228 (photo), 229–230, 230
        (photo)
    See also specific kinds
Vinaigrettes. See Salad dressings and vinaigrettes
Vodka
    Eye-Opening Bloody Marys, 205 (photo), 207

Walnuts
    Persimmon Walnut Upside-Down Cake, 87–88
    Spicy Glazed Walnuts, 95, 165
    Yankee Salad with Apple, Walnuts, and Blue
        Cheese, 30
Warm-weather holidays, 259–260
Water baths, 36
Wine
    Black Mustard Beef Tenderloin with Red Wine
        Sauce, 109, 140, 141 (photo)
    Blood Orange Mimosas, 204, 205 (photo)
    selecting the right wine, 132
    Sparkling Peach and Apricot Sangría, 261
    Strawberry Sparkling Wine Cocktail, 204
    Wine-Braised Artichokes, 153
    See also Champagne

Yankee Pot Roast, 228 (photo), 229–230, 230 (photo)
Yankee Salad with Apple, Walnuts, and Blue
    Cheese, 30

ABOUT THE AUTHOR

FOR OVER THIRTY YEARS, BRADLEY OGDEN, AN ACCLAIMED AMERICAN CHEF, has been creating extraordinary dishes for an enthusiastic public. Chef Ogden enjoys the reputation for being one of the country's most prolific and successful restaurateurs, while being at the vanguard of authentic American cuisine. As chef and cofounder of the Lark Creek Restaurant Group, he is the creative genius behind many award-winning restaurants such as Root 246 in Solvang; Fish Story in Napa; Moreton Fig in Los Angeles; Bradley Ogden, at Caesars Palace in Las Vegas; The Lark Creek Inn, Lark Creek Steak, The Tavern at Lark Creek, and One Market, in northern California; Parcel 104, in Santa Clara; and Yankee Pier Restaurants, located throughout the country.

His enduring success can be attributed to establishing and nurturing close relationships with many American farmers, ranchers, dairies, and fishermen, which allows him to bring the best farm-fresh ingredients to the table with dedication and culinary flair.

Chef Ogden's commitment to farm-to-table American cuisine has not gone unnoticed. He graduated with honors from the Culinary Institute of America (CIA) and received the Richard T. Keating Award for the student most likely to succeed. In 2000, the CIA again recognized Ogden for his achievements, presenting him with their Chef of the Year honor. Among Ogden's other numerous awards and honors, he was named Best California Chef by the James Beard Foundation, and he received the International Food Service Manufacturers Association Silver Plate Award for the Independent Restaurant category. Other awards include Who's Who of American Cooking by *Cooks* magazine, Great American Chefs by the International Wine and Food Society, the Golden Plate by the American Academy of Achievement, Star Chef of the Year in 2004 by the California Culinary Academy, and Epicure's Best Chef in 2003.

In 2004, his eponymous restaurant located at Caesars Palace received the James Beard Foundation's Best New Restaurant of the Year award, and also boasts a Mobil four-star award and a Michelin star. The restaurant has also been recognized as the Best of the Best from *Robb Report* and honored among American's Best Restaurants by *Gourmet*.

Chef Ogden now lives in California's central coast running his newest restaurant concept Root 246 in Solvang, staying true to his culinary roots and enjoying access to the most incredible farmers and food.